VOICES
FROM THE
JAPANESE CINEMA

Other Books by Joan Mellen

MARILYN MONROE

A FILM GUIDE TO THE BATTLE OF ALGIERS

WOMEN AND THEIR SEXUALITY IN THE NEW FILM

TAKING AIM: FILMS ABOUT POLITICS (forthcoming)

VOICES
FROM THE
JAPANESE
CINEMA

JOAN MELLEN

LIVERIGHT NEW YORK

PREFATORY NOTE

With the exception of the dialogue with Toichiro Narushima, which took place in New York, the following interviews were taped in Japan. Those conducted in Japanese were translated by Keiko Mochizuki, lecturer in Japanese at the University of California at Santa Barbara.

Copyright © 1975 by Joan Mellen

First Edition

Library of Congress Cataloging in Publication Data

Mellen, Joan.
  Voices from the Japanese cinema.

  Includes bibliographical references.
  CONTENTS: Daisuke Ito.—Akira Kurosawa.—Mme.
Kashiko Kawakita. [etc.]
  1. Moving-picture producers and directors—Japan—
Interviews. I. Title.
PN1998.A2M37 1975   791.43′023′0922   74–28197
ISBN 0–87140–604–7
ISBN 0–87140–101–0 pbk.

Published simultaneously in Canada
by George J. McLeod Limited, Toronto

Book designed by Jacques Chazaud
Typefaces used are Times Roman and Weiss
Manufactured by Vail-Ballou Press, Inc.

Printed in the United States of America
1 2 3 4 5 6 7 8 9 0

For
Mme. Kashiko Kawakita
and
Kyushiro Kusakabe

ACKNOWLEDGMENTS

Many people helped me warmly and unselfishly in creating my dialogue with Japanese artists. I wish particularly to thank

—in Japan: Mme. Kashiko Kawakita, one of the rarest women I have met and toward whom I have come to feel as a daughter; Kyushiro Kusakabe, who shepherded me everywhere in Tokyo, devoting many days, and without whom difficult access to many film professionals would have been impossible; Donald Richie, one of Japan's leading intellectuals and a generous friend, without whose pioneering works in the field this book would not have been conceived; Yoichi Matsue, producer of Kurosawa's *Dodes'ka-den* and *Dersu Uzala* and assistant director of *High and Low,* who provided an entrance to the world of Kurosawa; and the *Mainichi Shimbun* newspaper, which invited me to Japan and was my host throughout my stay.

—in the United States: I owe an enormous debt of gratitude to Keiko Mochizuki, who worked so painstakingly and ingeniously in translating and elucidating difficult Japanese tapes; to Gordon Hitchens for generously providing stills from his personal collection; to Charles Silver of the Film Study Center at the Museum of Modern Art for his help in research; and to many others such as Hajime Seki, formerly of *Mainichi* in New York; Kazuko Oshima, and Nammi Lee Miller, who assisted along the way.

—I would also like especially to thank my editor, Laurie Nevin Friedman, for so graciously establishing the kind of relationship that has become all too rare in publishing.

Finally, to Ralph Schoenman I owe once again my gratitude for the encouragement that sparks inspiration. He provided the best kind of help to me—that untrammeled by false consciousness about the limits of the possible.

CONTENTS

INTRODUCTION

A *gaijin no onna** in Japan

I traveled to Japan in the summer of 1972 at the invitation of the *Mainichi Shimbun* newspaper organization expecting, as a film critic, to meet Japanese artists and study at close range one of the world's greatest cinemas. Since the Second World War, the Japanese have produced a body of films and a host of fine directors rivaling, and perhaps surpassing their French, Italian, and American counterparts. Two peerless directors of the Japanese cinema were Ozu and Mizoguchi, both of whom began in the silent era. Their finest work occurred, however, during the postwar period. Akira Kurosawa, who remains the best known of Japanese directors in the West, made his great films, from *Rashomon* and *Seven Samurai* to *Yojimbo* and *Red Beard,* between 1945 and 1965.

Revitalized by the presence of these artists, the Japanese cinema expanded and grew, generating aesthetic space for masters as varied as Kon Ichikawa, Masaki Kobayashi, Kaneto Shindo, and Tadashi Imai. In addition, the early 1960s brought to the fore an extraordinary generation of filmmakers, all of whom became directors of important feature films. Hiroshi Teshigahara, who would later do *The Woman in the Dunes,* directed *Pitfall* in 1962. Susumu Hani made *Bad Boys* in 1960. Nagisa Oshima finished *A Town of Love and Hope* in 1959; *A Story of the Cruelty of Youth* and *The Tomb of the Sun* followed in 1960. Masahiro Shinoda showed *Youth in Fury* in 1960, and completed his first important film, *Pale*

---

* Foreign woman.

1

Flower, in 1964. Shohei Imamura came into his own in 1961 with *Pigs and Battleships.*

Yet most of these directors remain relatively unknown in the United States. And with the exception of Donald Richie's beautiful and unique books, little has been written about the Japanese cinema in English. Upon visiting Japan, I was armed with insights provided by Richie. I had seen most of the films of Kurosawa, many of those of Ozu and Mizoguchi, as well as some of Hani and Teshigahara. I knew enough when I went to Japan to be aware that a rich and indeed magnificent cinema awaited me. The many films that I viewed in Japan through the courtesy of the Japan Film Library Council and UniJapan Film confirmed what I had surmised. We, in the United States, have viewed so far only the tip of the iceberg, a merest sampling of the great films which form what Donald Richie has called the "renaissance" of the Japanese cinema from 1946 through the 1960s.

More than just viewing films, my aim in Japan was to meet the great directors and converse with them about their art. I wished to pursue how their films are received in Japan, the values and premises behind the Japanese director's conception of his art and how these differ from a Western approach. It is true of Europe and equally, if not more so, of Japan, that the Second World War and its devastation lie far closer to consciousness than in the United States. This has no doubt had been due to the fact that we alone of the nations involved did not endure the atrocities of war directly. And, of course, as the victors we did not suffer the national trauma experienced by the Japanese, followed by the albeit temporary demolition of their established institutions by an occupying power.

And the Japanese are also aware of the marked silence and indifference of the majority of foreign critics toward their remarkable culture—particularly their film art. From the Italian neorealists to the French New Wave, American critics have responded with often uncritical superlatives about European films of the postwar era; almost no critics have devoted their efforts to the Japanese film, which is so far superior in consistent quality to European cinema of the same period.

All foreign visitors to Japan are confronted in their attempts to make contact with the Japanese by a tradition of insularity. It is an isolation born of centuries when Western people and ideas were rigorously kept from penetrating Japanese culture. After the invasion by Portuguese missionaries in the sixteenth century, simultaneously bringing Christianity and the gun to Japan, the colonizing effort was suppressed and the country remained free of Western influence from 1608 to 1868, throughout the long years of rule by the Tokugawa dynasty.

When Commodore Perry arrived in Tokyo Bay determined to open, no matter the consequences, the lucrative market of Japan for Western capital, he was greeted by the swelling movement of *Jōi-i,* "Expel the Barbarians!" The *Jōi-i* movement was expressive of the fear among Japanese that foreign ideas would cause traditional discipline to be undermined. Without the willing subservience of individuals to a hierarchy, the cornerstone of the feudal Japanese social order, the ruling group feared a disintegration of its authority and total moral chaos. Quite rightly it dreaded the carving up of Japan by a militarily superior colonial power, and this it succeeded in preventing.

Townsend Harris, the first American consul to Japan, failing to appreciate the cultural trauma attendant upon the "opening" of the country, observed in his journal that "their great object appears to be to permit as little to be learned about their country as possible; and, to that end, all fraud, deceit, falsehood and even violence, is justifiable in their eyes." * Representing as he did an unwelcome foreign presence which had entered Japan by force and guile, his remarks, if accurate, ignored the cause and reflected a racial judgment designed to reinforce that feeling of superiority needed to justify Western ruthlessness.

There has thus always been in Japan a strong feeling that the adoption of foreign ways courts disaster, and that a Japanese can best find fulfillment by being as purely and passionately Japanese as is humanly possible. One might speculate that had feudalism not assumed the mantle of the nation's honor and identity at the time of the Meiji restoration, the Japanese themselves might have challenged it more vigorously. As it was, foreigners who wished only to exploit Japan attacked her institutions, causing the people to confuse the values of feudalism with being Japanese. Hence, even today, some of the most radical Japanese are afflicted by an ambivalence toward traditional Japanese habits and the sensibility born of the feudal era they might otherwise have rejected as retrograde. Yukio Mishima's suicide was at least partially in homage to this feudal past. His death by *seppuku* or *hara kiri* was a conscious act

---

* *The Complete Journal of Townsend Harris: First American Consul and Minister to Japan* (Rutland, Vermont, and Tokyo, Japan: Charles E. Tuttle Company, 1959), pp. 362–63.

of protest by a novelist who had become a militant advocate of restoring Japan's dignity and national honor through a return to the values of *bushido,* or the samurai spirit. He represented as well a neofascist current encouraged and fostered by Japan's new military establishment. As Jon Halliday and Gavan McCormack point out in *Japanese Imperialism Today,* Mishima's private army, the Tate no Kai, were trained and armed by the Japanese Self-Defense Forces and accorded quasi-official status.*

Osaka has traditionally been despised in Japan because it was there that the striving merchant class forged its dominance, weakening the power of the Tokugawa samurai. The extension to merchant industrialism, adopted to surmount Western technological advantage, has been regarded as representing the degradation of the national culture. Japanese are appalled by Tokyo, which is felt to be an abrasive industrial slag heap. The "national essence" seemed to be crumbling before a hated yet necessary utilitarianism and materialism. The Japanese are tormented by the knowledge that only this merchant industrialism, even as it despoils the society, has spared them the mode of colonial subjugation suffered throughout Asia.

The problem is that rejecting the technological amoralism imposed upon Japan by the foreigners and returning to what was uniquely "Japanese" meant, in the absence of anything else, a return to the harsh injustices of feudalism. Notoriously, there has been an absence of an alternative cultural vision among Japanese intellectuals who reject the ways of the present; it is instructive that this is as true for radical directors like Nagisa Oshima, who is interviewed here, as it is for neofascists like Mishima. But certainly among many of the directors I interviewed there remains the old contempt, samurai in origin, for the rising merchant class. It is a central emotion in Imai's *Muddy Waters,* in Kurosawa's *Yojimbo,* in Shindo's script for *A Pebble by the Wayside,* in Shinoda's *Double Suicide,* which closely adheres to the original play written by that stridently anti-middle-class playwright Chikamatsu. The descendant of the Edo merchant, Japan's modern "salary" or "company" man is satirized and subjected to intense critical scrutiny in films by directors young and old, from Kurosawa's *Ikiru, The Bad Sleep Well,* and *High and Low,* to Hani's *She and He* and Oshima's *Night and Fog in Japan.*

Because of the disruptive role played by foreign nations in Japa-

---

* (Hammondsworth, Middlesex, England: Penguin Books Ltd., 1973), pp. 91–92.

nese history and because of the ambivalence and trauma this engendered in the national psyche, a certain xenophobia remains part of the Japanese way. At its best it reflects a self-containment which views even the approval of the ''other'' as an intrusion; at its worst it produces a closed and cold wall, mistakenly confident of the inability of the foreigner to penetrate its ''inscrutability.'' As such it dangerously underestimates its presumed ''enemy'' and fails to distinguish between sympathetic individuals reaching out to Japan and foreign nation-states which have played an antagonistic role in Japanese history.

The early feeling of inferiority on the part of Japanese at the time of Commodore Perry and Townsend Harris and the fear of being ridiculed for old-fashioned ways by condescending foreigners produced its inverse within the same national consciousness. There remains a defensive contempt for foreigners still smoldering within the culture. The Japanese psychiatrist Takeo Doi describes in *The Anatomy of Dependence* this contradiction within a typical Japanese, ''who is pleasant in personal contacts, yet behaves with complete indifference toward outsiders who have no connection with him. He is diffident and circumspect in the place where he lives, yet in strange surroundings behaves just as the fancy takes him.'' *

It is also part of the old Japanese way that debate is considered a violation of decorum; to present one's ideas openly and in overt challenge to others, however civilly, represents a crude obtrusion of the self. The assertion by individuals of their personal and/or strongly felt attitudes is found to disturb the balance of proper intercourse. It breaches the very sanctity of the normal. Throughout the Tokugawa period competition was viewed as a form of social aggression. Until the Meiji restoration in 1868, when the outcast and essentially powerless emperor was restored to prominence, there was no word in Japanese for ''competition.'' The term had to be invented for the translation of Western books. Nor was there any way to express the term ''popular rights''; the word *minken* thus dates only from Meiji. In fact, only in the late nineteenth century did the concept of ''rights'' as distinct from ''obligations'' enter the culture with the newly coined word *kenri,* from *ken* for ''power'' or ''influence'' and *ri* for ''interest.'' By the beginning of the twentieth century there would still be no tradition of opposition and dissent in Japan.

One of the reasons Kurosawa so appeals to the Western filmgoer

---

* Faubian Bowers, quotation from *The Anatomy of Dependence* by Takeo Doi, *New York Times Sunday Magazine,* 15 July 1973.

is his implicit recognition of these ideas, so vital a part of the European and American Weltanschauung. In *High and Low,* which Kurosawa discusses at length in the interview, a kidnapper introduces the question of his rights as a human being: didn't he have the "right" to escape living in sweltering heat during the summer only to freeze in the winter trapped in a cramped three-tatami room? His wealthy industrialist victim lives in a white mansion high on a slope looking down upon him, and the film culminates in this executive's attempt to understand the motives of his antagonist.

The question of "right" also conflicts with the traditional notion of the family in Japan with its demand upon the individual for unquestioning fidelity to the hierarchy of authority. Before 1868 no member of a "house" or extended family could exercise separate property rights. An attack on this structure is the theme of one of Oshima's most brilliant films, *The Ceremony,* and it marks him as one of those young directors undividedly at war with the Japanese past.

Unlike the French and American revolutions, the Meiji restoration was not accompanied by a bourgeois revolution providing representative institutions, however controlled by the moneyed, or by a grant to individuals of "inalienable rights." The privilege of owning property by individuals was of course essential to the rise of capitalism, and this particular reform became synonymous with the restoration. But unlike the French Revolution, which involved mass upheaval, the Tokugawas were not overthrown by a rising bourgeoisie, but by equally feudal anti-Tokugawa forces centered around the Satsuma and Chōshū clans. The samurai class firmly retained its power.

Capitalism has always functioned in Japan under the power of the state and it developed side by side with feudal values. The "nation" has been treated with feudal fealty and deference. Individualism, a critical component of a rising bourgeoisie, has been absent, providing no space for a democracy. This is a point stressed in the interview with Daisuke Ito, who sought in *Bakumatsu* to dramatize the frustrations of the revolutionary Ryōma Sakamoto. Ryōma was left horrified by the unsatisfactory results of the great effort expended in the overthrow of the shogunate, and in depicting his despair Ito comments on the failure of the Meiji restoration.

What is striking about many of the directors interviewed for this volume is that they constitute a sector of the Japanese intelligentsia critical of traditional culture and authority. In this category fall artists as varied as Oshima and Kurosawa, Ito and Hani, Shindo and

Toshiro Mifune (*left*) and Tsutsomu Yamazaki (*right*) in Kurosawa's *High and Low*. "Didn't he have the 'right' to escape living in sweltering heat during the summer only to freeze in the winter, trapped in a cramped three-tatami room?"

Kobayashi, and Imai. The absence of a democratic wellspring in the culture has meant that conformity to tradition has always embodied for the Japanese a greater integrity than finding "one's own way." It expresses selflessness and sacrifice to the greater communal good as opposed to egoistic and selfish assertion. Harmony in the culture has thus been enmeshed with the notion of all maintaining their appropriate status and station. The interests, needs, or self-expression of the individual were not to be differentiated from those of the group and the authority which safeguards it. As Harris observed, "It would be an endless task to attempt to put down all the acts of a Japanese that are regulated by authority." * Certainly public speaking has traditionally been strange to the Japanese way. During early Meiji it was considered a shade indecorous for a man (let alone a woman!) to proclaim his ideas aloud.

* Harris, *The Complete Journal of Townsend Harris*, pp. 360–61.

Thus the critic, by his very function, represents a way of life that came to Japan only after 1868 with the fall of official feudalism. Just as feudal responses continue to haunt Japanese institutions, folkways too die hard. For a young critic, whether Japanese or foreign, to debate with passion and enthusiasm before his elders may not be a pleasing sight for the Japanese of the older generation who reached their maturity before the Second World War. If a Japanese so behaves, he may be marked as "un-Japanese." When a foreigner does so, particularly in confrontation with Japanese attempting to abide by the old ways, it is the height of disagreeableness, a veritable incitement to the worst expectations of foreign contumely.

The Japanese film director, therefore, responds to the foreign critic with some wariness. First, and this is also the result of the formalized and rigorous etiquette of Japanese culture, the unknown Western critic cannot easily approach a Japanese director for an interview without an introduction from a respected Japanese critic or friend. In my case, I was extremely lucky because my hosts at the *Mainichi Shimbun* introduced me to the fine critic and film producer Kyushiro Kusakabe, who is both well known and well loved by so many in the Japanese film world.

In the case of Akira Kurosawa, it was Mme. Kawakita who arranged our meeting. She is the curator of film of the Japan Film Library Council and the artistic spirit behind the Towa Film Company, which imports the best foreign films to Japan and enables the most distinguished Japanese films to be known abroad. Still, most directors, upon our introduction, remained uncertain of the sincerity of an American critic coming to Japan. Did I appreciate how fine a film art had been achieved in Japan and was I therefore worthy of unguarded discussion? Masaki Kobayashi began by asking me how many of his films I had seen and only after I had run down the list: *The Human Condition, Hara Kiri, Kwaidan, Rebellion, Inn of Evil,* etc., was he ready to proceed.

The issue of sincerity is not a slight one, particularly among younger directors whose work has gone unappreciated by Western critics. Most of these critics have felt able to come to terms with the Japanese film only by allowing the brilliance of older, established masters like Ozu, Kurosawa, and Naruse. Younger directors begin their work in the shadow of these great figures, as well as several lesser, if also brilliant, well-known practioners of the art like Ito, Kinugasa, Kinoshita, and Gosho. The new generation were understandably eager to open new byways for the Japanese film, and to expand it in areas hitherto neglected by their great predecessors.

Shinoda thus speaks quite typically of the need for a Japanese Ingmar Bergman. Hani and Oshima set all their films in the present and focus on the alienation and sense of futility afflicting the young in Japan. They each experiment with forms daringly new for the Japanese film and often with a semidocumentary approach. Both draw at least some of their inspiration from the French New Wave.

Oshima in particular was wary of a Western critic who would come to Japan with easy praise for the Kurosawas (who no longer need such recognition, having been acknowledged by the entire world), while their own work went ignored and misunderstood. Just as Virginia Woolf in her famous manifesto "Mr. Bennett and Mrs. Brown" was adamant about not having her novels and those of James Joyce subsumed under the aesthetic conventions of outdated sensibilities, like John Galsworthy, Arnold Bennett, and H. G. Wells, so artists like Oshima wish to distinguish themselves from what they consider to be tired forms endlessly duplicated by their elders.

Thus, in my praise for Kurosawa, and I had been invited to Japan on the strength of two articles I had written about the significance of Kurosawa's work, I was swiftly subject to suspicion. When Oshima asked me what my motives were in coming to Japan, he was really asking why I was taking so conservative a stance in allying myself with the past of the Japanese film rather than with its vital and living future.

It is also true that Kurosawa at the height of his career was very well financed by the Toho Company, whereas the directors who came into their own during the 1960s have been much less fortunate. As in the West, television has swept Japan, and the movie box office reflects the demise of film as a mass art. All of the younger directors, without exception, frequently must work independently, outside of the financing—and paternalism—of the "major companies." Their lot is not an easy one, either in terms of finding the money to make films or in achieving successful distribution.

The pornos and the *Yakuza,* or gangster pictures, continue to do well; the serious film, which was once the pride of Toho, Shochiku, and Daiei (the latter now bankrupt), must find meager outlets such as the Art Theatre Guild. Working under such handicaps clearly does not favor conditions under which an expensive, collective art like film can flourish.

It is especially important now to younger directors that their work gain the critical reputation abroad that they deserve. Because they have endured terrible financial strain at the very height of their careers, the younger Japanese directors are especially aware that genuine sympathy, especially from a foreigner, is possible only after a significant effort and with considerable knowledge. Why then should they not be wary of a young Western critic whose appreciation of the Japanese film, on the face of it, seems certain to be limited to the *jidai-geki* * of Kurosawa? It is as if a Japanese film critic were to arrive in the United States (an uncommon event, if not as unusual as the visit of an American critic to Japan) only to pour forth the long familiar praises of John Ford or William Wyler into the ears of a justifiably bewildered—if not irritated—Robert Altman.

But I was not only a foreign, Western critic in Japan. I was also a woman. Throughout most of Japanese history women were taught not to assert themselves. Women who did could only be degraded—loose women—or considered unfeminine and unseemly. Borrowing from the Chinese, the Japanese taught their women throughout the Tokugawa period the Confucian "three obediences": to her parents as a daughter, to her husband as a wife, and, during the last third of her existence, to her son as a mother. Even today in Japan when a male child is born the appropriate response is "congratulations for the prosperity of the 'Tanaka' family"; if the infant is female the wording alters: "It is a good thing that a first girl is born. We are hoping that the second child will be a boy."

If the first child is a girl, it is thought of as a test and practice in training for the raising of the real child, the boy. If a mother is blessed with three daughters, she ought to feel sorry for her husband and family who must bear this misfortune. Now, as in the Tokugawa period, the ideal of female beauty remains that a woman be gentle, quiet, graceful, and I fear, still, retiring and unobtrusive.

It was also only slightly more than a hundred years ago that adul-

---

* The *jidai-geki* is a period or historical film, a costume drama set in feudal times, before the Meiji restoration of 1868. It uses the past as a means of exposing the injustices of the present, and at its best it evokes a new interpretation of history by challenging accepted values, particularly those of *bushido*. The *jidai-geki*, as Donald Richie points out in his discussion of *Seven Samurai* in *The Films of Akira Kurosawa* (Berkeley and Los Angeles: University of California Press, 1965), is to be distinguished from the "*chambara* or simple sword-fight films" which might be compared with the more mindless of the American Westerns.

tery on the part of the wife was punishable by death. Later, during the early Meiji period a special class of novels called *Dokufumono* or "Works on Poisonous Women" were popular. The radical ultranationalists, despite their calls for "reform," predictably demanded a return to the feudal role for women. In Ikki Kita's *An Outline Plan for the Reorganization of Japan,* written in 1919, he stated: "Women will not have the right to participate in politics" because "anyone who has observed the stupid talkativeness of Western women or the piercing quarrels among Chinese women will be thankful that Japanese women have continued on the right path." * With fascist movements triumphing so early in the century, there was no room for the expression of anything but patriarchal attitudes toward women.

One of the most fascinating facts about Japan, however, is that it began as a matriarchy. Recorded history reveals a woman ruler in the third century in Japan named Himiko. She was the head of the largest tribe among the Japanese, the Yamatai or Yamato, which had a king who ruled for seventy or eighty years. But under his rule the nation fell into chaos and the people fought among themselves. And so they chose a queen, who was also a shaman. Himiko, however, was succeeded by a king, under whose power disarray once again resulted. Toyo, an adopted daughter of Himiko, who never married, took power; she too was succeeded by a man.

In the fourth and fifth centuries A.D., the Japanese emperor system, and with it an authoritarian patriarchy, was established. In our interview Masahiro Shinoda talks about his 1974 film *Himiko,* which centers on this ancient Japanese goddess and matriarch. That intellectuals should rediscover Himiko may point to a new consciousness in Japan about the capacities and powers of women, but it also remains true that the feeling that women must not assert themselves persist as a strong current in Japan.

Only 10 percent of Japanese women attend four-year colleges even now. And Japanese filmmakers of social conscience from Mizoguchi to Hani have frequently taken up the cause of Japanese women. It is an issue at the heart of any struggle to transcend the debilitating effects of Japanese feudalism and capitalism. The theme of the liberation of women was one of the requested film subjects emanating from General MacArthur's headquarters during

* Ryusaku Tsunoda, William Theodore de Bary and Donald Keene, comps., *Sources of Japanese Tradition* (New York: Columbia University Press, 1958), 2:275.

the American occupation, especially during the early period when its aim was a rapid "democratization." This amounted to a decartelization of the giant corporations, or *zaibatsu,* to rid Japan of its overtly troublesome feudal tendencies and its capacity to enter immediately into competition with American industry. In the 1970s it would take a contrived oil "crisis" to attempt the same end as the yen rose and the dollar sank on the international exchange—a difficult moment for Japan, which must import more than 99 percent of its crude petroleum. Just as there was very little sincerity in this "democratization," so too it has been easy to express a concern for the status of women, while silently, and in the actions of everyday life, endorsing the condition of women as it has been since feudal times.

The interviews with Sachiko Hidari and Setsu Asakura, both examples of the rare "new" Japanese woman, treat this problem in depth. An intense rapport was established, especially with Hidari, on the strength of the solidarity she felt with a foreign woman sincerely interested in the problems of women in Japan who have often felt despair and isolation in their struggle. The women's liberation movement reached Japan only in mid-1970. It now traverses a spectrum ranging from radical women who have taken jobs as bar hostesses, by way of understanding the struggles of their most oppressed sisters, to women whose ideas are similar to those of the National Organization of Women (NOW) in the United States. These latter stress such issues as the disparity between women's and men's wages in Japan. Women receive 48 percent less pay for similar work than do men, and there remain extraordinarily few jobs for women who are university graduates. In 1972 ten out of two thousand reporters at the *Asahi Shimbun* newspaper were women. At *Yomiuri,* another huge newspaper, there was one woman employed, after a history of sixteen years without a single woman in a professional capacity.

The interviews sometimes disclose explicit awareness on the part of the directors that their interlocutor is a foreign woman. They were thus especially concerned to discover the personal identity of their interviewer and from what explicit premises questions might spring. In part, feelings run high because of the general absorption and preoccupation among Japanese with the dilemma of identity—both as individuals and as representatives of a culture.

In Japan these two are often not distinguished. The Japanese have lived within a culture undergoing continual transformation since 1868; this has inspired a compelling need to discern what is uniquely Japanese. To many, as I have indicated, urbanization, capitalism, and the dissolution of feudal family relationships seem to have only a negative dimension—a violation by foreign ideas. They are disruptive of loyalty and propriety and they offer no new values to take the place of the old. This in turn has led many Japanese intellectuals to pessimism and indeed to despondency and the conviction that evils remain insoluble. Many have come to believe that the effort to change things for the better is futile. There is a profound nihilism at the center of what appears, on the surface, to be so hardheaded and pragmatic a culture.

The notion, however, that things will never be better than they are has been an attitude of Japanese culture for centuries. Nowhere is it more indubitably expressed than in the *Legacy of Ieyasu,* the first of the Tokugawa shoguns, who came to power in the first decade of the seventeenth century:

> Human life is like going on a long journey carrying a heavy load. You will not be disappointed if you think that hardship is the common lot. When desires arise in your heart, think back to times when you suffered distress.

At best, people are encouraged, stoically, to respond to failure and disappointment with an attitude of *mono no aware,* sad resignation before the unalterable injustices of human life. It is the great theme of Ozu, who finds bittersweet beauty as his characters yield to what Ieyasu called the "heavy load" of human existence. But other directors have felt differently, seeking to move beyond a legacy they feel has damaged the Japanese psyche and resulted in much self-hatred and a desperation resulting in cruelty.

The world described critically in the period films of Kobayashi, Shindo, and Imai is that of Ieyasu. It is a universe where once a law has been in force for a period of fifty years, it could not henceforth be amended, no matter how unjust or unworkable it proved. As they indicate in their interviews, it is the feudal vestiges in *modern* Japan to which they address themselves when they set their films in the past. This is a past in which, as Narushima describes, those who tried to revolt did not fare well. After the siege of Osaka in 1615, when Ieyasu finally consolidated his power, 100,000 were slaughtered. The Tokugawas dealt similarly with the Shimabara rebellion in 1637, and again in 1651 when they discovered a conspiracy against their rule.

The conviction that progress seems to be beyond the power of man, a root from which all modes of feudalism derive and retain

their strength, haunts the Japanese director. This is especially true
for Masahiro Shinoda. It leads in many to overbearing feelings of
claustrophobia about a fixed culture which oppresses but seems im-
penetrable and impervious to change. It involves a tension similar
to that described by Brecht in his poem about Japan called "The
Mask of Evil":

> On my wall hangs a Japanese carving.
> The mask of an evil demon, decorated with gold lacquer.
> Sympathetically I observe
> The swollen veins of the forehead, indicating
> What a strain it is to be evil.*

As a way out, as an escape from the irremediable, many younger
directors have sought to contrast "civilized," contemporary Japan
with the "primitive" rural byways where, these men suggest, peo-
ple may still be capable of simple, humane responses lost to the res-
ident of Tokyo who is often referred to in terms suggesting an
"urban neurotic." The fierce nationalism of the 1920s and 1930s
and the emergence of fascism contributed as well to a nostalgia for
the primitive and the unspoiled.

This impulse can be seen in so wide a variety of films that it rep-
resents a major tendency. It can be found in Hani's documentaries
about children, which we discussed together, as well as in films
like *Bride of the Andes* and *Bwana Toshi* set by Hani in technolog-
ically less advanced societies than Japan. It is a common theme for
Shindo, as *The Island* reveals. It forms the intellectual base of
Teshigahara's adaptation of Abé's *The Woman in the Dunes*. It is
the dominant idea of Narushima's *Time Within Memory;* it bril-
liantly comes to the fore in Imamura's *The Insect Woman* and
Kuragejima: Tales from a Southern Island; it emerges, only to be
rejected, in Shinoda's *Punishment Island* and *Himiko*. And it is at
the root of much of Yukio Mishima's psychology in such novels as
A Thirst for Love and *The Sound of Waves*.

As Mme. Kawakita stresses in her interview, World War II rep-
resents a major cultural turning point for the Japanese. New forms
of behavior were grafted onto the old, although the graft has only
partially taken. Beneath the surface the pervasive feelings of a pow-
erful feudal training persist. In the ensuing conflict, at once internal
and projected in her film art, Japan emerges in these interviews as
an irrepressibly intense and vital culture. At every instant of change

---

* Copyright © 1947 by Bertolt Brecht and H. R. Hays.

there is awareness of a self-reflective process. These directors convey a sense of Japan as a society continually questioning its validity and direction. One is left with the feeling that in all its turmoil, Japan is a culture straining for profound social change, a culture embued with a trembling energy.

Japan is no more a cultural monolith than is the United States or the Soviet Union. In Russia, official opinion persecuted and exiled Solzhenitsyn, yet a burgeoning dissident movement grows in opposition to the prevailing authoritarianism. Japan may retain its old feudal structures within the contemporary *zaibatsu* (the paternalistic corporation), but there are also those who resist the frantic pressure to submit. Women may not yet have freed themselves from the feudal definition of their roles, but many Japanese women, and men, like director Susumu Hani, continue to expose the inadequacy of the old view of woman's place. Nor are they content with the common, if indefensible, response that women, who customarily hold the family pursestrings and pay the bills, have therefore always possessed decisive or real power in the Japanese family. For what were their options except to aid in the carrying out of established ways? In fact, they were successfully required to act in direct conflict with their own personal development and became more stringently supportive of male dominance in all decisions than the men themselves. To do otherwise was to be cast aside, and in the past, as now, women who violate custom too extremely can suffer total isolation and disgrace.

The forced, harried modernization ushered in during the Meiji restoration caused Japanese culture to develop in a climate of frenetic economic pursuit. "Economic animal" is a cliché too readily attached to the Japanese. For it remains equally possible that the vitality of the culture will, perforce, result in new modes of social expression if and when large numbers of Japanese are freed from the repressive social institutions which have channeled Japanese energy into the commercial.

Japan's film art is a harbinger. Those in contemporary Japan who have already rejected the social order flourish and offer a hint of the scope of Japanese creative gifts which should blossom once freed from the pall of authoritarian tradition. The playwright-screenwriter-director Shuji Terayama is but one example.

During the late 1960s and early 1970s, another generation of directors surfaced, more overtly political than their elders, impatient of the oblique, and demanding solutions to the problems plaguing modern Japan. Noriaki Tsuchimoto created what Hani considers the finest postwar documentary in Japan. *Minamata* is about the new pollution, at once literal and metaphoric, in its depiction of the ravages of industrialism under Japanese capitalism. The film is about the gradual poisoning of the people of Minamata by mercury compounds left in the waste of a neighboring factory and entering the fish which formed the local diet.

Another filmmaker whose camera has pursued the outrages of modern Japan is Shinsuke Ogawa. His *Peasants of the Second Fortress* (and indeed all six films of his Narita airport series), slightly reminiscent in its vivid realism of Gillo Pontecorvo's *Battle of Algiers,* depicts the sit-in by local peasants who resist the construction of a new airport outside Tokyo which would, without their consent, take their homes. Ogawa's crew lived with the peasants throughout their protracted struggle and bloody clashes with army and police. The angle of the camera was always from behind the barricades and the camera itself was not at one remove, but functioned as the eyes of the peasants as they experienced their struggle.

Noriaki Hoshi has made two small documentary films whose themes are expressed in their titles: *Sunagawa—The Anti-War Groups in the Trenches* followed by *The Trenches—Continued.* Each protests the new militarization of Japan, first that of the Americans and now that of the Japanese military-industrial complex itself.

These films differ from their predecessors in that they are far more militant in intent and operate from the premise that films can change the world. They are based upon a solidarity between filmmaker and subject, and demand an equivalent response from the viewer. They are documentary in style; one of their central aesthetic tenets is a reluctance to cut, the better to provide an exhaustive sense of the moment-to-moment struggle of the protagonists.

In many instances they sacrifice professionalism for immediacy—a choice Jean-Luc Godard has made as well. A number of these films, like *Minamata, Peasants of the Second Fortress,* and Ogawa's best *Sanrizuka* film, *Heta Village,* are three hours long. The spirit of satire and redefinition remains a part of the Japanese film and these new documentarists far transcend the films of nihilists like Toshio Matsumoto and Akio Jissoji. Matsumoto in *Funeral Parade of Roses* and *Shura* and Jissoji in *This Transient Life* and *Mandala* remain content to take us nihilistically to the depths of ennui and pain without a glimpse of any means to redress evil.

In sharp contrast, the political documentarists view their work as

Ogawa's *Heta Buraku* (*Heta Village*). ''They are based upon a solidarity between filmmaker and subject. . . .''

direct vehicles for exploring "what is to be done." Another example is *Motoshin Kakarannu* (*You Don't Need Capital in This Business*). It treats prostitution in Okinawa by filming conversations with impoverished prostitutes, while imparting the mass hatred for the annexation of Okinawa by mainland Japan for large investment and exploitation. It is a theme dramatized as well by Oshima in *Dear Summer Sister,* one of the films he discusses at length in the interview.

One of the new documentaries about Okinawa is called *To Live.* Its subject is the island of Watakashito, where half the population committed suicide during the last days of fighting in the Second World War. The film is composed of interviews with the survivors in an effort to enter their experience and understand what had happened. The act of filmmaking in this instance altered historical knowledge. It had been accepted before the film that the commander of the Japanese defense forces gave the suicide order to the populace. This is thrown into doubt as the people discuss the event on camera. And by far the best of these films about Okinawa, Yoichi Higashi's *The Okinawa Retto,* is scathing in its exposure of both American and Japanese exploitation. Japan's attitude toward Okinawa is compared with that of a father who sold his daughter to a whorehouse and then, having used up the money, returns to ask for more. Shots of American F-105 jet fighter planes swooping down upon the sugar cane fields in bombing practice speak for themselves; the jets descend almost right over the people's heads. The nuclear-armed B-52 becomes a monstrous symbol of the all-pervasive American military presence. While the budgets of all these films are a fraction of those of big productions, the commitment to the discovery of truth and to protest intolerable aspects of Japanese life seems to be total on the part of everyone involved— the working crews, technicians, and "performers."

The Japanese film thus is experiencing continual renewal. Despite the shrinking market for films, important creative work abounds. Each generation defines itself in conscious reaction against forms forged by its predecessors. It is inconceivable, for example, that a sentimental Kinoshita-style family chronicle could be made in Japan today by one of these directors. Film is a touchstone of the pace of cultural change, part of the reason why cinema in Japan is so exciting a medium.

Shinsuke Ogawa's *Peasants of the Second Fortress.* "It is inconceivable, for example, that a sentimental Kinoshita-style family chronicle could be made in Japan today by one of these directors."

While the film industry in all countries has also been one of the most retrograde social forces, insinuating dominant and established values, film artists, like novelists and poets, are when they are at their vital best ahead of their time and project through their visions a society in embryo. The postwar generations of filmmakers in Japan introduce us to the tensions underlying the culture that exists—but signal as well new struggles for freedom and self-determination that presage the Japan of tomorrow.

ONE

DAISUKE ITO

INTRODUCTION

Daisuke Ito, born in 1898, is one of the grand old men of the Japanese cinema. He belongs to the golden age of the period or sword film, the true *jidai-geki,* and is considered by many to be one of the fathers of the genre. Ito was a pupil in Kaoru Osanai's original Shochiku Cinema Institute, which trained new people and developed new modes for the cinema in the early 1920s. Osanai had been one of the founders of the Shingeki movement in theater—a "modern" theater, noted for its realism. He had studied at the Moscow Art Theater and worked in Max Reinhardt's Berlin theater. Thus he returned to Japan with wide training and cosmopolitan ideas. In 1913 he introduced the Stanislavski method of acting to Japan, and his efforts and influence are reflected in a Shochiku prospectus of the early 1920s:

> The main purpose of this company will be the production of artistic films resembling the latest and most flourishing styles of the Occidental cinema; it will distribute these both at home and abroad; it will introduce the true state of our national life to foreign countries; and it will assist in international reconciliation both here and abroad.*

Ito's first interest was the theater itself, and he even acted in a production of *The Lower Depths,* a popular play in Japan. He

---

* Joseph L. Anderson and Donald Richie, *The Japanese Film: Art and Industry* (New York: Grove Press, 1960), p. 41.

joined the Shochiku Cinema Institute as a scriptwriter and became a director in 1924. In 1926 he established a relationship with actor Denjiro Okochi and the two went to the film company Nikkatsu, where Ito developed his conception of the "superman" or "nihilistic samurai"—a figure still seen so many years later in such epics as Kurosawa's *Yojimbo*.

Ito's nihilist samurai was, as he describes him in the interview, a "frustrated hero" who no longer believes in the meaning and values of his world but revolts against them. Society, rather than any individual or group, becomes his enemy and the target of Ito's social satire. It was through the genre of the period film that Ito tried to express his own revolutionary ideas at a time when censorship was very severe in Japanese cinema. Since he couldn't quite achieve left-wing films under these conditions, Ito made what were called *Keiko Eiga*, or movies "inclined to the left."

Ito combined his social criticism with an amount of gore later to be equaled only in the most crass of *chambara*, or mindless sword films. He began this tendency in the Japanese film and achieved it with style. In his 1922 script for *Don't Fall in Love* a pair of lovers commit suicide. The scene was staged on the second floor so that their blood could drip through the ceiling and down onto the first landing. (The technique would be used again in 1973 in *Don't Look Now*, a British film with Donald Sutherland and Julie Christie. It could hardly be called a *chambara*, but incorporated nonetheless something of Ito's influence.) In Ito's script for *Going Through Darkness*, as Joseph L. Anderson and Donald Richie describe it in their history of the Japanese film, *The Japanese Film: Art and Industry*, "a hunchbacked hero throws himself on the funeral pyre of his beloved for a final flaming embrace."

Ito's serious work began in 1927 when he started to combine serious thematic development and intense social criticism with the violence of his earlier efforts. Anderson and Richie fix the evolution of the Ito period film, with Ito creating the figure of the nihilistic samurai *before* he developed his social critique:

> In showing the nihilistic hero it was still necessary to have something for the hero to be nihilistic about, and consequently Ito's films became more and more critical of society as a whole, thus paving the way in the period-film for the left-wing tendency pictures which were to come.*

---

* Ibid., p. 65.

Actually, the very creation of the figure of the nihilistic samurai stemmed from Ito's sense of social injustice. The social critique was implicit in his choice of such a hero, and the development of the social criticism in his films was a result of his maturing as an artist.

In *Servant* (1927) Ito began the attack on the feudalism of the Tokugawa period which would be one of the primary themes of his career. His criticisms of feudal Japan and the utter break of his heroes with its values were absolute. The ferocity of Ito's social satire remains unmatched in subsequent Japanese period epics which drew their impetus from his early example. Perhaps this is why Ito remarks in the interview that although there are directors whose work he has admired, "no one follows me." He used the period film as a vehicle through which to lash out at contemporary social injustice in the hope that major film company executives, ever the watchful censors, might miss the bitter edge of his satire if it were disguised beneath the accouterments of the costume drama set in Tokugawa times.

Ito was not always successful in this dissembling aim. As Anderson and Richie point out about *A Diary of Chuji's Travels* (1927), "In contradistinction to almost all prior period-heroes, the heroes of these films neither defended nor ignored the social system, but were instead in full revolt against it." * He created heroes who were single-minded, as Anderson points out in a *Cinema Journal* essay, "Japanese Swordfighters and American Gunfighters." The hero of Ito's *Ooka's Trail* (1928), for example, was "the *rōnin* named Sazan [who] sacrifices everybody—enemies, friends, bystanders, lovers, and police—who would hold him back from his determined goal. In the character of Sazen Tange, *giri* and *ninjo* † are united. He chooses to be dominated by one obligation which is also his single *ninjo:* revenge. According to the particular plot of a picture, Sazen seeks either to destroy his father's murderers or to avenge himself against those who have ousted him from his clan." ‡

In Ito's famous film *Man-Slashing, Horse-Piercing Sword,* released in 1930, his intense class consciousness can be easily discerned. The plot concerns the protagonist's search for the murderer

---

* Ibid.

† *Giri,* or "duty," and *ninjo,* or "inclination." The conflict between the two forms one of the major themes of the Japanese cinema.

‡ Donald Richie, *Japanese Cinema: Film Style and National Character* (Garden City, New York: Anchor Books, 1971), p. 46.

of his father. He must steal from farmers to survive, but later he helps them in their fight against corrupt government officials. The local overlord against whom he directs his efforts turns out to be the same man he has been seeking all along.

Ito has said that he doesn't believe that *Man-Slashing, Horse-Piercing Sword* influenced Kurosawa in his conception of the brilliant *Seven Samurai,* but the plots of the two films do bear striking similarities. In the Kurosawa film there are also peasants whose harvest is stolen by down-and-out samurai, who have become bandits to survive, like the hero of *Man-Slashing, Horse-Piercing Sword.* And the main theme of the Kurosawa film concerns the collective effort of seven *rōnin* who volunteer to dedicate their efforts to help the farmers defeat their enemies. Ito, of course, is a much more revolutionary thinker than Kurosawa. *Seven Samurai* mourns the passing of the samurai class and presents the farmers as selfish and egocentric, although more fit for survival, since they still perform a useful function in a society which has ceased to need samurai.

None of Kurosawa's films approve the ideal of most of Ito's best work: his belief that "the privileged class should be abolished." With such far-reaching and radical views, as Anderson and Richie have pointed out, Ito did much to teach the Japanese cinema how to think for itself, as well as how to become a unique and self-fulfilling artistic form. Richie in his *Japanese Cinema* has described Ito in terms of his place in period cinema, the richest genre of the Japanese film:

> Japanese cinema . . . offers a long and distinguished line of period films in which history is treated as contemporary. From Masahiro Makino's *The Street of Masterless Samurai* (*Roningai,* 1928) through the period films of Daisuke Ito, Hiroshi Inagaki, Mansaku Itami, Sadao Yamanaka, through Kurosawa's *Seven Samurai,* Kobayashi's *Hara Kiri,* (and) Shinoda's *Assassination,* the finest period pictures have been those in which the past is presented with a concern for detail and a feeling for actuality which most other countries reserve only for their films about contemporary life.*

Ito continued making period films throughout the Second World War. In 1942 he made *Kurama Tengu Appears in Yokohama* about a group of *rōnin* who break up a gang of smugglers. In 1944 he

---

* Ibid.

chose a similar plot with *International Smuggling Gang* set in the period when Yokohama had just been opened as a port. In keeping with the needs of wartime propaganda, the film showed the British running an opium smuggling ring which was used to subdue Japan.

After the war, Ito still made period films, including the huge box-office success *Five Men from Edo* (1951), which used devices which have since become clichés of the form and satisfied a huge postwar appetite for the genre. In 1950 he directed the first part of an adaptation of Victor Hugo's *Les Misérables,* aimed at the growing international market for Japanese films. It was by and large unsuccessful, although it did feature Sessue Hayakawa as Jean Valjean.

In the 1950s Ito remade several of his earlier successful period films. *Servant* became in 1955 *The Servant's Neck,* and in 1955 Ito also remade *The Life of a Woman in the Meiji Era,* the original of which was directed by Tomotaka Tasaka before the war. By this time Ito had long since become a commercial director of period films and these new efforts lacked the verve and passion of his earlier works. For this reason his fineness as a film stylist escaped critics who were heaping praise on younger directors. Richard N. Tucker, in *Japan: Film Image,* makes this point:

> Looking at his work today is still a shock, for not only are his actors superbly skilled in the handling of the curved blade but his audacious use of the camera is startingly modern. With a sure choreographic touch he slides his camera into furious battles, catches the essential action and pulls back again at high speed. Modern techniques have hardly improved on Ito's work.*

Recent *chambara,* such as the Zatoichi blind-samurai series, lack both the depth of commitment and the artistic energy of Ito's best films.

The interview with Ito, held at Ito's home in Kyoto, to which he has retired, was punctuated by cloudbursts and loud sounds of thunder. At one point he remarked, "The weather is rough today, like the assassination of Ryōma." With the years he has become somewhat deaf and this added to the difficulty of communication, although Ito spoke with vibrant enthusiasm about his long career. Reminiscing, he spoke of his youth, "gone forever with the good memories of Old Meiji," and quoted a little saying often recited by

---

* (London: Studio Vista, 1973), p. 113.

old-timers who grew up during the Meiji era (1868–1912): "*Furuki yoki Meiji wa toku narinikeri,*"—"Oh, good old memories, the Meiji era is gone, it only remains in our thoughts." He reflected a frequent nostalgia among people of his age for what are remembered as the sweet times of the Meiji period.

Daisuke Ito with the cast and crew of *Bakumatsu*. "If I had made *Bakumatsu* before the war, I wouldn't have been able to show the manner in which Ryōma Sakamoto was critical of the imperial system."

INTERVIEW WITH
DAISUKE ITO

Mellen: Can you tell me something about your family and educational background?

Ito: I come from a samurai family. My father was a vassal of the Tokugawa family. In 1868 he joined the Shôgitai, a force formed by the discontented Tokugawa vassals who were against the opening of the Edo castle. He was defeated in the battle. As a result his family had the misfortune of being broken up. From the time I was a child I was brought up in a samurai environment. When I was a boy my father told me the following story. When he reached the age of five, he was given a small sword; samurai were supposed to hold two swords, a large and a small. He was taught to kill anybody who would disgrace his family. He was also taught to kill himself with the very same sword in atonement for his sin after killing somebody. A five-year-old child doesn't know chalk from cheese. However, here lies the true spirit of hara kiri.

I was a lover of the drama from the time I was a teen-ager. When I was in high school I sent some of my works to Kaoru Osanai, who was a great leader of the *Shingeki,* or "new drama," and had founded two theaters in Tokyo. I began to correspond with him. After I graduated from high school I became his disciple and started my career as a scenario writer. At first I studied theatrical productions, but later when my master became an advisor to the Shochiku company, I also switched from the theater to the movies. There were moving pictures at that time, but no modern movies and dramas. At that time the Shochiku company was employing actresses for the first time in Japan. Before that all female characters had been impersonated by well-trained actors, as in the Kabuki theater.

Mellen: Why did you take up the "samurai" or period film so exclusively?

Ito: First of all, my family background explains this. Second, in those days all healthy young men plunged themselves into the left-wing movement. And they died one after another. I myself sympathized with left-wing ideas and so I wanted to be like them. However, my physical weakness prevented me from doing so. That's why I have survived until today. Moreover, I had no courage to

27

become involved on the left. At that time I was under the influence of Christianity. As a high school kid, I read and reread the Bible until I became a Christian, although I didn't go to church. I was a Christian until I was twenty or so. Then I began to harbor doubts about the teachings of Jesus Christ. They seemed to me too "just" and too strict. However it doesn't mean that I gave up Christianity completely. Even today I am not free from it, although *"old Meiji is gone."* * Third, I attempted to rebel against the political reality of Japan at the time under the mask of period pieces. At that time there was strong oppression and no freedom of expression. It was only through costume plays that I could incorporate revolutionary ideas into my films. I was basically a left-wing person, so naturally I put my ideas into practice by taking the theme of revolution in my works as a substitute for personal action.

Mellen: What would you say is the main theme in all your films?

Ito: My main theme, in a word, is class struggle. At present my works have lost significance because the situation has changed a great deal and people are enjoying freedom of thought. I am critical of the present left-wing movement. Young radicals of today are fickle and frivolous. They should be more thoughtful. I was an angry young man. However, with old age I have become cowardly.

Mellen: How would you describe your approach to film as an artist?

Ito: My principle is not to tell a lie—both in real life and in my work. I try to be honest and vehement. My life has been full of trials, the life of a struggle against oppression. I am also a doting writer and director. I dote on my characters. I can't see them calmly and objectively, for they are my own shadows. The heroes I created are all "frustrated heroes," whose ambitions were not achieved—be they samurai, merchants, or proletarians. I enjoy shedding sentimental tears with my heroes who fought with the world and died under an unlucky star. I find in them an outlet for my unrequited wrath. It is a sort of empathy. The spirit of the samurai and the teachings of Christ still dog my steps.

Mellen: What were your characters revolting against?

Ito: Against oppressive governmental power. I chose all my main characters from the common people—merchants, townspeople, etc. All are proletarians. In the case of samurai, they are mainly unemployed samurai or *rōnin*. Before the last war, governmental sup-

---

* What Ito means here is that he cannot help but retain the romantic values of his youth, including the ideals of Christianity, although the period of their currency, the early optimistic days of the Meiji resoration, is long gone.

pression of the arts was terrible. In one of my films the townspeople attacked the men bearing lanterns which signified that they were policemen. These lanterns bore the inscription *Goyoo,* or "on authority," and the men who carried them were obviously working for the Tokugawa government. People knew that my protagonists, who killed these men with lanterns, were cutting up police very much like those in their own towns. They cheered loudly. Before and during the war people were never allowed to express their hatred of the authoritarian power. Whatever the police said or did, the people obeyed. It was natural in this context that people would cheer the actions of common men revolting so freely against this tyrannical rule. In period films we were allowed to show such scenes.

Mellen: How would you contrast the ideas permitted before the war with those allowed after it?

Ito: If I had made *Bakumatsu* before the war, I wouldn't have been able to show the manner in which Ryōma Sakamoto was critical of the imperial system. Ryōma Sakamoto was a rebel whose dream was to bring down the oppressive Tokugawa rule and truly to emancipate people. Japanese commoners were heavily tied down by the class distinctions of *shi* (samurai), *nō* (farmers), *kō* (artisans), and *shō* (merchants).

Making *Bakumatsu* in 1970 I was able overtly to show Ryōma discussing his real dream of revolution—establishing a society that doesn't separate people on the basis of social class. His friend Nakaoka advises him not to mention such things before others or he will be assassinated by his own class. These words were the actual words of Sakamoto himself. He wrote, "I have such crazy ideas, and they try to assert themselves. They must be locked up in a jail." Such ideas would certainly not have been permitted in a film before the war.

At the beginning of *Bakumatsu* a townsman goes out into the rain in wooden clogs, although a member of his class was not permitted to wear clogs. A samurai mercilessly kills him merely because he does not act in accordance with his appropriate social standing. Ryōma realized at that time that his own samurai class should be abolished; he later extended this idea and came to the conclusion that both the emperor and the Tokugawa shogunate should also be overthrown. My belief in social equality runs as an undercurrent in all my films.

Mellen: Do you believe that Japanese society today needs another revolutionary figure like Ryōma?

Ito: I don't think there is an urgent need now. However, the society is changing fast. There is a strong tendency to believe that because the emperor is only a symbolic figure, with no real political power at all, we can do away with him. I am not suprised that a large number of people now believe this. Ryōma called for this a hundred years ago and we are still debating his words. At least now we have removed the image of the emperor as a living god. At the time of the restoration they overthrew the Tokugawas, but they raised the emperor to the same position; in the end it amounted to the same thing. Ryōma's question arose: What should we do with the emperor? He is indeed the frustrated hero in an exasperating era.

Mellen: Can you speak about some of your earliest films?

Ito: My films were labeled *Keiko Eiga,* films with a tendency toward the left rather than being strictly left-wing films. *Shinsei [New Life]* was my virgin film. It was Shochiku's first piece. This film described a young Catholic priest who was expelled from the church because of his love affair, and afterwards experienced the sweetness and bitterness of life. In the end he decided to devote himself to a labor movement. Since then I have produced about ninety films in fifty-one years. *Shinsei* represented my own new life. *Bakumatsu* [1970] is my latest film. It is two years old and I hadn't done a film for six or seven years before that. I am afraid it is a failure as a work of art. My physical condition made it impossible for me to do enough retakes to be satisfied with the results. This film suggests the abolition of the caste system, including the emperor system. Ryōma Sakamoto was assassinated because he spoke the truth. The film ends with the question of what will Japan do with the emperor after abolishing the feudal system. I myself don't find the Meiji restoration a source of progress for Japan. The Emperor Meiji was called a living god. He plunged the people into a dangerous war in which they fought in the name of the emperor. In this sense the Meiji restoration had a bad effect on Japan. At present I don't feel a need for individual revolution. I don't know what the statistics show. However, the political situation is changing and becoming better. Something, perhaps an invisible revolution, has been in progress. I support the emperor system under the new constitution, although I am basically against the class system. However, the present emperor is the symbol of the state and has no authority. Thus there is no *raison d'être* for him. And this is what Ryōma was concerned about one hundred years ago. Ryōma is also a frustrated hero. The last scene of *Bakumatsu* gives a vivid account of this. Ryōma fell after he received the fatal wound, but he managed to lift himself up once. I symbolized his spiritual rise in that scene. We did not do a very good job, and probably it failed to convey enough feeling.

Zanjin Zamba Ken [*Man-Slashing, Horse-Piercing Sword*, 1930] was a successful work. I don't think this had any effect on Kurosawa's *Seven Samurai* although many people say so. This was the first film that dealt with a peasant riot. The plot is as follows: one day a *rōnin* saw a persimmon tree and tried to get some persimmons with a bamboo pole. Then he found himself surrounded by poor peasants. He was regarded as a thief by them and dragged into the neighboring village with his arms lashed horizontally to the bamboo pole. In this village, which was ruled by a bad lord, he was badly maltreated. At the sight of this the peasants felt sorry for him and succeeded in helping him escape. This proved to be the beginning of their riot. In the end they won and peace was restored in their village. But in the last scene the *rōnin* suggests that this is not the end of the struggle. He says, "There is still a village beyond the mountains which must be mended like ours."

Rōnin Chuya [1930] is the story of two *rōnin* who plotted the overthrow of the Tokugawa government, and were detected and crucified. The slogan "the privileged classes must be done away with" was the order of the day. Chuya Marubashi was the samurai who inspired the revolt against the Tokugawa family in 1650. He was widely acknowledged as an excellent swordsman and a true samurai. He was joined by Shosetsu Yuhi, a man of letters, who especially excelled in the tactics of war. Their conspiracy was found out by spies of the Tokugawa government and both men were executed. However, their act was an inspiration to many silent, discontented men in Japan and the incident became the basis for a famous Kabuki play. Audiences especially cheered for Chuya Marubashi, who was rare in remaining a true samurai in a stifling era.

Among the other works taking up the revolutionary theme were *Gero* [*Servant*, 1927], *Issatsu-Tassho-ken* * [1929], *Konokubi Ichimangoku* † [1963, the last *Keiko Eiga*], *Hangyakuji*,‡ and so on.

Mellen: Have any of your films been censored?

---

* Literally, *Kill-One-Man, Let-Many-Live Sword*.

† Literally, *This Head Is Wanted for 10,000 Goku*, featuring the famous and popular period film actor Hashizo Okawa. During the Tokugawa era, each feudal lord was given land by the Tokugawas measured in terms of the amount of rice the land produced. The unit of income of the samurai class was the tax paid by the farmers in rice; the *goku* was the unit used to measure the rice and thus the size of the land.

‡ Literally, *Rebel* or *Rebels*.

Ito: There are very few films that escape censorship. I can't mention any particular one I feel most regretful about. Many of my films were cut to pieces. Period films were censored in many cases by the executives of the movie company itself, so there was no way to resist. One of my films that was censored was *Chikeburi-Takadanobaba* [1927]. The hero of this film is Yasubei Horibe, who belongs to Echigo, the present Niigata prefecture. Because he was critical of the policies of his clan, he was considered an outlaw. He left Echigo with some sake and a sake cup. On the way he happened to pass by a *Kôjin-sama* * on which was carved three monkeys, one of which holds its hands over its eyes, another over its ears, and the other over it mouth, symbolizing the precept "See no evil, hear no evil, speak no evil." When he saw it, he poured some sake over the *Kôjin-sama,* saying, "I have been mistaken so far. I'll correct my way of living. I'll close my eyes like this monkey, even if I don't like the ways of the world!" He started to leave but suddenly turned around. "Bakayaro!" ["You fool!" or "Damn you!"] he shouted, "I'll say wrong is wrong. I won't forgive whatever is wrong." And he threw his sake bottle onto the *Kôjin-sama.* This part was passed when the film was at the scenario stage, but not for the final version. They asked me where I got this idea. "Nowhere," was my answer. "I thought of it." "Such an idea can be found in the tactics of the Communist countries," was their assertion. This part was removed on the ground that I took advantage even of *Kôjin-sama* in order to inspire antireligious ideas, which, they asserted, stemmed from the secret ranks of the left wing. However, the *Benshi,* the narrator for silent films, was allowed to tell the whole story. Here is another example, which was censored by G.H.Q. after the war. *Osho* was the name of the film. This is the story of a man who was addicted to *Shôgi* [Japanese chess] and paid no attention to his family. That made his wife decide to commit a railroad suicide with their eight-year-old daughter. When they were walking on the railroad tracks they heard a train whistle in the distance. Then the little girl began to sing a song called "One Whistle at Shinbashi." The last line of

---

* *Kôjin-sama* are small stone carvings, which may take many shapes. Sometimes they are images of gods, sometimes of people, and sometimes of animals. The nature of this image worship entails a simple animism. When people felt the need for guardian spirits to protect them from the invasion of evil, they put these stone carved images in strategic areas. Many are placed along the roads to protect travelers. Every village used to have one in the shape of a small child to protect the village children against disease.

the second stanza of the song was frowned upon by the G.H.Q. of
the American occupation. The entire second stanza is as follows:

> On the right is Takanawa
> (Where there is) Sengaku-ji
> The grave of 47 *Rōnin*
> Snow still remains even after it has melted
> Their names will be remembered forever
> (for many generations to come)

At that time anything reminiscent of the old Japan was considered
undesirable for the democratization of Japan. In short, it was the
occupation's resistance to the old morals of Japan. As a matter of
fact, however, the context of the scene made it impossible to blue-
pencil the song. So they managed to deaden the song by making the
sound of the approaching train louder.

Mellen: Who are the directors, past and present, in the Japanese
film whom you have admired?

Ito: There is no film director who follows in my footsteps.
But politically I can sympathize with Imai, who produced *Bushido
Zankoku Monogatari* [*Bushido Samurai Saga,* 1963] recently. I
like Shinoda very much, and he likes me, although historically we
don't have very much in common. He is not a left-wing man. He is
more of an artist. He loves films to such an extent that he steeps
himself in them. He is a hard worker and his study is not superfi-
cial. He doesn't try to reveal social questions but rather exposes hu-
manity. Technically, I, an old man, am no match for him. Satsuo
Yamamoto is another man whose work I like. He is definitely left-
wing. He has his own production company and is doing a pretty
good job in spite of his poverty. He is strong and steady as a person
and so are his ideas, although I may be praising him too much. One
of his recent works is *Sensô-jyo.*

Mellen: What is your opinion of Kurosawa's work?

Ito: He is, of course, an artist, although he hasn't much to do with
left-wing ideas.

Mellen: Don't you think Kurosawa has made films that are critical
of social injustice?

Ito: I think that underlying all his work is Dostoevski with his love
for mankind. This surfaces from time to time in Kurosawa's work.
He has a definite hatred for social injustice and he has said many
times that he is protesting against the social evils inflicted upon his
fellow human beings, but I cannot classify him as a left-wing direc-
tor. My theme is personal rebellion and its defeat. My main charac-
ters were all defeated by the weight of the time. [Laughs]

Mellen: Even though it does not succeed, you show the need to rebel.

Ito: Yes. But probably I am too involved with the fate of my characters. My heart and tears are wholly with them. I cannot detach myself as Kurosawa does. Kurosawa's objectivity separates my work from his. The tragedies of my characters overwhelm me. For this reason, I consider Kurosawa a finer artist than I.

Mellen: So you love the main characters in your films too much?

Ito: That is right. I enjoy crying with them and crying for them. I know that their dreams are never to be fulfilled. So, I cry for them. In this way I sublimate my anger. It reflects again my personal life: I have always been thwarted by physical weakness. I could not go forward under my own flag, so to speak; I had to say something in my own way. My works are reflections of my life. The characters I produce in my scripts and on screen are my children. I love them intensely.

Mellen: Nagisa Oshima is considered to be the most radical political filmmaker of the contemporary Japanese cinema.

Ito: I don't value him so highly. In his case, will takes precedence. He is self-satisfied and has more ideas than skill. Moreover, his films are difficult for us to understand, and much more so for foreigners. Compared to Oshima, Yamamoto has solid skills and is a mature person. His political thinking is solid, also, although at times his ideas come on too strongly.

Mellen: Among foreign directors who has interested you?

Ito: I like Eisenstein, Chaplin, and so on.

Mellen: How do you see the future of the Japanese film?

Ito: Good films cannot be produced by the present big movie companies. It is hard, however, to depend only on art theaters. But however small a production company may be, I respect it as long as it produces a good film. It would be ideal to make a film in a production company of one's own, even on a small scale.

Mellen: Have you ever set up your own production company?

Ito: I set up my own productions twice in the early Showa period [around 1926]. Each time I did, it was forcibly crushed. I had a hard time of it. Since then I haven't made the same attempt. As far as the adaptation of period films to the theater is concerned, everything is going well. It is easier to present them in the theater because I write a scenario taking the limitations of the stage into consideration anyway. The greatest difficulty I had in making a big film was my poor health. In the TV age, another difficulty lies in the decision regarding the cast. It is hard to get together actors and actresses who are suitable for television.

Mellen: In what have you been interested in recent years? How do you see contemporary Japanese society?

Ito: I have been very interested in the problem of public hazards. The Ashio Copper Mine copper poisoning incident (1891–1906) caught my attention very early and has since developed into a major social problem. And labor disputes arose after that in 1907, 1919, and 1921. Shôzô Tanaka, a member of the Diet, plus the sufferers, presented the case to the Diet and clashed with the police and the army. I wanted to make a film about this, but I couldn't. Now I can't bring myself to do it because it is the talk of the town and is taken up by the newspapers every day.

TWO

AKIRA
KUROSAWA

INTRODUCTION

With the deaths of Kenji Mizoguchi in 1956 and of Yasujiro Ozu and Mikio Naruse in the sixties, Akira Kurosawa remains the sole living master of the Japanese film. In the West his reputation ranks with those of the greatest practitioners of cinema: John Ford, Orson Welles, Luis Buñuel, and Roberto Rossellini. It was through the works of Kurosawa, which seem so "Western" to the occidental audience, that the Japanese film first became known abroad.

Even with the current rise to prominence of Ozu, Kurosawa is still the symbol of the Japanese film at its best. It is possible to draw a line from Kurosawa's finest film, *Seven Samurai* (1954), which Donald Richie has called the greatest Japanese film ever made, back to Daisuke Ito's *Man-Slashing, Horse-Piercing Sword* (1930). But if Ito created the genre of the *jidai-geki*, Kurosawa perfected the form and gave it so deep a historical resonance that each of his *jidai-geki* has contained within it the entire progress of Japan from feudal to modern times.

Kurosawa's first film, *Sanshiro Sugata* (1943), was also a *jidai-geki* and was made during the war. Since then he has completed twenty-four films, with *Dodes'ka-den* in 1970 his first in color. Kurosawa became known abroad only with *Rashomon* (1950), which, against the wishes of the Daiei film company for whom it was made, was sent to the Venice Film Festival of 1951. Japanese critics, fearing Western condescension, attributed *Rashomon*'s receiving the Golden Lion for best film to its "exoticism." Even

Akira Kurosawa on the set of *Sanjuro*.

37

today the film retains only a minimal reputation in Japan among film people.

Together with *Seven Samurai,* Kurosawa is personally most fond of *Ikiru* (1952), the story of a government bureaucrat who, upon learning that he has terminal cancer, decides to perform one meaningful act before his death. Cutting through red tape, he builds a playground for neighborhood children in what was a disease-breeding swamp.

One of the best of the Japanese film critics, Tadao Sato, has said that Kurosawa's work suffered a marked decline after *Record of a Living Being* (1955), his film about a man's fear of a new atomic attack on Japan. Sato argues that Kurosawa relied afterward upon the "superman" samurai, leaving behind his earlier ethical concerns. It is an opinion echoed by the English critic Richard N. Tucker in *Japan: Film Image:*

> A close regard for the central characters within Kurosawa's world will show that in every case there is a relationship which is in essence feudal. The master-pupil situation, one in which values of humanist tendencies are slowly absorbed by the pupil through observation of the master, is central to each of the films culminating in what is probably Kurosawa's greatest film, *Red Beard.**

Sato, of course, locates Kurosawa's finest work in the period of *Seven Samurai,* but he displays, in common with Tucker, an uneasiness about the films of the late fifties. Tucker, in particular, has difficulty with what Richie has praised as the "humanism" of Kurosawa. Tucker even goes so far as to challenge Richie's contention that Kurosawa's ethical preoccupation and feeling for the distinctive value of the ordinary man are deeper than those of Kobayashi and Ichikawa. According to Tucker, "There are other film-makers who have a clearer regard for the individual in Japanese society, the individual free from the constraints of a feudal relationship" † than Kurosawa. He cites Ichikawa and Kobayashi, but his argument could perhaps be made more effectively through a different contrast. Kurosawa, preeminently a man of his generation, can be distinguished from directors like Hani and Oshima, who aspire to expose feudal remnants within *contemporary* Japan.

Careful attention reveals, Sato's schema notwithstanding, that much of Kurosawa's most subtle and deeply felt social criticism is

---

* (London: Studio Vista, 1973), p. 83.
† Ibid.

to be found in his work designated by Sato as exhausted in sensibility and theme. At least three masterpieces, *Yojimbo* (1961), *Sanjuro* (1962), and *High and Low* (1963), occur within this period. In *Yojimbo* and *Sanjuro* Kurosawa discovers Japan through critical moments of transition in Japanese history when decaying values have lost their universal acceptance and new modes have neither clearly emerged nor fully displaced the old. *High and Low,* unlike the others, is set in the present and recalls the vibrant Marxism of Kurosawa's youthful work, *No Regrets for Our Youth* (1946). It depicts the inevitable hostility in modern capitalist society between rich and poor, "high and low."

A young medical intern, intending to abduct the son of a wealthy shoe manufacturer, accidentally kidnaps the chauffeur's son but demands the ransom money nonetheless. The sum is so high that it would ruin Gondo, the businessman. Tested in this manner, he decides to ransom the boy. But in so doing, he transcends his class role and recreates his own humanity.

Sato has accused Kurosawa of an incongruity in this film. He contends that the intern, assured of a lucrative and prestigious station upon the completion of his training, would not risk a certain future in a futile act. Kurosawa is more subtle and penetrating than his critics. He conveys both the psychology of desperation and the embittering disillusionment of the young intern who must gaze up at Gondo's extravagant, inaccessible white mansion from his miserable three-tatami room. Stifling in summer and freezing in winter, he is incensed by the suffering he now experiences and can no longer aspire to a high place in the social hierarchy. It is present pain that fuels his hatred for Gondo.

After *Red Beard* (1965) five years elapsed before Kurosawa's next film, *Dodes'ka-den*. It lacks a linear narrative line, but instead contains many small episodes in the lives of Japan's poor who live as neighbors in a slum. Japanese critic Masahiro Ogi greeted it as a "song of fantasy" in his "Kurosawa, *Dodes'ka-den* and Japanese Culture," which appeared in *Kinema Jumpo:*

> . . . it is a fairy tale in which all the smells of the real world have been eliminated. In this deodorized and objectified microcosm, an ardent affection for humanity crystalizes in the beauty of gratuitous love: this is Kurosawa's new achievement. It strives to make its exaggerations seem natural but it is completely different from naturalistic realism.

Through a non-naturalistic use of color, theatrical painted sets, and stylized acting Kurosawa finds an aesthetic equivalent for the lives

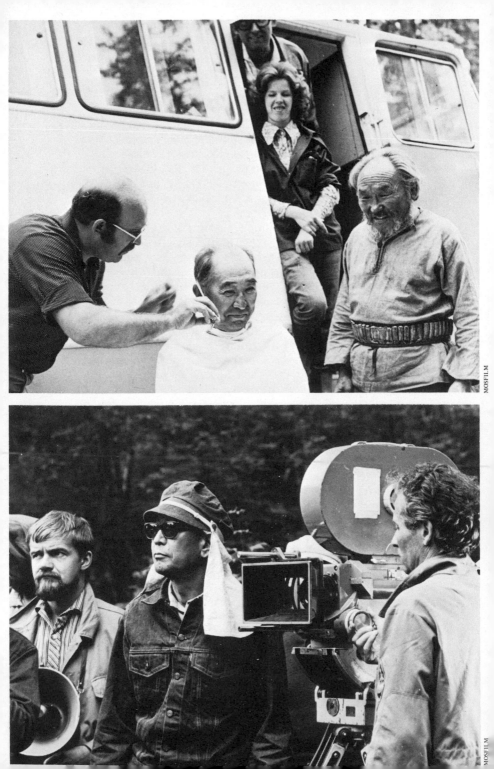

of his characters, people for whom illusion has replaced the harsh
and unbearable realities of the "objective" world.

Kurosawa has said that the greatest influence upon his work has
been John Ford, and many critics have been overly quick to assert
that Kurosawa produces "Westerns" in a Japanese setting. But
Kurosawa's influence upon foreign directors has been far more
profound. *The Magnificent Seven,* John Sturges's remake of *Seven
Samurai,* is one obvious example. Another is Sergio Leone's *A
Fistful of Dollars,* derived from *Yojimbo.*

Kurosawa has no direct disciples in Japan, further evidence of
his uniqueness as a director; but his influence continues to pervade
the Japanese film. If younger directors like Masahiro Shinoda de-
clare their autonomy from a master like Kurosawa, Shinoda's *As-
sassination,* a *jidai-geki* set at the time of the Meiji restoration,
would nonetheless have been inconceivable without him. Even the
rhythmic sound of the coffin maker in Shinoda's *Buraikan* recalls
the hammering of coffins in Kurosawa's *Yojimbo,* set also during
the last days of the Edo * period. Those like Kihachi Okamoto,
who have turned out *jidai-geki* according to pattern, have even used
Kurosawa's Toshiro Mifune in their starting roles, hoping that the
resonance he achieved in the Kurosawa films would rub off on their
own.

And directors like Daisuke Ito, with humility, point out that
while they too made *jidai-geki,* it was Kurosawa who raised the
form to an art. Masaki Kobayashi is perhaps the cleverest of the re-
cipients of Kurosawa's influence. Kobayashi's *Rebellion* and *Hara
Kiri,* both dramas excoriating the outrages and injustice of feudal
Japan, would have been unthinkable without him.

Although Kurosawa has been compared to Ozu by critics such as
Tucker as the "left" in contrast to Ozu's "right," Kurosawa as
often affirms Japanese values as he revolts against them. He is not
an opponent of tradition per se, but is rather concerned to distin-
guish the cultural and moral values of Japanese history and identity
from the social institutions that deform them. Ozu, for that matter,
does not lend himself to so schematic a formula. If Ozu mourns the

---

* The Tokugawa period (1603–1868) is also known as the Edo period since the
Tokugawas made their capital at Edo (now Tokyo).

Kurosawa on the set of *Dersu Uzala* in the U.S.S.R., 1974. Looking on
(*above*) is Maxim Munzuk, who plays the title role.

fixed roles of the past in comparison with the disarray and cultural decay of the industrial present, it is not without an ironic attitude toward those rigidly encased in the old ways.

Kurosawa is thus only superficially "Western" in his themes. The clash between "appearance and reality" or "seeming and being," categories through which Donald Richie has viewed Kurosawa, represent but one strand of his art. Equally, his admiration for Russian writers and Dostoevski in particular, and his having filmed both *The Idiot* and *The Lower Depths,* is but one facet of his work. Kurosawa transcends all easy categories. He is one of the few artists to achieve international communication while at the same time remaining true to his own highly distinctive and insular national culture.

INTERVIEW WITH
AKIRA KUROSAWA

Mme. Kawakita: Mr. Kurosawa finds what Japanese critics have been saying about him very strange.*

Mellen: Not what I have written or said in that debate? Oh, that is good! Mr. Sato was so angry with my views about you that he brought back three books he had originally intended to give me as gifts. [Laughter from everyone] To be appreciated by foreigners has made your situation in Japan difficult, hasn't it?

Kurosawa: Yes, to some extent I have to agree with you about that.

Mellen: Do you feel *Dodes'ka-den* represents a new direction in your work, or does it recapitulate earlier moral concerns?

Kurosawa: I think the film arose out of the latter. The production and theme were conceived very naturally. Approaching a more mature age myself, and with the world situation being what it is at this time, the idea grew within me. I did not intend to create something new or something unfamiliar to me.

Mellen: Is the character of Mr. Tamba in *Dodes'ka-den* a correction of the old pilgrim Luka in *The Lower Depths?*

Kurosawa: No, I don't think so. The original plays are two different things, written by different writers with intentions of expressing two different points of view. I consider Tamba to be quite a different person, having a different soul from Luka's. I didn't have *The Lower Depths* in mind while I was making this film.

Mellen: To me, Tamba is a much more realistic force than Luka was regarding the problems of the slum people. Confronted by similar situations, Luka tells the people to have faith that their lives can be different while Tamba accepts the problems and the people as they are.

Kurosawa: I see it this way. Luka and Tamba are quite different. To me, Luka is not really a good, honest person. I detect a dark side, probably something that happened to him in his past. Compared to Luka, Tamba is an artisan who has lived every day honestly. He has matured as an honest, good fellow throughout his life, and he has reached the position of the mature, experienced elder.

---

* A debate about the current status of the Japanese film in which I participated with Nagisa Oshima, Tadao Sato, and Michitaro Tada in Kyoto, August, 1972.

43

Mellen: Yet it is ironic that in *The Lower Depths* it is the landlord, an evil character, who tells us that Luka is not such a good man. We doubt his judgment somehow.

Kurosawa: Yes.

Mellen: Is there any reason why you did not use color in your previous films with the exception of that one puff of smoke in *High and Low?* Are your moral concerns better expressed in black and white than in color?

Kurosawa: Yes, to some extent. However, I felt that I was a novice regarding color and my cameramen did not seem to know color very well either. Now I am more familiar with the use of color and I have met a brilliant cameraman named Takao Saito who has been diligently researching the right color techniques. My own volition and his coincided, so we produced the film in color.

Mme. Kawakita: Kurosawa is very particular and very exact about color. He is also a painter.

Mellen: I understand that you are deeply interested in Dostoevski. But Dostoevski at the end of his novels always tried to reconcile the reader to very orthodox, conservative ideas such as the Russian Orthodox Church or Russian patriotism. You never give an easy answer in your films. What attracted you to Dostoevski?

Kurosawa: I am no authority on Dostoevski. I am an admirer of his, but if I may say so, I don't think he is religious deep down in his heart. He appears to be very religious on the surface, however.

Mellen: I showed *The Idiot* to my students. They liked individual scenes, certain moments, but couldn't put the film together as a whole. Is it correct to see *Yojimbo, High and Low,* and *The Bad Sleep Well* as anticapitalist films delineating the endemic corruption of big business?

Kurosawa: [Laughing] Well, I did not want to say so formally. I always have many issues about which I am angry, including capitalism. Although I don't intend explicitly to put my feelings and principles into the films, these angers slowly seep through. They naturally penetrate my filmmaking.

Mellen: Tadao Sato mentioned that you were a Marxist before the war.

Kurosawa: In my youth the situation of society was much worse than it is now. I experienced being a sort of Marxist. It was very fashionable among the youth. For one thing, we couldn't get jobs after graduation from the university. There was a fever among young people. They did not know how to use their energies. I would say that almost all the intellectual urban youth in that period were at one time or another Marxists. They were not satisfied with the government and its policies. I was one of them. In reflection, we were also enjoying the thrill of being Marxists. But it is doubtful that I was a true Marxist, although I had that tendency.

Mme. Kawakita: What about now?

Kurosawa: I still lean toward these ideas. I probably have Marxist ideas somewhere in me. When I was involved in the Marxist movement I fell ill. I sort of dropped out as a young Marxist because of my health. I had to stay in bed for about one year. During that period literally all of my Marxist friends were arrested and dispersed. This occurred before I was twenty years old. I guess I was about eighteen.

Mellen: Such feelings are still manifest in a film like *No Regrets for Our Youth.*

Kurosawa: I became sort of nostalgic for the time of my youth after I saw it recently. I missed this period of my life while I was making that film.

Mellen: Did you wish to be back again?

Mme. Kawakita: No, he just became nostalgic.

Kurosawa: Almost all the Japanese film directors who are my contemporaries were more or less Marxists and had similar experiences. The only two who remained Communists until now are Satsuo Yamamoto, who made *War and Peace* [*Senso to Heiwa,* 1947], and Imai Sho-chan.* I guess these two are the only ones. The rest of us are all ex-Communists.

Mellen: Yes, but Tadashi Imai seems to have forgotten how to make movies. [Kurosawa and Mme. Kawakita laugh.]

Mme. Kawakita: What film do you have in mind?

Mellen: The most recent film about young navy recruits sent to Iwo Jima. That was embarrassing.

Mme. Kawakita: [to Kurosawa] She was not impressed at all. She is talking about *Kaigun Tokubetsu Nenshôhei* [*Eternal Cause*].

Kurosawa: I have not seen it yet.

Mellen: I wanted to sympathize with it before I saw the film, but I could not. It was too simplistic. I think Kobayashi is more modern and mature.

Kurosawa: Where films are concerned, if you set out to convey some special message or thesis you will become narrow and rigid. I think it is true for any other creative work as well.

Mellen: One of my debates with Mr. Sato regarded the role of the

---

* Tadashi Imai. *Chan* is a Japanese endearment used for close friends, children, etc. *Sho* is the nickname for Tadashi.

police in *High and Low*. I argued that the police detective played by Tatsuya Nakadai was so anxious to capture the criminal that he did not care about how many people died or how much damage he did. All he wanted was to nail the criminal. He was therefore responsible for the death of the woman who died of drug poisoning. He himself was cruel in his belief that since Gondo had lost his money, the criminal must pay with his life. But Mr. Sato argued that the detective was thoroughly dedicated to his duty and his devotion to his job would justify his behavior. Which do you think more nearly correct?

Kurosawa: I better tell you the background of this film. The original book was written by Ed McBain. It was not particularly well written. But the setting of the story was shocking to me. If someone can perform a kidnapping on that basis, he could simply snatch any child and demand that the nation or the prime minister pay the ransom. It would create an entirely new technique for this kind of crime. Moreover, Japanese criminal laws against kidnapping are very lenient. They don't pay much attention to the lives of the victims. I felt that I had to do something about this situation. To stress this point I had to make the pursuit by the police very cruel, and very severe. In some cases I have felt myself that the pursuit was too relentless.

Mellen: I see, so I was wrong. [Laughs]

Kurosawa: I certainly agree with your point that the police detective used inhuman methods to track down the criminals. These were part of an overreaction, but the nature of the crime was extremely cruel, and clever in the worst sense.

Mellen: Yet you also show so much sympathy in the film toward the kidnapper.

Kurosawa: It is very funny, but I just cannot help it. I always think even the worst criminal should have his say. I tried to avoid these sympathetic feelings, but this much slipped from my hand. Originally I tried various types of music while Yamazaki, the kidnapper, was walking toward his house. Well, some other music I chose to be heard over the radio in that scene evoked much more sympathy so that the audience would really feel, "Oh, what a helpless fellow." I finally settled on the *Trout* of Schubert. It was not my real intention to make the criminal sympathetic, but as a director it came naturally to me to be sympathetic toward an oppressed person. As a result, the effect was not one of total detachment, was it? [Laughs]

Mme. Kawakita: So you had understanding and sympathy for his background and his misfortune?

Takashi Shimura as Watanabe in Kurosawa's *Ikiru*.

Kurosawa: Partially. But one of the main reasons why I could not hate him enough was the fact that I had used Yamazaki to play that role. He had a very strong personality and it was his first screen role. He was a small figure in a theatrical company up to this time. He was so fresh and energetic that I did not want to repress these qualities. I experienced the same thing when I made *Drunken Angel.* In that movie Mifune was playing a no-good man, but his charm, energy, and freshness overtook the main theme, even overshadowing Shimura's role. I couldn't suppress Mifune and his part became bigger and bigger. I wonder if any director could for that matter. I saw the same quality in Yamazaki. Well, if you try to be sadistic toward this man, you really cannot help being also a little bit sympathetic. I simply couldn't help it.

Mellen: It is very interesting. His personality takes over the film at the end.

Kurosawa: In a way, these happenings are miscalculations on my part. Both Mifune and Yamazaki made their debuts in these films, and I knew that their freshness and personalities were not to be ignored. They were so overwhelming that I couldn't control them. The audience caught on right away and sympathized with them. I should say that when the forms of drama are altered because of the actors' personalities it should be considered the director's fault, his miscalculation. Probably I was wrong. I should have started out from the planning stage itself and considered the actor's personality more carefully. This is my view in retrospect.

Mme. Kawakita: I don't think as a critic and a spectator that it should be called a miscalculation.

Mellen: No, I don't think so either. It made *High and Low* a masterpiece.

Kurosawa: Well, at least I followed my own natural feelings. I hope you are right.

Mellen: With this ambiguity, the end of the movie imparted another, larger dimension to the story. The final outcome pleased me very much.

Kurosawa: Let me tell you one backstage story about that ending scene. Actually I shot another scene after the confrontation between Mifune and Yamazaki in the prison. We shot some long footage

Toshiro Mifune in *Seven Samurai* (*above*) and *Record of a Living Being* (*below*). "I wanted to say that after everything the peasants were the stronger, closely clinging to the earth. . . . It is the samurai who were the weak because they were being blown by the winds of time."

showing Nakadai and Mifune walking while thinking about Yama-
zaki. The two were full of unhappy feelings, despite having suc-
ceeded in their mission. To take this scene, we had made a huge
set. They were about to part and they felt his shadow behind them.
They couldn't forget him.

Yoichi Matsue [assistant Director for *High and Low* and producer of
Dodes 'ka-den; he had accompanied Kurosawa to the interview.]:
Yes, we had spent about two weeks on this scene. But Mr. Kuro-
sawa felt that the scene between Yamazaki and Mifune in the jail is
really the end of the picture so he decided not to use the additional
scene.

Mellen: The detective must leave the film at the moment when
Mifune and Nakadai, Detective Tokura, walk down the corridor of
the prison. The people who are cleaning the floor bow their heads
because the detective represents the control of society over all poor
people who are like the prisoner. That is his moral role and he can
be no more than that; the image sums up his identity. The last
confrontation in the film must be between Mifune and the kidnap-
per. The detective's role is finished. The problem of the remainder
of the film is between these two other people: the kidnapper and his
victim.

Kurosawa: At the time Yamazaki was cut off, and Mifune's face
remained reflected in the glass, I knew that I had said all I wanted
to say. So I cut off all the remaining scenes, which were superflu-
ous. My assistant art director scolded me. [Laughs]

Mellen: Was Nakadai unhappy with that conclusion?

Kurosawa: I should think so, because I focused on Mifune alone.
[Laughs]

Mellen: Here is another argument that I had. Mr. Tada said that the
end of *Seven Samurai,* when the peasants begin their song and plant
their rice, represents a return to peasant tradition. Do you agree
with that?

Mme. Kawakita: Do you know Mr. Tada?

Kurosawa: No, I don't know him. I have read what he wrote about
my films again and again, but I do not understand what he meant.
He said something to the effect that the peasants were a weak lot
and that they were stupid. On the contrary, I wanted to say that
after everything the peasants were the stronger, closely clinging to
the earth. Rather, it is the samurai who were weak because they
were being blown by the winds of time. They won the battle for the
peasants, but then they were dismissed and went away. The peas-
ants remained to till the earth. I made Shimura say at the end, "We

have lost again." So I thought I laid out my thoughts rather plainly. However, Mr. Tada and Mr. Sato insist that my view toward the peasants is otherwise. I just don't understand them.

Mme. Kawakita: Isn't that the Mr. Sato who wrote that the peasant is stupid in Kurosawa's view?

Matsue: That is right.

Mellen: I am very glad to hear that.

Mme. Kawakita: It must be some kind of misunderstanding. Is it true he wrote such things in his book?

Mellen: I had the feeling that whatever I said, he would say the opposite. He didn't want to occupy the same critical space.

Kurosawa: There is one more thing I should like to add. Many critics try overly to elucidate my ideas or intention. They try to nail down every scene with an explanation. I object to this practice. The film is a whole entity. I don't know myself what my message is within a particular sequence. There are scenes which I play down, not saying anything, or rather, in which I conceal my real view. But somewhere in the film the director's real intention surfaces. On many occasions I myself am completely unaware of this expression in a particular scene. Well, sometimes my peasants act silly, being real peasants. Sometimes they may act like warriors, but this is not my real concept in that film. I almost consider this attitude of critics disrespectful. I have been dismissed by many of them. It is a strange attitude among Japanese film critics. They analyze films too easily, saying that my intention was such-and-such. Japanese critics like to put me in one category and dismiss my films in this way. I have felt that my works are more nuanced and complex, and they have analyzed them too simplistically. [Laughs]

Mellen: In *Seven Samurai* the samurai are able to go beyond their social class by helping the peasants. I may be wrong, but is the help of the samurai for the peasants the result of a moment in history when they can transcend their class? Is it simply because they have no alternative?

Mme. Kawakita: Right. Out of their compassion for the peasants, they helped them, going beyond their class role.

Kurosawa: Yes, in the end they helped the peasants because they had to. However, in the beginning their intentions were mixed. The samurai were preoccupied with themselves, not so much with helping the peasants out of compassion. Kikuchiyo, played by Mifune, was the ideal go-between—the samurai brought up among peasants. As time went on, both sides, samurai and peasants, had come down to the very basic human condition where they had to fight together

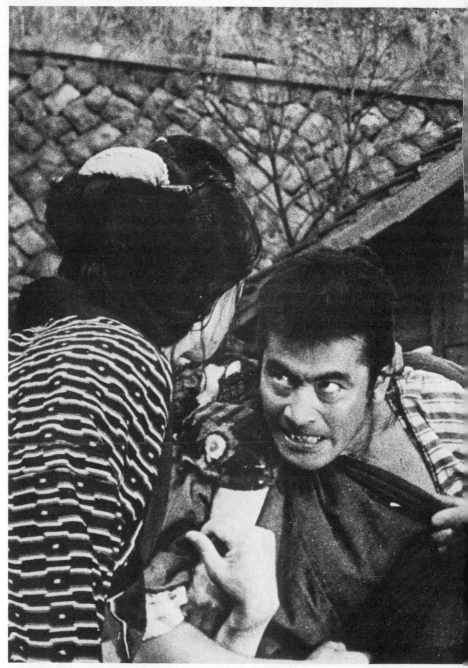

Toshiro Mifune in *The Lower Depths*. "It is a strange attitude among Japanese film critics. They analyze films too easily, saying that my intention was such-and-such. Japanese critics like to put me in one category and dismiss my films in this way. I have felt that my works are more nuanced and complex, and they have analyzed them too simplistically."

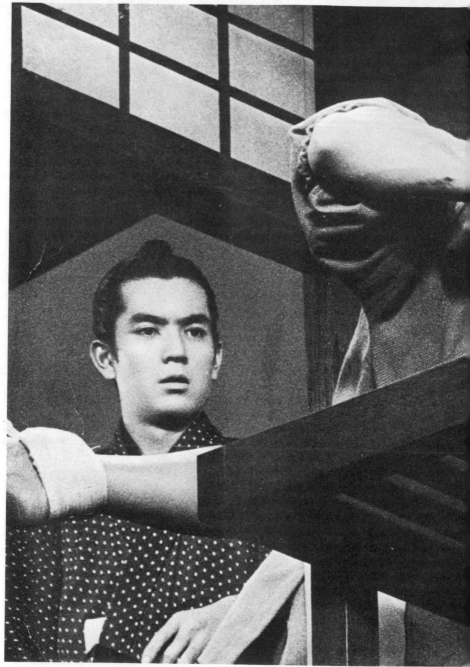

TOHO INTERNATIONAL

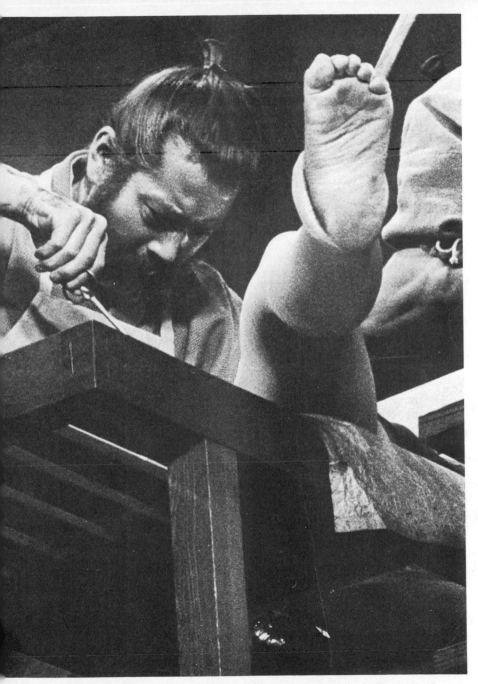
Mifune as Red Beard. His disciple, played by Yuzo Kayama, looks on.

to fend off an enemy. Do you remember the battles in the hard rain? Everybody had to fight for himself. They all melted into the same class.

Mellen: In the very beginning of the film isn't Shimura able to change his class when he cuts his braid to save the baby? Isn't he already going beyond the samurai distinction?

Kurosawa: Not so. Being a samurai, although he was a jobless *rōnin*, he had the natural moral obligation to help the peasants under that circumstance. [A baby had been kidnapped by a thief and held hostage in a small hut.] As the samurai class is superior to any other, they felt the duty of being guardians of society. So when the commoners could not handle a situation, they had to use their good judgment.

Mellen: I see. It was still a reflection of the old samurai code, of *bushido.*

Kurosawa: Right. The samurai class had sort of a moral code to help the helpless.

Mellen: But some samurai had refused to help the group of peasants.

Kurosawa: I was revealing there the worst side of the samurai class. Some ambitious samurai were naturally intent on only advancing their own careers and did not pay any attention to the weak and the needy. At the time there were many samurai who were traveling all over Japan in order to find better employment under more powerful lords. These seven samurai are the real samurai, but in the worldly sense there was something missing in them because they couldn't get jobs and further their careers.*

Mellen: The thing that was "lacking" in them was a moral center.

Kurosawa: These seven samurai were the real samurai who responded to need. They were the truly good samurai.

Mellen: Here is a question which has interested me for a long time. Many of your films like *Yojimbo* deal with transitional moments in history when old values are no longer useful and new values have not yet come into being. Is this a conscious theme in your films? Is

---

* The era was the end of the sixteenth century; right after, the old regime of Toyotomi was defeated by the rising Tokugawa clan, which ruled Japan from 1603 to 1868. During the unsettling takeover period, most powerful clans in Japan were forced to take sides, and after the decisive battles were won by the Tokugawas, nearly half of the samurai on the defeated Toyotomi side were thrown out into the world without employment. Thus, many samurai were forced to search for new masters. Many unemployed samurai, no doubt with low moral discipline and status, became bandits out of the sheer struggle for survival.

Toshiro Mifune visits Kurosawa in Arseniev, U.S.S.R., 1974. At the right, Yoichi Matsue, producer of *Dersu Uzala*.

this treatment of transitional societies a means of drawing parallels to contemporary Japanese society? Did you have such an intention in making *Yojimbo?*

Kurosawa: Well, my original idea in making *Yojimbo* was much simpler. I was so fed up with the world of the *Yakuza.** So in order to attack their evil and irrationality, and thoroughly mess them up, I brought in the super-samurai played by Mifune. He was himself an outsider, a kind of outlaw, which enabled him to act flexibly, if sometimes recklessly. Only such a samurai of the imagination, much more powerful than a real samurai, could mess up these gangsters. The film sort of evolved from there. [Laugh]

Mellen: Do these gangsters represent what the society will become in the future? Isn't the *yojimbo,* or bodyguard, a moral spirit reacting against the process of history?

---

* Gangsters, similar to the Mafia here. They were traditionally illegal gamblers with a long history of possessing an underground world of their own.

Kurosawa: In this period the samurai themselves had gone through quite a change. The samurai in *Yojimbo* is not the same as the samurai in *Seven Samurai*. During the peaceful era of Tokugawa those who had secured their jobs long ago had ceased to be warriors. They had become administrators or white-collar workers, what we would call "salaried men." Those who were out of jobs were to remain permanently unemployed. Their hope had completely vanished. So they had to take a job, any job available, and some became the bodyguards of gamblers.

Mellen: Wasn't the *yojimbo* looked down upon by the peasants at the beginning of the film when he came into the village? He is referred to as a "dog" by one of the peasants.

Kurosawa: The villagers at first thought he was another samurai or jobless *rōnin* who would probably bring more harm to their lives and that he would be employed by the gamblers. So they detested him.

Mme. Kawakita: Mr. Kurosawa is tired after the operation. Perhaps we should stop for now.

Mellen: Oh, I completely understand. You know, there is so much I would love to discuss with you. It's a rare opportunity.

THREE

MME. KASHIKO
KAWAKITA

INTRODUCTION

The Towa Company is the largest organization dedicated to importing foreign films into Japan. But Towa is more than just a commercial apparatus for the distribution of films. It has set itself the cultural tasks of making Japanese cinema known and valued abroad and of introducing foreign cinema to an insular Japan.

It was founded in 1928 by Nagamasa Kawakita, who had studied in China and in Europe, where he had been struck by the provincialism characterizing the Japanese approach to things foreign. And so he began to import Western films to Japan, an activity in which he is still engaged.

Kawakita has also, in his long career, been sensitive to the stereotyped attitude of Westerners toward Japan. Joseph L. Anderson and Donald Richie point out, in their history of the Japanese film, that when Japanese films were first being considered for foreign audiences, Kawakita urged that "the first exported Japanese films should be travelogues and that subsequent non-travelogue features should insist upon an amount of scenery," * so alien and exotic did things Japanese seem to Westerners.

Kawakita's wife, Mme. Kashiko Kawakita, is one of the most remarkable women of Japanese—or of any—culture. Of a generation when the very idea and possibility of women taking public initiative was unheard of, she has been the single most significant fig-

---

* Joseph L. Anderson and Donald Richie, *The Japanese Film: Art and Industry* (New York: Grove Press, 1960), p. 23.

Mme. Kashiko Kawakita.

ure in shaping the taste of Westerners toward Japan through its remarkable cinema. She has been the force at Towa, openly acknowledged, who has personally taken the most important Japanese films for critical viewing abroad, as she has selected European and American films for import into Japan. Working as her husband's partner and equal, she has transcended every social pressure in advancing the cause of film directors; she has also convinced the Japanese of the relevance of serious European and American films to their own experience.

Because she has not worked "behind the scenes," or generated her influence through the more acceptable mediation of her husband's voice and station, she has come to be acknowledged in Japan as the grand persona of Japanese film art. Like Madame de Staël, she is referred to everywhere as Madame Kawakita; the honorific has become part of her name. It expresses the recognition she has earned by her perseverance, judgment, and, particularly, her achievement in altering the international image of Japan.

Mme. Kawakita continues to select films for import to Japan, traveling each year to the major film festivals at Cannes, Venice, Moscow, and elsewhere to view the new works of important directors in world cinema. As Nagamasa Kawakita has admitted, she makes the aesthetic decisions, he the financial ones; and he has stressed that her judgment in films is more knowing than his.

Mme. Kawakita is now involved in creating an archive for the Japanese film in the manner of Henri Langlois's Paris Cinémathèque. It is an especially important task, as so many Japanese films were destroyed over the years through fire, air raids, general neglect, and ineffective cataloging. Rare masterpieces are even now "discovered" in mismarked cans. Sometimes, unfortunately, they emerge in so damaged a state that they remain, to all intents and purposes, "lost." These include works by great masters such as Mizoguchi and Ozu. In recognition of her work as an archivist of film, Mme. Kawakita has been appointed curator of the Japan Film Library Council.

At the international film festivals she has attended for so many years, Mme. Kawakita is admired by film people for her wit, charm, savoir faire, and shrewdness as a critic. Her husband headed a film section in occupied Shanghai during the war, where he made 160 very popular films. Mme. Kawakita learned Chinese during their stay and she is fluent as well in Russian, English, French, Italian, Spanish, and other languages. Mme. Kawakita would be a unique figure in any culture, but she is especially outstanding in Japan, where the defined role of woman has been that of passive recipient of values rather than the creator of them.

In 1974 Mme. Kawakita brought a festival of twenty films by younger Japanese directors to the Paris Cinémathèque, the National Film Theatre of London, the Conservatory of Cinematographic Arts of Canada in Montreal, and the Japan Society in New York, where Japanese "film weeks" were held. The films included recent and important work of Shinoda, Oshima, Imamura, and Hani, among others.

INTERVIEW WITH
MME. KASHIKO KAWAKITA

Mellen: Can you tell me something about yourself, your life as a young girl, and your studies. Were you a typical Japanese girl of your time?

Kawakita: [Laughter] Oh! It was such a long time ago. I've almost forgotten it.

Mellen: Was it different from the life of the ordinary young girl at the time?

Kawakita: Not very different, but I think one of the reasons why I feel more liberal and free from the so-called family tradition is that I graduated from a mission school, a Dutch-American mission school in Yokohama. The whole atmosphere was quite different from that of the ordinary girls' school founded by the Japanese government. Maybe it affected my way of thinking and my way of living.

Mellen: How did you happen to go there and not to a more traditional school?

Kawakita: I was, of course, too young to consider this question for myself, but my grandfather was a schoolmaster in the governmental primary schools. He had the idea that in the future everyone must learn English and must have a more international education. So he advised my father to let me go to that school. The school still exists and has had its one hundredth anniversary. It is the oldest girls' school and even now it is considered quite democratic. But in my time there were many American missionaries and very few students, so we were all very close to each other. I enjoyed my school days very much.

Mellen: Was it what we would call a college or university?

Kawakita: It was a middle school and sort of college combined. It was a seven-year course, quite long—just for the girls. At that time five years was the usual, followed by two or three years for college.

Mellen: Did your family expect you to become a traditional Japanese housewife?

Kawakita: No, I don't think so. I had only sisters and I am the eldest. We had some family trouble and my father left the family when I was quite young so I had to work.

Mellen: Because you were the eldest you were automatically out in the world?

Kawakita: Yes, I had to be.

Mellen: What did you work at?

Kawakita: I learned a little English stenography and typewriting at the YWCA in Yokohama after graduating from school. I was also teaching English, a very primary course, at the YWCA. One day my teacher of stenography told me that I was good enough to get a job, although I didn't agree. But anyway that teacher showed me the *Japan Times* advertisements. There was a small company that wanted a secretary. The teacher said, "Why don't you apply?" So I went there and that was the Towa Company. [Laughter] Quite coincidental! And now I'm almost at the top beside my husband!

Mellen: Was he working here at that time?

Kawakita: Yes, he founded it as a very, very small company. At that time there were only three people working for Towa. He was quite young, twenty-six, and he had just come back from abroad and founded the Towa Company. So he needed a secretary. And I became his secretary. I was very fond of films from childhood. In Yokohama, my home, I always went to the very newest American and European films. And I had the impression that movies were very important not only for artistic purposes, but also for the mass media and for international knowledge. It was when I saw Flaherty's *Nanook of the North,* when I was thirteen or fourteen, that I realized this. That film was so impressive. I was amazed that just by seeing it, I could get in touch with those people in the North and we could know their way of living, how they felt about their family life, their dogs, and so on. Since that time I always wanted to work in the field of film. And then I came to this company and I saw its prospectus and that its job was to import and to export films. I was very pleased.

Mellen: It must have seemed perfect.

Kawakita: Yes. I thought I would try very hard to work with that company. And we worked very, very hard for several years. And then Mr. Kawakita asked me to be his wife. So we got married, but we kept on working together. Now my main work is for the film library business and I have rather little to do with my husband's business of importing and distributing foreign films. But I still go to almost all the film festivals and see films to help decide whether they are suitable for Japan.

Mellen: That must be the most enjoyable arrangement: to make the decisions and not to have to do the work. Pure enjoyment.

Kawakita: But you know this is not pure enjoyment at all. Sometimes we find very good films, but they are so uncommercial for Japan. That is my agony.

Mellen: I gathered from Kon Ichikawa, who hadn't seen it, that *The Conformist* hasn't been shown in Japan. Is this true?

Kawakita: The Italian film? It was distributed by an American company. I liked the film and we wanted to take it, but the company people didn't approve of it, making it very difficult for business. Then some American company took it and it was shown here. But not successfully. I'm so often away from Japan that sometimes I don't know when a film opens, how it was released, and how it does. I don't think it was a great success, although some critics appreciated it very much.

Mellen: What is your work now with the Film Library?

Kawakita: Did you know we have a National Film Center?

Mellen: Yes, I've been going there in the afternoons. I've seen *No Regrets for Our Youth, A Man Vanished, The Origin of Sex, Pigs and Battleships, Red Desire to Kill,* and some others.

One of my most successful interviews was with Daisuke Ito in Kyoto. He had not been well, was suffering from kidney trouble, and had in fact stopped working. He was completely charming and very kind and cooperative. There was a thunderstorm during the interview, the lights went out, and yet he continued in the dark because my recorder worked on a battery. It was in a very remote part of Kyoto and it seemed that as soon as the thunder started, the lights went out.

Kawakita: I think in general that the older Japanese people are nicer. Japanese before the war and Japanese after the war are completely different.

Mellen: Of course some of the younger directors like Mr. Shinoda have been extremely nice too. When I was leaving the screening of *Sapporo Winter Olympics* he came especially to the elevator to say goodbye. I was so surprised I didn't have a chance to tell him how much I enjoyed the film.

Kawakita: He's polite and he knows how to behave. Some people don't.

Mellen: How do you account for the absence of critical enthusiasm in Japan for Shinoda's *Buraikan?* My interpreter, Mrs. Hoshikawa, noticed a resemblance between the visual style of the film and that of a well-known Edo period printmaker named Eikan and she enjoyed the film very much.

Kawakita: Perhaps the general public enjoyed it more than the critics. Each year there is a ten-best films selection by the critics and *Buraikan* wasn't chosen at all, even among the ten. Donald Richie and I were quite angry about that and we tried very hard to make the foreigners see it. I think most foreigners appreciated it much more than the Japanese.

Mellen: I consider it a great work of art. When you're in the presence of a great work of art, you know it.

Kawakita: Yes, you feel it immediately.

Mellen: The minute that it came on, you could see how carefully it was photographed, how beautiful the visual style was. I saw Shinoda's more recent film *Silence* at the Japan Society in New York, which was less fine. At the time I hadn't seen anything else by Shinoda and I wondered why it was being shown. One wonders whether in *Silence* the subject of the treatment of the Christian missionaries and the Japanese response to Christian ideas might not have been too complex for screen treatment. And perhaps the failure of the film comes from Shinoda's not being critical enough of the Catholics in Japan.

Kawakita: Yes. And he doesn't know enough about the Catholics.

Mellen: Shouldn't he have been much more hostile to the Catholics as foreign invaders coming to Japan? The film doesn't take a clear stand on this crucial question.

Kawakita: Yes, yes, that's right. Because the author [Shusaku Endo] of the original novel upon which the film was based is a Catholic. And so the film just stands in between. Shinoda tried, at least in the last scene, which was completely changed from the original story, and there was a big row between the author and Shinoda but finally Shinoda insisted. But that was the only place, the only scene in which he could make a change. The other scenes just follow the original story. It was really a very difficult situation in which to make this kind of film.

Mellen: Of course it was a good idea, and he took quite a risk in trying to film so difficult a subject in the first place.

Kawakita: Yes, it was quite courageous of him and that film was chosen by the critics here as the best film of the year. Here the standards are different from international standards of criticism. I think most of the Japanese critics are very hard.

Mellen: Is Mrs. Shibata your only child?

Kawakita: Yes, she is.

Mellen: She's in the same business, isn't she?

Kawakita: Yes, but her line is a little different and she deals more with the noncommercial side of filmmaking.

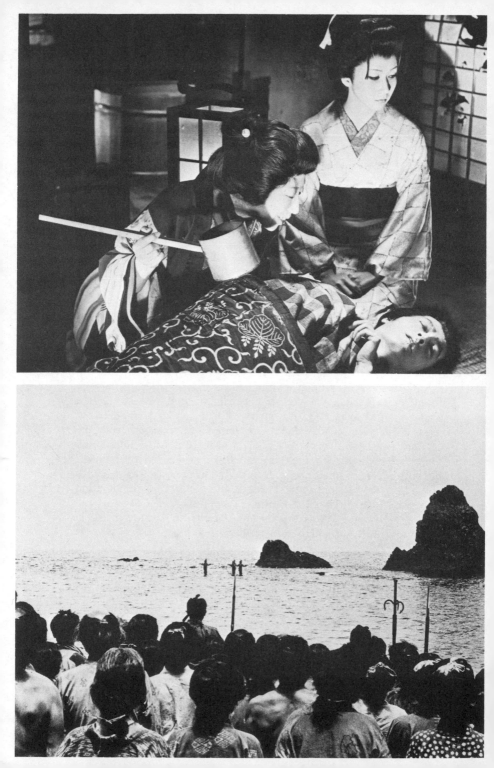

Mellen: This makes it more difficult for her.

Kawakita: I admire their courage. One of their main business lines is to export Oshima's films. He is a very interesting person and very talented.

Mellen: Did your daughter go to a university here in Tokyo?

Kawakita: No, she also had a very strange type of education, more strange than mine. When she was fifteen she went to England for ballet lessons. At that time she was very keen on ballet and music. She went to a ballet-music school. But then for some reason or other she gave it up. Then she went to London—the ballet school was in Kent. In London she went to a sort of finishing school. And then she went to Paris and learned French. She also went to Italy—Perugia—and learned Italian. So she speaks those languages quite well. She came back to Japan after four years.

Mellen: Did you see each other during all that time?

Kawakita: My job allowed me to go abroad often and on one occasion I lived with her in London. We rented a flat and lived together, so it wasn't too bad. But she was away from Japan for four years.

Mellen: Wasn't it very unusual for a Japanese girl to live on her own at so young an age?

Kawakita: Yes, quite unusual for a young Japanese girl. She was nineteen when she came back. And then she got married (Shibata is her second husband). She had learned more about life than I. She married a very handsome Japanese actor, a very talented man named Itami. He's still active, but mostly on television. After seven years of marriage they broke up. It is not a legal marriage with Shibata—they just live together.

Mellen: But she calls herself Mrs. Shibata.

Kawakita: She is called Mrs. Shibata, but her proper name is still Kawakita, Kazuko. But everyone calls her Mrs. Shibata because they live together and work together. He's such a nice man, I like him very much. He's very studious and he's very good at selling Oshima's films.

Mellen: Does she have any children?

Kawakita: No, no children.

Mellen: I'm struck by how unusual her experience must have been. It might be less unusual now.

Kawakita: Yes, for young people to go abroad and study just after

Shinoda's *Buraikan* (*above*), with Tatsuya Nakadai and Shima Iwashita, and *Silence* (*below*). "Here the standards are different from international standards of criticism. I think most of the Japanese critics are very hard."

the war was very difficult because of the problem of foreign currency. She is quite international.

Mellen: She looks very international.

Kawakita: She is a bit of a hippy.

Mellen: When I met her I thought, she has you as an example, but it must also be very difficult for her. She might have had the desire to emulate you. And this might explain why she was away for such a long time.

Kawakita: Maybe. And after that too. It explains her interest in film now. And here I am, I'm also in film and her father is quite outstanding in the film business and so her situation was very difficult. I understand that and I sympathize with her. And so she must do something different from our work. And she must not be dependent upon us. But it is very difficult for her to be free of our influence.

Mellen: Perhaps she should have done something completely different, the ballet perhaps, although that's a hard life.

Kawakita: Quite difficult and I think her heart was not strong enough for that. And now I think she's quite happy. Although she is also in films, her line is quite different. She imports most of the Godard films and we never touch those. [Laughter] I think our ways are separate.

Mellen: Yet she does the same kind of thing, importing and exporting films.

Kawakita: Yes, but they are very limited. So far they import almost only Godard and export almost only Oshima.

Mellen: To make money she must really expand.

Kawakita: To make money, yes. But I don't think they care so much about money so long as they can make a living. And so they do what they like. She goes to America quite often. Donald Richie has been especially good to her.

Mellen: He loves Japan so much and he has so much goodwill toward Japan.

Kawakita: He has made so many good friends among the Japanese. To me also he is most helpful and a good friend.

Mellen: In connection with the Museum of Modern Art? [Donald Richie had recently resigned from his job as curator of film for MOMA.]

Kawakita: We do about the same job. We sent most of the films to Richie at the time of his Museum of Modern Art film retrospective. We worked very closely together.

Mellen: He asked me if I liked you and when I told him that I did, then he liked me. That's how he decided. It's such a closed world. He told me that you drove him home from the *Sapporo Olympic* movie and that he had dinner with you that week.

Kawakita: [Laughter] Oh, is that so? You're quite well informed.

Mellen: He wants to be accepted by the Japanese people.

Kawakita: But we are all very grateful to him. You know it's mainly through him and his books that Japanese films are more known outside Japan. We are quite indebted to him.

Mellen: It's been his life's work. He's written some novels that I've discovered in bookshops here in English. One is called *Companions of the Holiday*. It's about a group of servants who have the house to themselves when the mistress of the house goes away, and about the intrigue in the kitchen.

Kawakita: [Laughter] Oh, is that his novel? I haven't read that. Another novel he wrote is about the Inland Sea.*

Mellen: He reveals so much of himself. When I asked him about that book he said, "But no one Japanese would believe that the 'I' in the novel is really me." [Laughter]

Kawakita: Is that so? Do you know his wife?

Mellen: She's in the United States, isn't she?

Kawakita: Yes, in New York and she writes very well. Her name is Mary Evans.

Mellen: He mentioned her at a party we attended at Setsu Asakura's house. An interesting game was played there. Everyone was asked to draw on a piece of paper a house, a body of water, a tree, and a snake, and Donald collected all the drawings. Then he gave a psychological characterization of each person based upon the relationships of the objects in his drawing. It was fascinating.

---

* The best description of this area comes in Donald Richie's *The Inland Sea* (New York and Tokyo: John Weatherhill, Inc., 1971): "The Inland Sea is a nearly landlocked, lakelike body of water bounded by three of Japan's four major islands. It is entered through but four narrow straits, three opening to the south into the Pacific Ocean and one—called Kammon or Barrier Gate—to the west into the narrow sea that separates Japan from Korea and the rest of Asia. . . . it has been called the Aegean of the East. There are, however, differences. The Greek islands are few, and they stand from the sea as though with an effort, as though to indicate the water's great depth. The islands of the shallow Inland Sea are different. They are small, and there are many—hundreds of them, so many that a full count has never been made, or certainly not one that everyone can agree upon. They rise gracefully from this protected, stormless sea, as if they had just emerged, their beaches, piers, harbors all intact. Some have springs, most have wells; many are covered with forest, almost all have trees or bushes. A castaway, given the choice between a Greek and a Japanese island, would swim toward the latter. It looks like a place where it would be nice to live."

How would Japanese ladies, living in a more traditional way, view your life?

Kawakita: [Laughter] I don't know. Because I don't really make many friends. My job keeps me too busy. I go to the office and I go back home. I make friends only among film people and most of these are men. So I have very few Japanese women as friends. I don't know.

Mellen: How do your sisters feel about your success?

Kawakita: One of my sisters is dead and the other, my younger sister, keeps a home for me. Otherwise I couldn't come out to the office every day. She is doing my housework. I feel quite happy and indebted to her.

Mellen: She is, of course, a part of your life.

Kawakita: She is really very nice and she is the manager of the whole family. My husband and I go abroad very often and we need someone to take care of the household and be there.

Mellen: Are you interested in the women's liberation movement at all?

Kawakita: I don't quite understand exactly what women's liberation means for Japan or in general. What do they aim at?

Mellen: They aim for women to be complete human beings, to have the confidence to make the decisions that affect their lives, to make their own choices, to be able to be free enough to choose any work, to have the confidence to pursue work successfully, and to be creative persons without the need to be dependent on a man's opinion or ideas.

Kawakita: Financially. But I think to some extent Japanese women, particularly after the war, have been getting those equalities. Even before the war the Japanese housewives were quite strong. They were quite influential over their households, families, and husbands. It looks as if Japanese women before the war were so obedient, so subdued, that they couldn't express any opinions of their own, but in fact it wasn't like that. I think it all depends on the ability of the individual woman, the housewife herself. If the woman is more clever and more capable than her husband or father, I think more or less she can get what she wants.

Mellen: Become something?

Kawakita: Become something, yes.

Mellen: I was so surprised to find that this is a very separate society. The women have their own world. At least this is the impression that some women gave me. The men go out by themselves in the evening and the women have separate friends. I was invited to a women's liberation group meeting way out in one of the suburbs of Tokyo.

Kawakita: Are there such groups? I didn't know.

Mellen: They were all professional women. One was a reporter for *Asahi Shimbun,* two were in publishing. There were fourteen in the group in all. Another was a producer of television shows. They invited me to the meeting and described their own lives. The woman from *Asahi* said, "I rarely have dinner with my husband. He has his friends, his separate life, and I have my work and my own life."

Kawakita: I see, yes.

Mellen: I hadn't really perceived how much that's true here. Do you think so?

Kawakita: Yes, I think in general that is true because that woman working on a newspaper is leading quite an irregular life and so she doesn't have much opportunity to have dinner with her husband, while her husband must have a different job and often he must entertain his clients at parties. Yes, I think that is true.

Mellen: In Kyoto I was invited to a bar and a geisha house by some professors who were supposed to be discussing a book contract for one of them. Their wives were nowhere to be seen.

[Laughter and a break for a *sushi* lunch]

FOUR

KANETO
SHINDO
INTRODUCTION

Like Kobayashi, Kaneto Shindo belongs to the middle group of Japanese directors, the generation after that of Akira Kurosawa. But although he is younger, Shindo actually began his film career in 1934, before Kurosawa, as an assistant art director. His family were rich landlords who had suffered bankruptcy and become farmers—a dislocation which caused the family to break up. Leading Japanese film critic Tadao Sato views Shindo's experience as that of "a typically tragic Japanese family," and part of the explanation why a central theme in Shindo's work is the reconstruction of the family.

This is especially true of *Sorrow Is Only for Woman* (also known as *Only Women Have Trouble*) made in 1958. It concludes when the heroine comes to the realization that it may not be wisest after all to restore the family. Drawing upon his childhood and youth, Shindo has frequently treated rural Japanese and their problems in his films. Sato has observed:

> Contemporary Japan has developed from an agricultural into an industrial country. Many agricultural people moved to cities and threw themselves into new precarious lives. Kaneto Shindo's style of camera work comes from his intention to conquer such uneasiness by depicting the perseverance and persistence of farmers.

Until the early 1950s, Shindo worked exclusively as a screenwriter; even after he became a director he continued to write scripts

72

for other people. He has written screenplays for Mizoguchi, Kinoshita, Ichikawa, and, most frequently, for Yoshimura. Two of his best-known scripts are *A Pebble by the Wayside* (1960) for Seiji Hisamatsu, and Imai's *Night Drum* (1958).

In 1951 Shindo made his first film with his own company, the Kindai Eiga Kyokai. It was called *The Story of a Beloved Wife,* and became a film much admired in Japan. Anderson and Richie in *The Japanese Film* credit it with "opening up a new genre concerned with the characterization of wives as individuals." Shindo's *Epitome* (1953) was also a critical success. It exposed the sordid life of the geisha and has been described by Sato as "a really magnificent work." In 1954 Shindo made *Gutter,* excoriating social maltreatment of the mentally retarded. Anderson and Richie regard it as "one of the best of the *lumpen-mono*"—films concerned with the degrading lives of the lumpen proletariat.

Having established a reputation as a passionate social critic, Shindo was invited in 1952 by the Japan Teachers' Union to produce a film about the atomic bomb. The result was *The Children of the Atom Bomb,* a semidocumentary centering on a teacher who, having moved away, returns to Hiroshima to track down each of her former pupils who had been caught in the attack. The film has been praised by Donald Richie as "a quiet, muted, deeply-felt picture." Through its use of real orphans and actual victims, Richie suggests, Shindo's reenactment "rises to something approximating the horror of the bombing when he reconstructs . . . the five minutes just prior to the detonation." Richie adds that the power of this sequence "is somewhat mitigated by [Shindo's] curiously stylized reconstruction of the holocaust itself."

Actually, Shindo's use of Soviet-style montage during the moments preceding the attack provides a beautiful equivalent for the fragmentation of reality about to occur. The film is not sentimental, but the Japan Teachers' Union thought differently. Extremely disappointed, they contended that Shindo had "reduced the story to a tear-jerker and destroyed its political orientation." They felt it was insufficiently critical of the United States military and the circumstances leading to the use of atomic weapons against Japanese civilians. Instead, they used Hideo Sekigawa's *Hiroshima.* This film was closer to their purpose, with its portrayal of the atomic attack as a scientific experiment in which the United States government perceived the Japanese as animals upon which to experiment. In one scene American tourists arrive to buy souvenir bones of A-bomb victims.

Shindo is best known in the United States for another semidocumentary, *The Island* (1960). It is the story of a poor rural couple living with their children on a barren island in the Inland Sea, an island that lacks a water supply of its own. Twice a day the two must clamber down from the steep cliff of their home and row to the mainland where they fill buckets with fresh water, returning to trudge step by step up the steep incline of their island, ever careful not to spill a drop of the precious liquid carried in two buckets on the ends of a shoulder pole. The journey to fetch and retrieve water occupies their lives with the exception of one brief outing to the mainland. The routine is broken only by the sickness and death of their older boy. Not a word of dialogue is spoken throughout the entire film, for their very existence precludes the energy and indulgent luxury of conversation.

The film met with instant approval from foreign critics. Bosley Crowther in *The New York Times* spoke of "a sense of the pride and pathos in primitive life," and admired the pictorial quality of the film:

> The eloquence is in the fidelity, the solidity and clarity with which Kaneto Shindo . . . has embraced the rhythmic beauty of the landscape and the mountain-fringed waters of the bay and the rhythmic toil of his people. . . .*

Stanley Kauffmann in *The New Republic* has also appreciated the intense beauty of the film:

> *The Island* fixes it all: the odd security of knowing exactly their position—on the bottom and ceaselessly struggling; the beauty of their interdependence. . . . This is more than a *Man-of-Aran* combat with the elements. It is a fully realized little epic of the family as the last and the first barrier against chaos: a way of life that needs no rationale, that is its own purpose.
>
> To see how their world meshes—the difficulties met and shared without comment, the children running (*always* running) to do their own appointed tasks—is to perceive the strength in order. Each of the four is a pillar of their common, small universe. It is impossible to imagine these children growing up lost or bewildered; and it is no bourgeois beatifica-

---

* Copyright © 1962 by The New York Times Company. Reprinted by permission.

tion to say the film lays bare the secret of this impoverished family: they are happy.*

Richard N. Tucker, in his book *Japan: Film Image,* echoes this view:

> He observes these struggling people in life and death and by his superbly controlled images and narrative pace enlarges their plight to represent that of the whole Japanese people.†

Not all Western critics were equally enthusiastic about *The Island.* Richie, although he had also called it Shindo's best film, suggests that *The Island* "combines basic superficiality and basic honesty in a way this critic is much more likely to call typically American than typically Japanese," a point of view developed at length by Pauline Kael. Ms. Kael examines the near unanimous praise received by *The Island* and contends that it was found a "masterpiece" because "it is so ponderously, pretentiously simple." Kael argues against what she believes to be inverted condescension concealed in such praise. It is a view shared by many Japanese who resent those who affect to believe that removing "the non-essentials of civilization and personality," as Kael puts it, automatically leads to something profound and of importance. Rather, argues Kael in *Kiss Kiss Bang Bang,* the result is

> . . . something so barren that those who praise it seem to be asserting proof of virtue, of moral superiority over those of us who are bored by false purity . . . if this island family—so sure of their relationship to each other and to the earth and water and plants that they have nothing to say—ever figure out how to get a pipeline in from the mainland, they'll be liberated from that primal struggle with the elements and soon they'll be on their path to conversation and what—in Kaneto Shindo's view—is, I suppose, sophistication, corruption and decadence.‡

Many Japanese critics felt embarrassed by the amount of attention *The Island* received in the West. They were suspicious of a certain sense of superiority in those critics who saw in the portrayal

---

* See also Stanley Kauffmann, *A World on Film* (New York: Harper and Row), pp. 386–387.

† (London: Studio Vista, 1973), p. 129.

‡ (New York: Bantam Books, 1971), p. 357.

of the primitive life of these islanders something typical beneath the
"civilized" veneer of contemporary Japan. This sentiment has been
clearly expressed by Michitaro Tada, a professor at Kyoto Univer-
sity, who described at our Kyoto panel discussion the reactions of
people he met in Paris to *The Island:*

> Whenever they saw a Japanese, myself included, they
> would ask him his impressions of *The Island*. I was very em-
> barrassed by that. The French seemed to think that the Japa-
> nese are as foolish and without questions about the circum-
> stances of their lives as the characters in that film. They
> seemed to prefer approaching the Japanese as a primitive peo-
> ple rather than as a technologically sophisticated one. That
> was their way of dealing with the Japanese—through a sympa-
> thy with the primitive. Certainly if people of other countries
> believe that all Japanese live on that kind of island with that
> way of life, there is a severe communication gap.

Film director Nagisa Oshima also shared the view that foreign
acclaim of *The Island* reflected "the image foreign people hold of
the Japanese." Oshima stresses that he personally "did not find the
film interesting at all."

In 1964, after years of making films centered on social observa-
tion, Shindo underwent a dramatic change in style and subject mat-
ter, placing the stress in his films on the erotic and its role in our
lives. It was a departure which brought him something less than
sympathy from critics. Donald Richie in particular regarded this in
his *Japanese Cinema* as indicative of a dead-end reached by
Shindo, caused by the limited political quality of his films up to
1964:

> At their worst the films make one wonder how much is true
> social criticism and how much is political propaganda. As with
> Hideo Sekigawa, Satsuo Yamamoto, Fumio Kamei, during
> this period, the party line is never completely invisible and any
> audience naturally feels manipulated when the purpose of the
> director becomes this noticeable.*

Richie comments that many of these directors did a *volte-face* simi-
lar to that of Shindo. He observes "that although sex and politics
are bedfellows is not a new observation . . . given the formerly al-

---

* (Garden City, New York: Anchor Books, 1971), p. 168.

most suspiciously pure pictures of Shindo, the re-evaluation came with a certain suddenness.'' Richie is suggesting that Shindo's focus on the anatomy of sex is cynical, a function of career or the attempt to draw interest, by conjunction, to his political work. Yet Shindo seems to be trying to relate distortions in sex and emotion to social ill-usage.

The first film in this group was the visually exquisite *Onibaba* (1963), which treats two women during wartime left to survive as they will. One is the daughter-in-law of the other. Together they kill dying samurai and strip their bodies of armor to sell for rice. When a neighbor returns from the war to the deserted village, the daughter-in-law begins a sexual relationship with him. Her panic-stricken mother-in-law, fearing that she will be left alone to starve, resorts to pretending to be a demon and scares the girl at night with a monstrous mask. The sexual and the social are brilliantly interwoven in a haunting metaphor of the distortions of the psyche by social decay. Many European critics, like Arne Svensson in his *Screen Series: Japan,* have noted the subtle and resonant force of Shindo's conception:

> Shindo depicts a period of bestial killing and animal sexual-
> ity in his ghost story. In the daytime an idyllic sun glitters in
> the water, but at night a lurking full moon gives the film the
> tone of a legend.*

Richard N. Tucker has noted that in *Onibaba* "the introduction of eroticism blended with sadism radically altered the somewhat detached approach of his former work.''

Shindo, however, followed *Onibaba* with less successful films such as *Lost Sex* (1966), *The Origin of Sex* (1967), and *Naked Nineteen-Year-Olds* (1970), whose titles betray their relative lack of merit. Tucker, like Richie, notes a substantially decreased power in Shindo's films as he entered his "erotic" period:

> Unfortunately, he tended towards sentimentality in these
> later films and did not manage to convey a genuine under-
> standing of the sexual drives within a small society as was
> shown by Imamura in *The Pornographer* (1966).†

Others, like Oshima, who view Shindo with more hostility and less esteem, argue that he was merely moving "from his early simplis-

---

* (New York: A. S. Barnes & Co., 1971), pp. 77–78.
† Tucker, Japan: Film Image, pp. 129–30.

tic Marxism'' to a different subject matter, while continuing to lack those basic characteristics necessary for a creative filmmaker.

In the late sixties Shindo began making thrillers, two of which, *Kagero* (*Heatwave Island*, 1969) and *Live Today, Die Tomorrow* (1970), have received very favorable critical response. The latter, as Tucker describes it, contains "a searching socio-political examination of the individual human being." * In this film the lumpen hero, Michio, steals a revolver from an American naval camp. The act is symbolic both of his oppression and of its partial cause. Michio's criminal nature is explained by Shindo through his character's life history. With no prospects, he has been everything from laundryman to waiter to murderer. His death at the end was presaged by his childhood when he and his siblings were abandoned and left to starve by their mother, who fled with her two youngest children. Shindo thus locates the causes of Michio's development as a murderer in his life experience; he does not create a preordainedly vicious character.

Kagero has been highly praised by both Richie and Tucker. Its locale is again the Inland Sea, the same setting as *The Island*. Ten years have elapsed and the people who might have been the heroes of the earlier film have moved to the cities. Lacking skills, they are absorbed inevitably into the lumpen proletariat as petty criminals, prostitutes, and dealers in drugs. Richie holds that the film far transcends the level of melodrama:

> From the brilliant opening it becomes apparent that he is making a statement on the relation between love and death; from other parts of the film ("cops are poor—criminals are poor: it is the poor chasing the poor") it is apparent that a social statement is being made; finally, Shindo is making a film about what happens when sudden affluence reaches a simple people.

The treatment of sex in Shindo's films was never exploitative or gratuitous. It has been employed by the director as a means of looking into the heart of the human being and of exploring human nature in general. At their best, Shindo's films now involve a merging of the sexual with the social. His radical perception isolates man's sexual life in the context of his role as a member of a specific social class. *Kuroneko* (1968), for example, is brilliant in its treatment of the conflict between Oedipal and upwardly mobile social drives.

---

* Ibid.

For Shindo our passions as biological beings and our ambitions as members of social classes, which give specific and distorted form to those drives, induce an endless struggle within the unconscious. Those moments in his films when this warfare is visualized and brought to conscious life raise his work to the level of the highest art.

INTERVIEW WITH
KANETO SHINDO

Mellen: I find the social dimension of your films very complex and interesting. Would you describe how in your films you depict the class struggle as it has appeared both in history and in society?

Shindo: Speaking about *Onibaba* in particular, my main historical interest focuses on ordinary people . . . their energy to carry themselves beyond the predicaments they encounter daily. I wish to describe the struggles of the so-called common people which usually never appear in recorded history. This is why I made *Onibaba*. My mind was always on the commoners, not on the lords, politicians, or anyone of name and fame. I wanted to convey the lives of down-to-earth people who have to live like weeds.

Mellen: In the setting of *Onibaba* I noticed that the people seemed very small, moving around a lake where the reeds were very tall and imposing.

Shindo: Yes, the tall, swaying reeds are my symbol of the world, the society which surrounds people. In *Kuroneko* bushes are used for the same symbolic end. Tall, dense, swaying reeds represent the world in which these commoners live and to which the eyes of lords and politicians do not reach. My eyes, or rather the camera's eye, is fixed to view the world from the very lowest level of society, not from the top.

Mellen: Do you consider yourself a Marxist?

Shindo: Ah, Marxist! I am a believer in socialism. I can say that I am a socialist.

Mellen: One can see your very strong sense of the class struggle both in *Kuroneko* and in *Onibaba*. There is a powerful separation in *Onibaba* between the woman and her daughter-in-law and the rich samurai who has come to die.

Shindo: If you have to look at society through the eyes of those placed on its bottom level, you cannot escape the fact that you must experience and perceive everything with a sense of the political struggle between classes. This sets the general political background of the film.

Mellen: Is it your class consciousness which inspires you as a filmmaker?

Shindo: Yes, I cannot but be class conscious. However, I should like to point out here that first I am an artist, not a politician, so I do not see the class struggle as it appears in the political arena. I like to see and describe it as it affects the individual human being, in his daily life. I like to look into the political and class struggle with the eyes of an objective artist. It is so easy to view social conflict with political idealism, or at least with the tainted eyes of political desire. I strive to avoid this by all means. After all, struggles are endemic to our society with its many faults and contradictions. But I do not hold the view that the artist should accept or merely present society as it is. I am saying that, with an artist's eyes, I would like to see problems as they face working people who are the protagonists in my films. I am interested in the way they overcome their difficulties; at least I like to evoke the hope of overcoming, some prospect for the future.

Mellen: Does any character in *Kuroneko* * represent the director?

Shindo: My sympathies are expressed through the peasant mother who is slaughtered with her daughter-in-law at the beginning of the film. In *Onibaba,* again, the mother is myself.

Mellen: Yet in *Onibaba* you punish the mother at the end by having her become afflicted with a horrible skin infection.

Shindo: Through punishment I wanted her to escape the confines of her own old world, in fact for both women to escape. I punished her, but this punishment is not a kind which ends her world; it does not involve the overt force of punishment alone. I meant this punishment to be a spiritual one, so that through suffering I could reveal the real soul of the mother herself. Afer her recovery, we, the mother and the director, are ready for the next step into a new world, the stage which might take us to a new future.

Mellen: You, as the director, at the moment her face is destroyed, are still sympathizing with the mother, rather than with the daughter-in-law, who has the right to live her own life and remarry, rather than be forced to work for this old woman who is not even her own mother?

Shindo: Yes, because she is myself. I am Onibaba.

Mellen: You did not blame her for preventing her daughter-in-law from running away to find a new man?

Shindo: No, I prevented it to heighten the issue between them. As far as the story line is concerned the mother was punished because she tried to stop the girl from finding a new man. But behind the

---

* *Kuroneko* again deals with a woman and her daughter-in-law who are raped by marauding soldiers. Their house is then set on fire and they perish. Yet they return to the world as revenging spirits waylaying samurai and drawing them to a mysterious hut in the woods where the younger woman seduces and then kills them. One of these samurai turns out to be the woman's son returning from the wars.

Kaneto Shindo on the set of *Onibaba*.

surface drama there is a story other than the one we are now discussing. It is that everyone in my films, the mother and the daughter-in-law in this case, is invariably an outcast of society. They are people totally abandoned, outside society's political protection. Among these outcasts I wanted to capture their immense energy for survival. Obviously the mother has done very cruel things, like preventing her daughter-in-law from finding another man. She is punished for these acts, but the punishment is an expression of the uncontrollable events which these people meet in their actual lives. My next suggestion is that the destroyed face * is not the end of her world. This miserable face will dry later and she will find the day

---

* To scare her daughter-in-law and prevent her from going out at night, the woman puts on the mask of a samurai who had a leprous skin infection; the night is rainy, the mask doesn't come off, and when it does (with the aid of a hatchet), the woman's face is bleeding, scabbed, blistered, and decaying, like that of the samurai she killed.

Jitsuko Yoshimura and Nobuko Otowa (*above*) and Jitsuko Yoshimura and Kei Sato as Hachi (*below*) in Shindo's *Onibaba*. "They are people totally abandoned, outside society's political protection."

From *Onibaba:* on the left is Jitsuko Yoshimura as the daughter-in-law; on the right, Nobuko Otowa as the mother. "Among these outcasts I wanted to capture their immense energy for survival."

to live again. She has to find it. By destroying her face, I said something about the beginning of a new life for people who are assaulted by unexpected social events.

Mellen: The important thing is for the mother to survive?

Shindo: Yes.

Mellen: Is it similar to the situation in *The Island?*

Shindo: In that film I expressed the very same thing, but in a more quiet manner. *Onibaba* is an old Japanese folk tale, probably a Buddhist tale. I made it into a dramatic, dynamic drama.

Mellen: Are you then adapting Buddhist lore to your own particular style of social expression?

Shindo: I adapted the story into a script resonant with the spirit of modern man. It is a modern version of an old traditional story.

Mellen: But infused with your class consciousness?

Shindo: Yes, I would agree with that. Through the eyes of modern man, I would put it.

Mellen: Was there anyone in particular who inspired you to go into the field of film?

Shindo: There were some. But more than anything else I was interested in the "image." To me "imagery," with its deep associations and imaginative richness, provides a powerful, eloquent medium. Filmmaking is one form of visual imagery, and also an art. I was deeply interested in creating within this art form. In Japan there is a proverb which says "the eye can express as much as the mouth can." [Laughter]

Mellen: Didn't you start first as a screenwriter and only later become a director?

Shindo: Yes, I wrote scenarios first. However, to me the director and the scriptwriter should be one. At least ideally. In actuality in Japan, in the filmmaking world, they were and still are considered to be separate skills. I wrote scripts for a long time and gradually became dissatisfied. So I turned to directing.

Mellen: Were there any older Japanese directors who influenced you?

Shindo: Mizoguchi was the major influence.

Mellen: Did you work with him personally?

Shindo: I was his chief assistant director.

Mellen: On which films?

Shindo: Aienkyo [*The Gorge Between Love and Hate,* 1936], *Genroku Chushingura* [*The Loyal Forty-seven Rōnin of the Genroku Era,* 1942] . . .

Kyushiro Kusakabe: Aienkyo was an old, good film, wasn't it? Fumiko Yamaji was the actress in it.

Shindo: That's right. I cannot recall exactly, but it must have been made around Showa 12 or 13.* At the time of *Genroku Chushingura* I was the art director as well as the chief assistant director for Mizoguchi.

Mellen: Which are your favorite Mizoguchi films?

Shindo: Well, *Ugetsu Monogatari* [1953] and *Saikaku Ichidai Onna* [*The Life of Oharu,* 1952].

Mellen: My favorite is *A Story from Chikamatsu* [*Chikamatsu Monogatari,* 1954].

Shindo: Yes, *Chikamatsu* was a good film. I recall now. Mizoguchi was pretty bad at the very first and became good. In the middle of his career he became bad again for a long time. Just before his death [in 1956] he was so good, he became superb. When I had the honor of assisting him as his chief assistant director, it was already close to the end of his career.

Mellen: I've always thought that his last two films, before *Street of Shame, The Empress Yang Kwei Fei* [1955] and *Shin Heike Monogatari* [*New Tales of the Taira Clan,* 1955] represented something of a decline for Mizoguchi.

Shindo: You are right. Comparing these two to *Chikamatsu Monogatari* or some of his best films, they show a lesser quality. I can explain the reason now. Mizoguchi was in need of money at that time and he was bent upon making some out of his last films.

Mellen: Right at the end of such a long career. How sad!

Shindo: Oharu was the film into which Mizoguchi poured everything he had. He was really working hard on it but not for the money.

Mellen: I hope this question is not out of line. Some say that in your career you have two distinct periods: political work, in which films like *Children of Hiroshima* stand out, and the films dealing explicitly with sex. How do you explain your sudden interest in making films about sex? For instance, in the panel discussion I participated in for the *Mainichi Shimbun* in Kyoto, Professor Tada of Kyoto University tried to argue that with these latter films you descended greatly in the level of your work.

Shindo: Well, what shall I say? Political things such as class con-

---

* In the Japanese calendar Showa would represent the second quarter of the twentieth century. Shindo remembers *Aienkyo* as being made in 1937 or 1938.

sciousness or class struggle or other aspects of social existence really come down to the problem of man alone. So I am essentially interested in the individual human being. I have to observe closely what a man or woman is. In this process I discovered the powerful, very fundamental force in man which sustains his survival and which can be called sexual energy.

Mellen: I don't quite understand. Are you saying that sex expresses, beyond individual need, the vitality of a social class, its capacity to survive?

Shindo: Let's state the whole thing from the beginning. What I meant was that I am interested in man, the solitary person who is placed in the midst of chaotic surroundings, and when I try to grasp and unfold the problems of society which surround him, I have to know what is within man himself. I cannot escape from looking more closely into what is the essence, the root existence of man. This led me to locate the vital energy of man. This energy to live is expressed for many in the sexual drive. I consider the focal point of a man's existence to be in sex. This is the basis of my interest.

Mellen: Is it sex as it expresses raw human nature, or sex as it is organized socially by the culture?

Shindo: Well . . . the sex I have in mind here is not the sex enjoyed behind closed doors. My idea of sex is nothing but the expression of the vitality of man, his urge for survival.

Mellen: Do you feel that your interest in sex is in any way a result of a lack of faith in political action as the means to survival? Is your despair over the possibility of socialism, for example, involved?

Shindo: Now I understand what you are getting at. Well, the answer is no! It is not any lack of faith in political activity or its possibilities. Rather, I should put it that I do not look at political activity as it appears in our society because I am not essentially a politician. I like to observe politics and then articulate my ideas through the eyes of ordinary common people who have their own faults and the merits of human nature as well. This is why I am interested in the individual man, and this interest leads me to explore his sexuality.

Mellen: Then this theme of sex does not, as some have tried to say, mean that you reject the possibility of political action in the world?

Shindo: Oh, no. I am not at all pessimistic about political struggle. It is just that as a film director I try to perceive the political in a purer untainted way. In the process of looking into political issues, I pursue man's problems closely. And in order to delve into an individual problem I then directly connect back to its social implication. There is an interaction. Actually I am very much saying something about political activity through the illumination of one man.

Mellen: Is this artistic quest more interesting to you than the actual pursuit of political goals would be?

Shindo: I think so. But you should not forget that we are dealing intimately with the political when scrutinizing a man's individual nature, needs, and problems.

Mellen: In many films of yours the same people work again and again, including the technicians. And you have created a company of actors and actresses who work closely with you. Do you feel this is a successful means of filmmaking in Japan?

Shindo: Yes, it is. I believe, as a director, that having a group of people who can trust each other while working on a film is a very good thing, if it does not exceed a certain degree. Any creative group activity has to depend on mutual trust and understanding among the members.

Mellen: Do you still work for the big production companies in Japan? I am not very familiar with your particular situation.

Shindo: No, I am working for myself right now. We have been working for our own production company alone for some time, twenty-three years.

Kusakabe: Let me explain here. Since Shindo began making films, he has always worked for the Kindai Eiga [Modern Film] Production Company, which he himself organized. There was only one movie which he made outside it. That was *Aisai Monogatari* [*Story of a Beloved Wife,* 1951, Shindo's first film]. However, there were many occasions when films made by Shindo under Kindai Eiga were distributed by other major film companies, like Toho, Shochiku, and so on.

Mellen: Have you had any experience with censorship?

Shindo: No, I don't think I have. There were times when the hands with the scissors got very close to us, though. [Laughter] But we always fought.

Kusakabe: I can explain more. The very name "Shindo" has been effective with those men who perform censorship. His films always had a formidable reputation as works of art, so people were rather careful with what they did to Shindo's films. Naturally, his films are in no way the same as commercial pornographic films.

Mellen: A more specific problem. Can you describe how you contrasted moments of sound with moments of silence in *Kuroneko?* Are there any specific points where the sound stops completely?

Shindo: Let me see . . . I cannot recall now exactly where and in what scenes I have used silence. But I see film as an art of "montage" which consists of a dialectic or interaction between the movement and nonmovement of the image. Probably in order to sustain the even tempo of the film, I have used this idea in the soundtrack. The sudden moments of silence are to heighten the effect of the montage through contrast.

Mellen: Do you yourself do the editing for your films?

Shindo: Yes, I do it myself. I have an editor. But generally in Japan today directors spend a great deal of time editing the so-called quality films.

Mellen: I was intrigued by the use of the cat as a symbol in *Kuroneko.* The cat seemed to accompany the demon woman and I felt that this represented some aspect of Japanese culture with which I was not familiar. What is the force of the cat as a symbol in this film?

Shindo: Let me see. The idea of the cat came to me because the original story was based upon an old Japanese folk tale called "The Cat's Revenge." It was at least partly based on that story. I liked the idea of using the cat because I could thus express the very low position in society which certain people occupy by using so useless and low an animal as the cat.*

Mellen: The same emotional level is expressed both by the cat and by your human beings?

Shindo: No, it is not at the level of emotion. Only the cat can occupy such a low position in our society. I wanted a strong expression of the degradation of the common man's life in our culture. I hope you understand this point.

Mellen: Is there a Freudian aspect to the relationship between the mother and son in *Kuroneko?* Although as a demon the mother must kill her son, she doesn't want to do it, and the son seems to recognize his mother through the demon.

Shindo: Yes, there is. There is a strong Freudian influence throughout all my work. I have one question. In the United States is there any Freudian influence in films?

Mellen: I would say that it is a minimal one. Italian directors like

---

* The cat is considered a much less valuable animal when compared to other more useful ones in Japan. Its social status, as well, is very low compared to other animals, perhaps analogous to that of the rat in our culture, because the cat, being so lazy, failed to arrive at Buddha's funeral on time. Much to his disgrace, he never earned a position as one of the twelve animals who represent the twelve years of the Oriental calendar. In ancient times the cat was a symbol of lack of value or merit. This is not so true anymore as their popularity as house pets has increased.

Bertolucci, Petri, Visconti, Fellini are much more interested in Freud than American directors.

Shindo: Yes, I agree, particularly in the case of Visconti.

Mellen: When the son in *Kuroneko* opens the door to his mother at the end of the film do you feel that his desire to rise in society and be accepted as a feudal lord transcends his Freudian Oedipal impulse toward his mother?

Shindo: Even at the end of the film this conflict remains unresolved.

Mellen: Do you fear that when you treat extreme scenes such as rape, murder, insanity, starvation, etc., your films have a tendency toward melodrama? Do you consider this a danger?

Shindo: No, I am not bothered by the use of extremes.

Mellen: In Japanese films is it true that melodrama is not considered bad?

Shindo: I should like to state here my opinion of what melodrama is. I consider melodrama to be a story or situation created artificially with the sole purpose of attracting an audience's attention. This is contrived very conveniently. If you want to depict a truthful drama, it is permissible to use any means available. Here I mean any possible dramatic situation, including the extreme examples you mentioned. However, this is the area in which true artists are separated from professional craftsmen. If the director, the "creator," intends to produce a truly artistic work, he must carefully choose the most suitable dramatic situation from the many possibilities. This selection is in the director's hands entirely, and the choice determines how fine an artist he is.

Mellen: Then you believe that melodrama per se is not bad, but what counts is how appropriate it is to the needs of the subject?

Shindo: It all depends on the context of the film and what other ideas and devices are employed in it. If you talk of the style of a film, the content often decides the style.

Mellen: Is there any special reason why you, as well as other Japanese filmmakers, favor historical settings and legends, fables and old stories for your plots?

Shindo: Well, essentially this is because I am a Japanese. We select certain old stories which have sufficient modern application; I should say stories which have universal and modern implications. I choose one or two out of hundreds. Many are useless for my filmmaking. I am sure that this process of selection must be the same for filmmakers throughout the world.

Mellen: Do Japanese filmmakers choose historical settings so often because the Japanese feel close to their history? There is not much distance between past and present?

Shindo: When I want to dissect a modern problem, I actually find many similar problems in ancient days. In fact, without the many outer layers of so-called modern civilization, the themes I find in old stories are more clear-cut. They are so visible and extreme. I am not saying that all historical eras are similar to today. But by using a comprehensible social structure such as we had in the past, it is much easier for me to convey or recreate modern situations.

Mellen: Why do you think so many Japanese directors, including Imamura and yourself, treat the relationship or conflict between civilization and an earlier primitive life? Your *Island* is a renowned example.

Shindo: Yes, that tendency has been rather popular among Japanese filmmakers for the past five or six years. The reason is that since the latter half of the nineteenth century, we have been witnessing the weakening of the human mind. I think this is a universal problem. Consequently, modern men, and I for one, are in the process of reevaluating primitive man's energy and identity. This is a very central question.

Mellen: You try to recover what is human in a time when people are not acting like human beings? What is your point of view as the director in *Live Today, Die Tomorrow* toward the criminal in modern society?

Shindo: In this the protagonist is the pus of a rotten society.

Mellen: An example of the social disease? Do you sympathize with him?

Shindo: I stand on the same ground as the protagonist.

Mellen: Thinking about *Kuroneko* and Shinoda's *Buraikan,* I am interested in the attitude toward the criminal. The criminal is an example of vitality deflected against the society. Do you consider this an example of the vitality which human beings have for survival?

Shindo: To oppose the law?

Mellen: Yes.

Shindo: You cannot forget here that filmmaking is first of all an art. So, in taking an extreme case like the criminal, you can achieve a strong impact on a society which holds to a deceptive "common sense" about the legal versus the illegal. You are illuminating something for the audience in the form of a strong and shocking expression. You should not use criminal violence just for the sake of titillation.

Mellen: There is one more specific question I have. Why does the

blind beggar Iwakichi sacrifice himself in *Children of Hiroshima?*
Shindo: This requires a very Japanese interpretation. His act is a
protest. Iwakichi is a weak, meek person and so his expression of
meager resistance can only be self-sacrifice. If he were a strong
man, he probably would have fought gallantly.
Mellen: Resistance to what?
Shindo: To those people and the many outrageous acts and situa-
tions in the world which originally led to the idea of and finally car-
rying out the bombing. You know that his resistance was indeed
vain.
Mellen: Are there any Western directors whom you still admire,
past or present?
Shindo: Yes, the American Orson Welles and the Russian Eisen-
stein. They are the best. There are more as well—the Frenchman
Godard.
Mellen: Do you still like Godard—the recent political films?
Shindo: I like his earlier films. It seems to me that he has changed
very much in his later work; the earlier Godard has vanished.
Mellen: Do you believe any of the young Japanese directors are
doing socially interesting films? Are there any directors whom it
would be important to include in any discussion of the social con-
sciousness present in the contemporary Japanese film?
Shindo: Yes, I can think of several. Nagisa Oshima, Masahiro
Shinoda, Shohei Imamura, and many more, too many.
Mellen: How about Teshigahara?
Shindo: Yes, of course. He is interesting. I admire many young
directors. Among older directors, I admire Mizoguchi most.
Mellen: Not Kurosawa?
Shindo: Oh, yes. I admire him also [Laughs]
Kusakabe: But of course each has his own shining talent. These
people are, including Kurosawa, the really talented directors Japan
is proud of. They are first-class in the international sense.
Shindo: I read your article about Kurosawa. It was well done.
Mellen: Did you think it was correct?
Kusakabe: Yes, it was correct. It was well written.
Mellen: Because Oshima and Tadao Sato thought I was wrong.
Kusakabe [to Shindo]: Oshima-san and Sato-san didn't agree with
her. [Both laugh] I think she was disappointed.
Shindo: You should not worry about their attempts at refutation.
You know each has his own opinion.
Kusakabe [in English]: Everybody has a different position, a dif-
ferent viewpoint.

Mellen: I felt as if I had much more sympathy with Kurosawa than they did. They seemed more conservative.

Shindo: At present Kurosawa is not very active, so many people say this and that about him, but one must agree that he is indeed a rare talent among us and we will not have anyone like him in the near future. He is a renowned director throughout the world.

Mellen: In the panel discussion we had, they couldn't admit that Kurosawa was an international figure who belonged to the whole world.

Shindo: Oh, well, I firmly believe everybody secretly admits he is, although they won't want to say so at times.

Kusakabe: I think so too.

Shindo: It is disgusting that now Japanese people are wholly against authority or rather anything that even looks like an establishment. I agree to some extent, but they should not be swept away by this kind of generalization. Good is good no matter how established it is.

FIVE

TADASHI IMAI

INTRODUCTION

As yet little known in the United States, Tadashi Imai stands out as one of the directors most sympathetic to those suffering from feudal oppression. In Japan he is praised for his compassion for the downtrodden and his reputation is high even among conservative and conventional critics—despite his membership in the Communist Party. Imai's *Muddy Waters* (*Nigorie,* 1953), a three-part film based upon stories of Ichiyo Higuchi, has been shown abroad; it is a moving exposé of the cruel persistence of feudal values during the Meiji era.

The first episode of *Muddy Waters*, "The Thirteenth Night," concerns a woman who returns to her parents' house, determined to live no longer with her adulterous husband. On this moonlit night her father sends her back to her husband. While returning she meets an old school friend, now a down-and-out rickshaw man, with whom she passes a few moments' respite before she must resume her hated journey. The second part treats a maid indentured to an unfeeling mistress from whom she shudders to borrow money for her needy family. Finally she steals it, but escapes detection because the son of the house is equally repelled by his mother and filches the rest of the money, making it seem as if he took it all. The maid's "crime" is attributed to him as well.

In the third segment a prostitute is murdered by one of her married clients who is jealous because she has at last met a man who may free her from the degrading life she despises. Each of the film's components exposes in its own way how cheaply women are held in Meiji Japan, a surrogate for the Japan of the present. They are shown, despite their varied circumstances, as ultimately powerless to make any of the decisions which can alter the ensnaring patterns of their lives.

Imai's father was chief priest at the Reisen-in Memorial Hall at Shōun-ji. Until World War II, this was the hereditary temple of the noble Matsudaira family, a great historical name among the feudal aristocracy. Imai's reaction against his traditional family and its conservatism was expressed in his radical activities while he was in college. These included a famous protest against the removal of Dr. Yukitoki Takikawa from the faculty of law at Kyoto University.

Imai, like many Japanese directors from Mizoguchi to Kurosawa, had neither planned nor aspired to be a film director. He has expounded upon the manner in which he was slowly drawn to the film industry in the periodical *Eiga-no-Tomo:*

> My original intention certainly was not a career in the film industry. I liked history and my big ambition was to devote my life to the study of oriental history. When that plan was ruined by my imprisonment in my university days, I approached my father with the idea of getting into movies or journalism. To my knowledge he had not seen a movie more than twice in his whole life and his answer came as a pleasant surprise to me. "If you want so much to be in the movies," he said, "well, try and make yourself a person like Shimazu or Kinugasa." Heaven knows how he ever came to know those names!

Imai made his first films during World War II, although the period of his greatest creativity did not begin until the fifties. The wartime films were made in the service of a group which ruled Japan in a manner antithetical to Imai's espoused beliefs—an anomaly which has not gone unnoticed by Joseph L. Anderson and Donald Richie in their history of the Japanese film:

> Imai was just as dedicated to the Imperial cause during the war as he was to the Communist cause both before and after it. In way of explanation one can only again call attention to the Japanese genius for the *volte-face,* and for the completely apolitical quality of the Japanese character.*

Probably this performance on Imai's part had far less to do with the Japanese character than it did with the politics of nationalism which

---

* *The Japanese Film: Art and Industry* (New York: Grove Press, 1960), p. 387.

must have been stronger in Imai than his radical convictions. The films of Oshima, among others, bear witness against the appropriateness of this apolitical designation when applied to the Japanese film director.

Imai's later activities returned him to social commitment. The onset of the cold war precipitated a "red purge," an outgrowth of the famous 1948 strike at the Toho Film Company. Imai was blacklisted in the film industry. Having in the interim formally become a member of the Communist Party, he had to start from scratch to find backing for his films. In 1951 his *Dokkoi Ikiteru (And Yet We Live)* became the first Japanese movie made outside the control of large capital, a considerable breakthrough for all independent and avant-garde directors in Japan.

During the 1950s, Imai was influenced by several Italian neorealist directors, particularly De Sica, then entering his most productive period. *Until the Day We Meet Again* (1950) had a wartime setting, the hero dying at the front and the heroine in an air raid. It was patterned after *Brief Encounter* and was made without a completed scenario. Each day writers would turn out for Imai scenes which were filmed piece by piece.

Although Japanese critics refer to Imai's style as *nakanai* realism (realism without tears), certain of Imai's works do border on the sentimental. This is true particularly of *The Tower of Lilies* (1953), which treats the deaths of a group of schoolgirl-nurses during an American invasion. In their name a monument called the Tower of Lilies is erected, from which the film takes it title.

Imai's finest work includes *Darkness at Noon* (1956), which bears no relation to the Koestler novel. Its subject is an actual case wherein five boys were charged with murder. The film was made during the trial and argued for the innocence of the boys. It had trouble gaining release precisely because the case was still pending before the Japanese courts. The critic Akira Iwasaki called *Darkness at Noon* "the Japanese Sacco and Vanzetti, Tom Mooney and Rosenberg cases all rolled into one." But Imai emphatically repudiates the notion that his films have either been conceived for or provide any function as propaganda. His desire, he continually stresses, is "to make films not for cliques but for the entire film audience. I want everyone to find something they can like in my pictures."

Another of Imai's distinguished works was *Night Drum* (1958), a film also about the condition of women in Japan, which developed the theme of the intertwining of adultery and feudalism. *Night Drum* was based upon a play by the classical master of Japanese theater and literature Monzaemon Chikamatsu. But Imai's purpose, unlike Chikamatsu's, was to unfold the manner in which feudal values remain a vital intrinsic component of Japanese society, part of the psychological and social fabric of life in Japan. At the film's end the husband kills his wife and her lover—the accepted reaction to adultery. But in *Night Drum* this traditional conclusion is invoked only, as Donald Richie has observed, because Imai has "brought [the husband] to question everything which his society has made him do."

Imai has received the highest praise from Japanese film critics, consistently responding to the unpretentious quality of his films, his directness and lack of pseudo-profundity or extraneous stylistic ploys. His sincerity in speaking for the victims of Japanese social injustice has won over critics who would not normally be disposed to approve. Akira Aoji expressed this forthrightly in the *Chūō Kōron* magazine:

The movie world . . . is a hangout of bluffing cheaters. Director Tadashi Imai, with his characteristic sincerity and honesty, is a rarity in that world. He is upright and advances steadily with such care as one would lavish in piling up bricks one upon another. He is a man who has absolutely nothing to do with bluffing or cheating, such as is described by the old phrase, "intimidate others by wearing the mask of a devil."

Imai provides a sense of relief from posturing and inflated stylistics designed to conceal a paucity of thought, genuine emotion, or real commitment. Susumu Okada's description of Imai in the *Kinema Jumpo* characterizes the attitude of many Japanese film people, critics included, toward his work:

At the time when the storm of the "red purge" was raging, Imai was living in a dark house situated right below a cliff at Meguro. Whenever I visited him there, I found him sitting quietly in a room upstairs. He struck me alternately as being lost in reverie, thinking seriously about something, and trying to visualize his plan for the coming age. I also have found him like that at the second floor of a certain tea house near Namiki-dōri Street at Ginza, sitting and staring blankly at the people walking in the street below. In such moments Imai looks so intimate and so likable. This warm human touch often shows itself spontaneously in an ordinary shot in one of his films—the ability to move the audience without much effort is one factor that makes up Imai's happiness.

Donald Richie, however, particularly in his *Japanese Cinema,* has been a dissenting voice in this adulatory assessment of the work of Imai: "Imai's films are almost without style. His only 'style' is found in the content." * In the early book with Anderson, Richie argued that Imai "is resolutely political and [his message] continues to indicate the limitations of the director." † Imai's own description of his method of work seems to support Richie's contention that his films divide into an uneasy dichotomy between form and content:

> In my work, I never decide in advance on elaborate continuity. As we come to each scene, while we are shooting I decide how I'll do it. When the day's shooting is over and the next day's schedule is decided upon, without thinking any more about it I go to bed. The next day, on the shooting site before work begins, I talk things over in general with the actors. By the time everything is ready to go, I know how I'm going to do it.

Imai, however, has been defended by European critics like Max Tessier, in his *Dossiers du Cinema (Cinéastes II)*, who share with the Japanese an ease with Imai's point of view:

> Si les options d'Imai le mènent parfois à préférer la propagande à l'art, et le didactisme au simple constat, son humanisme sincère le garde toujours des tentations dangereuses du dogmatisme.‡

Tessier contends that Imai's realism functions first as a mirror of reality, but second and more importantly as "une pierre lancée contre ce miroir"—a stone thrown against this mirror.

Imai depicts harsh reality and social injustice with meticulous accuracy before proceeding to assail it. Richie holds, in Tessier's view, "that Imai, like Yoshimura or Yamamoto, lacks a distinctive style and give more importance to what he says than to the manner in which he says it." But, answers Tessier, this is an unwarranted and pejorative judgment, since when great auteur-directors identify themselves with a preexisting style in their films, their style inevitably precedes any idea or ideology:

---

* (Garden City, New York: Anchor Books, 1971), p. 126.

† Anderson and Richie, *The Japanese Film,* p. 385.

‡ If Imai's options lead him at times to prefer propaganda to art and the didacticism of simple statement, his sincere humanism always protects him from the dangerous temptations of dogmatism.

Cet aspect fondamental d'Imai explique le mépris ironique dans lequel la plupart des jeunes cinéastes, tels Oshima ou Yoshida, tiennent son oeuvre: il est clair qu'elle a trop bien correspondu à un type de pensée et d'esthétique pour continuer à exercer une influence profonde sur une génération qui, d'une manière générale, se moque du réalisme social.*

To those like Tessier, writing in 1971, the aestheticism of the *nouvelle vague*—both French and Japanese—has come to seem tedious and repetitious, its absorption with style for its own sake barely able to conceal a poverty of social perception. For such critics, Imai's social concerns reemerge as refreshing. His objections to contemporary Japan and in particular to the peculiar lack of resistance of the populace to the authorities, especially during the last war, constitute a vital and significant force on the side of change in both Japanese cinema and in a barely postfeudal society.

---

* This fundamental aspect of Imai's work explains the ironic contempt in which the majority of young filmmakers, like Oshima or Yoshida, hold his work: it is clear that this corresponds as well to a type of thought and aesthetic which continues to exercise a profound influence on a generation which may in a general way mock social realism.

INTERVIEW WITH
TADASHI IMAI

Mellen: Why did you decide to make a film about Iwo Jima in 1972?

Imai: The film was not originated by me. The scenario was handed to me and I was requested to make it. That was my only reason.

Mellen: I understand there is a great deal of anti-American feeling among Japanese youth today. Do you think this film might contribute to that climate? Do you think there may be a danger in contributing to blind anti-Americanism, which would even include the left in America?

Imai: No, I don't think so. To me, the military power of America during the Second World War served to liberate the Japanese people. The Japanese were utterly oppressed by military fascism by the end of the war. America created democracy in Japan.

Mellen: Would you still hold to this view?

Imai: Yes, indeed I believe in this argument. Before the war, Germany, Italy, and Japan represented the fascist nations. Like it or not, history proves that American military power was the greatest force involved in liberating us from fascism and liberating the entire era from fascism. I had no intention of inciting or emphasizing anti-Americanism per se in this film. But, of course, one has to expose elsewhere the historical role performed by the United States military power in the present.

Mellen: Today some Americans are trying to liberate our country from American militarism with domestic fascist overtones.

Is it true that you were once arrested for belonging to a leftist study group when you were in high school? Do you remember anything about that group?

Imai: I don't know if you could call them leftists; they were just a bunch of students who wanted to read Marx, Lenin, etc. The time was such that even to do this simple thing, we had to be secretive. The governmental oppression was complete. I was arrested, charged with being a member of the reading group, and locked up in jail.

Mellen: What was the year?

Imai: I was seventeen years old. It was Showa 4th year [1929].

Mellen: When did you join the Communist Party?

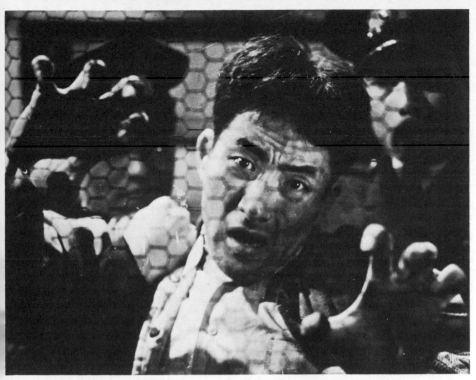

Kojiro Kusanagi in *Darkness at Noon*. "Like it or not, history proves that American military power was the greatest force involved in liberating us from fascism and liberating the entire era from fascism."

Imai: I became a member officially after the last war. I was a member of Kyosan-shugi Seinen Domei [Young People's Communist Alliance] before the war ended. This was a secret organization and I was a member from the age of seventeen.

Mellen: Are you still a member of the Japanese Communist Party?

Imai: Yes, officially I have membership, but it is more appropriate to say that my position in the party is that of a sympathizer.

Mellen: What kind of films did you make during the war?

Imai: We were only allowed to make films with military themes and heroes, or about conventional middle-class citizens. I didn't do much work. During the last two years of the war, I made no films at all.

Imai on the set of *Eternal Cause*. "The military power of America during the second World War served to liberate the Japanese people. . . . America created democracy in Japan."

Mellen: Were any of your films censored during that period?

Imai: I don't recall my films actually being cut, but the censor checked all films at the point of the scenario writing.

Mellen: Who did the checking?

Imai: There was Naimucho [the Ministry of Domestic Affairs]; they were the directors of the police system in Japan at that time.

Mellen: Can you describe the historical background to your making the film *An Enemy of the People* [*Minshu no Teki,* 1946]?

Imai: After the war, the occupation army created the CI & E * located at General MacArthur's headquarters. It was the organization which controlled the information flow in Japan. The CI & E had a movie division in it and they did all the censoring of film scenarios. During the first three years of the occupation, America, through MacArthur, had a plan to spread "democracy" in Japan, and many so-called leftists worked in that division. Anyway, the CI & E film division dispatched several officers to the large Japanese film companies. The directors and scenario writers were gathered together and we were ordered to make six kinds of films. I have forgotten what the six were, but they included (1) movies criticizing the Japanese imperial system, (2) movies attacking the activities of the Japanese *zaibatsu* † or cartel families during the war, (3) autobiographies of Japanese revolutionaries who were annihilated, like Takeji Kobayashi, who was tortured and killed by the police during the war, and Hidemi Ozaki, (4), films encouraging and urging coal miners and other sectors of labor to expand economic

---

* Civil Information and Education Section (CI & E). In March of 1946 the Civil Information and Education Section of the American occupation assumed the responsibility of viewing and passing judgment on all completed films in Japan. No films could be released without its approval. CI & E was particularly against the making of period films, which it confused with an endorsement of feudalism. From 1945 on prohibited subjects included "anything infused with militarism, revenge, nationalism or anti-foreignism, distortion of history, approval of religious or racial discrimination, favoring or approving feudal loyalty or treating human life lightly; direct or indirect approval of suicide, approval of the oppression or degradation of wives, admiration of cruelty or unjust violence, anti-democratic opinion, exploitation of children, etc." CI & E also relied on the officers of the Japan Motion Picture and Drama Employees Union to draw up a list of the industry's "war criminals." See Anderson and Richie, *The Japanese Film,* pp. 159–180.

† The *zaibatsu* were giant industrial and financial conglomerates controlled and dominated by families, such as Mitsui and Mitsubishi. They began as humble merchants during the Tokugawa era, but rapidly became economic giants who controlled virtually every manufacturing industry after the Meiji era. The government played a decisive role in allowing their growth into such an enormous power within fifty years.

production in Japan so that Japanese industry might recover. I cannot recall the last two categories. But anyway, in accordance with these guidelines the companies summoned many young film directors and instructed them to carry out these projects. I was still a beginner at Toho at that time, and they made me do *An Enemy of the People*. I am sure you know *Waga Seishun ni Kuinashi* [*No Regrets for Our Youth*] of Kurosawa. He made this film based upon the life of Hidemi Ozaki, one of the persecuted revolutionaries of Japan. No one had the guts to make a film critical of the emperor so we tacitly dropped this and made films that fit into the permitted categories. It seems somewhat funny in retrospect. Several officers gathered together the board of directors of the company, directors, scenario writers, assistants, everybody, and gave us a few long speeches. They threatened us, saying that if we didn't cooperate, they would immediately shut down the place. We cooperated.

Mellen: I don't quite understand why the American military asked for films attacking the huge companies since the American economic system has a similar structure in which large conglomerates exercise complete control of the economy and even the political process, not so different from the *zaibatsu* * and even their German counterparts, the Krupps.

---

* MacArthur immediately divided the *zaibatsu* into many small companies. Mitsui, for example, was broken into some fifty companies. This was probably done to prevent or retard competition with United States industry. After Japan asserted her independence, these companies came back again under the same old banner to occupy the same essential position as the *zaibatsu*.

During the first three years of American occupation of Japan, MacArthur set about to remove the power of the feudal conglomerates, which had created a fascist power and a military state. He sought to democratize the form of rule without altering its essential structure. The ancillary purpose of this policy was to curb the industrial expansion of Japan into American economic markets. MacArthur could not achieve these ends without the collaboration of those components of the left willing to support his democratic antifeudal and anticartel "reforms." He approached trade unionists, socialists, and those communists willing to support his creation of representative forms. Paradoxically, he therefore came to be regarded as "socialistic" by the Japanese old guard. Thus once the parameters of reform were agreed, MacArthur supported union organization, and even the Socialist and Communist parties in forming an opposition to the old order. Land reform was imposed on the countryside and the tenant farmer system was abolished. Villagers were educated to engage in politics. The moment, however, that the rank and file of these parties began to press for a true political voice and leadership in the new government, the occupation initiated a vast purge, "red hunt," and repression. Thousands were fired or blacklisted. The socialists and communists who helped MacArthur "democratize" feudal power found the *zaibatsu* regrouping into political parties where they now adopted more flexible techniques of rule.

Imai: You see, they asked us to make films which revealed the exploitation of people and the cruelty of the big *zaibatsu* to the masses. As I mentioned before, their main purpose was to make Japan a democratic nation as soon as possible, so they apparently used every possible means to do it. Filmmakers were to be useful in the rapid development of democracy in Japan.

Mellen: Is there a particular definition of "democracy" which you explore in your own films?

Imai: Oh, that is a difficult question. All I can say is that to me democracy is the realization of government "by the people, of the people and for the people." [Laughs]

Mellen: Could you describe something of *An Enemy of the People,* which you made so soon after the end of the war? It is often written about when your films are discussed.

Imai: I don't recall it much. I didn't think that it was much of a movie. [Laughs] It was the story of workers placed under very severe working conditions during the war. After the war they stand up for themselves and organize a union. This organization of unions was one of the major recommendations of the CI & E, so I had guidelines. [Laughs] Many labor unions were organized through the solicitation of the occupation army. That was one of their central policies. We encouraged it in the movie industry.

Mellen: Is that so!

Imai: I can hardly recommend this film myself. [Laughs]

Mellen: Would you say that the essential theme of your films is the struggle between the ruling class and the working class?

Imai: No, not so much the class struggle. This theme is more appropriate to the works of Satsuo Yamamoto. I cannot formulate the theme of my work very well, but after perusing my films and listening to critics talking about my films, it seems to me that my work is centered on human tragedies—those created by the weight of war, poverty, and social oppression. I think I can designate these as "social evils."

Mellen: I understand that in your new film about the young sailors the human relationship between the naval officers and the young conscripts is the main theme. Certain things were expected of the officers that should not have been expected of the poor peasant boys who became sailors without fully realizing what was going on. Even at the conclusion of the film the distinction between officers and young conscripts remains the same.

Imai: You could say that is one dimension of the film. However, my main subject is the humanity of those officers drafted from the universities who could not prevent the tragedy of the war. Young boys were conditioned by their families to fight for their country and to die proudly. The student-soldiers tried to treat these boys humanely; these young officers know themselves that they are powerless to alter the fate of these young boys in Japan. Humaneness is good, but under certain circumstances it cannot in itself help people. I think this was the reality of that period during the war.

Mellen: Do you sympathize with the character called Kudo?

Imai: Yes. Kudo comes from a dirt-poor village. He feels and understands very well the backgrounds of the young boys, and between him and the boy soldiers there is a very poignant, strong emotion. He seriously sets out to teach them that the poor have to be self-reliant and self-esteeming. He tries to make them realize that to be born poor is not a crime as long as they are willing to open up their own world with their own hands. But in the end he fails. The poor finally have no one but themselves on whom to rely. They should use their own energy to gain their share of the world and not permit themselves to be used endlessly as tools of the ruling class. The central tragedy of Kudo is that he himself is the victim of an age which succeeded in brainwashing the entire population of Japan. Kudo doesn't really doubt the war itself. And there my second theme emerges. If you oppose the war, your opposition has to begin long, long before the war actually starts. It is already too late to stop a war-making machine when the actual fighting has started. Japan as well as Germany learned that.

Mellen: Do you wish to influence your audience toward any action or any particular point of view?

Imai: I usually do not attempt this. I don't think it is good technique to shout messages. Such an attitude would be inappropriate to film or any serious art form. What I try to do is to show, to unfold, a direction which seems to be the most reasonable. I usually stop there. If a person infers the necessity of political action, that is his decision. Some people may not see my films in that way, and that is fine. Their sensibility will be affected differently. Some are alert and some are not.

Mellen: Donald Richie criticized *Here Is a Spring* [*Koko ni Izumu Ari,* 1955] and *Darkness at Noon* on the grounds that they suggest that workers need intellectuals to point a right direction, to show them the way. Do you have any comment?

Imai: Oh, Donald Richie. Yes, I have heard of him. I have never met him, but I understand he is very much against communism. He must have thought that my films were trying to teach an audience something about communism. He is not correct. I may believe in a set of ideas, but I don't use a figure in my films to articulate my own beliefs. Chekhov warned against this and I agree with him. The writer should not transmit his own ideology through the mouths of his characters.

Mellen: What techniques of filmmaking do you think appropriate for a political film director? This would apply not only to your own films, but also to those of Godard, Costa-Gavras, Bertolucci, and other radical European directors.

Imai: As for the style of Godard, his early films were excellent—employing new techniques and breaking with traditional methods. He showed us how fresh a movie could be. Especially his *Katteni Shiyagare!* [Literally, "Do as You Wish!" Probably *My Life to Live*] But now these new methods have become part of film tradition and we have to seek continuously for something more. This is the difficulty of filmmaking or of any art.

Mellen: Are there any techniques or is there a style appropriate for the political filmmaker? Godard's early films were not political in sensibility or subject. Let me give you an example. Don't scenes of violence and melodrama, because they substitute gratuitous violence or explicit action for the unfolding of events within the drama, subvert the meaning a director wishes to convey? And wouldn't melodrama therefore be inappropriate to a political film, although so many political films have an inordinate amount of violence in them? In most of these films violent scenes are used simply to attract the attention of the audience. Do you use any techniques to foster the audience's interest in the political aspects of your movies?

Imai: I don't fully understand your question. Are you asking if there is any special technique which I use in my political movies? If that is your question, the answer is no. I am not conscious of any special technique. The success of a political film depends on the keenness of the director's understanding of society. Obviously the movie, political or not, is the product of the moviemaker's viewpoint; the expression of his ideas could take many forms. I was very impressed by *The Battle of Algiers*. It was a good revolutionary film. Do you mean films like this when you speak of political films?

Mellen: Yes. Actually I spent some time in Italy with Pontecorvo, the director of that movie, and I've written a book about it.

Imai: Oh, is that so? That is very nice. I was very impressed by that film.

Mellen: Are you interested in any of the Japanese police films that came after your *Darkness at Noon?* I am thinking of Oshima's

Death by Hanging or even Kurosawa's *High and Low*. Do you see any similarity between these films and your film?
Imai: I did deal with this area in *Darkness at Noon*. This is the story of four young men who were arrested, tortured, and forced to confess to a crime which they didn't commit. They were sentenced to the death penalty. The film was made about seventeen or eighteen years ago. I don't think there is much similarity between this film and the Kurosawa or Oshima films.
Mellen: For what crime were these four young men arrested?
Imai: Nothing in the way of political charges. They happened to be sort of juvenile delinquents. They were known as "bad boys" and had been marked by the police for some time. But they were not antiestablishment in any way. When the police were faced with an unsolved murder, these young men were framed. This story was based on an incident which actually happened.
Mellen: Is there any Japanese director in the history of the Japanese film whom you admire or with whom you have felt sympathy?
Imai: Yes, many. All those considered first-class in this industry have something to offer. Each has some special virtue from which we all can learn. It is true of all outstanding directors in the international sense as well.
Mellen: From a political point of view, have you felt a special affinity for any of these Japanese directors?
Imai: The word "political" is difficult to define. It can be broad, meaning "social." "Social" can be "political."
Mellen: What I had in mind was someone understanding the relationship between social groups and society, including even the relationship between an individual and history, not political in the sense of parties.
Imai: I see. With this in mind, I have much respect for Satsuo Yamamoto. If you ask me about Western filmmakers who contributed much to the film as we know it today, I would mention Eisenstein, Chaplin, Disney, and so on. I admire them very much for their innovations and for their inventiveness.
Mellen: Are there any contemporary Japanese filmmakers whom you admire?
Imai: He is not "modern," since he is my contemporary. It is peculiar he was not recognized outside Japan, but I have great admiration for Keisuke Kinoshita.*

---

* Keisuke Kinoshita has long been one of the highly respected middle-rank Japanese directors, enjoying enormous popularity with Japanese audiences. His earlier

Mellen: What is your impression of the status of women in Japan today, as distinct from the way women are represented in your film *Muddy Waters* [*Nigorie*]?

Imai: Well, the status of Japanese women has progressed enormously since then and especially since the war. Not many Japanese men, however, have advanced much in their hearts, and in some cases this remains true of women. In their minds they know women have to be respected, but they don't act accordingly. Woman's status in Japan is not very high yet, certainly not to the extent I had expected it would be by this time.

Mellen: What action do you recommend to Japanese women to alter this situation?

Imai: Well, it is not so much a case of methods. First, women themselves have to realize their problems and become conscious of them. Much will follow upon this.

Mellen: As individuals?

Imai: Yes, as individuals at first.

Mellen: And then to establish some movement or organization?

Imai: Possibly, but to me the most important thing for women to overcome is the old definition of who they are, what they should be, their sense of reality. I am speaking of average Japanese women who might say, "I don't want to see cruel films," and they refuse to watch films about the atomic bomb. When women behave in a frivolous way, they destroy their own potential role and position in society.

Mellen: Is it that they don't think in terms of causes?

Imai: Yes, and they avoid looking at the reality of the world.

Mellen: Since many of your films have been made against feudalism in Japan, do you think feudal elements remain today?

Imai: Yes, mainly in human relationships. For example, there is a modern "swinging" labor union man, in fact the president of the union here at Toho. He was patted on the shoulder by the Toho company president and the president asked him, "How are things going?" The union leader was deeply impressed by the fact that the president knew him and talked to him personally in such a friendly manner. Japanese people are traditionally weak when confronted by someone in authority, especially their superiors.

---

films, like *Carmen Comes Home* (1951) and *Candle in the Wind* (1957), attacked, or at least questioned, traditional norms. His much less interesting later films, like *The Ballad of Narayama* (1958) and *The River Fuefuki* (1960), a tediously sentimental family chronicle, began more and more to endorse, at least implicitly, the family system and the old ways.

Mellen: In other words, could we say that he cares more about being recognized by the president of the Toho company than about the workers whom he represents in the union?

Imai: Right! Many Japanese would reject this view and they say so periodically, but in reality they have a soft corner in their minds when it comes to authority or hierarchy in society.

Mellen: They are not always conscious of it?

Imai: Yes. Not too long ago I made a movie called *Cruel Story* [*Bushido Zankoku Monogatari*], about the cruelty involved in being a warrior. This film deals with modern soldiers who, on a conscious level, are modern men, yet they act very differently, exposing their feudal ways of thought and the feudalism among the Japanese people. The movie was well received both in Japan and abroad.

Mellen: In *Satagashi ga Kowareru Toki* [*When the Cookie Crumbles,* 1967], your film about the death of Marilyn Monroe, set in Japan, how did you handle the similarities between Japan and the United States?

Imai: This film was based on a story written by one of the leading authoresses of Japan. The story evolves around an actress who is somewhat like Marilyn Monroe. I was asked to make the film by Daiei. Well, I am one of those Japanese directors who cannot afford to make only the films I want to make, so I accepted. In some respects I enjoyed making it, but it is not a film I really want to talk about.

Mellen: I see; so this film is not one in which you chose to show any cultural similarities between the United States and Japan?

Imai: No. Directors in Japan are not very wealthy and often they have to do films they don't especially like.

Mellen: Do you write most of your scripts?

Imai: No, I usually don't write.

Mellen: Which do you like best among all your films?

Imai: I'm often asked which I like best. To tell the truth none of them really satisfies me. Every time a day's shooting schedule ends, I have many ideas about improving this scene or that. But in practice you cannot retake many shots. As I think back over my films, those unutilized ideas come back to my mind as accumulated regrets. In fact, I try not to think too much about my past work. Probably I will not have one film of which I can say, "This is my masterpiece." I usually go to see the finished film once as a matter of responsibility. Afterwards I will not see it again. One day I was talking about this to Kurosawa-san and he said he doesn't even see the preview of his films. He finishes his film in the darkroom and that is the end of his seeing that film. [Laughs]

Mellen: Then he never sees his films?

Imai: No, he doesn't. [Laughs]

Mellen: Do you take a large hand in the editing of your films?

Imai: No. In Japan we have an editor. I usually work with him, asking this and that. I review his work many times.

Mellen: Do you have any thoughts about the conflict between the "advanced" and the "primitive" which has become a frequent theme in contemporary Japanese films?

Imai: Can you give me an example of this theme?

Mellen: The Insect Woman of Imamura or *The Woman in the Dunes* of Teshigahara.

Imai: Oh, I see. I understand that Imamura is especially keen on this theme, but I don't think that it is the main theme in *Woman in the Dunes* or that other directors in Japan are interested in it.

Mellen: What is your opinion of the prevalence of pornographic films in Japan today?

Imai: I don't know whether this is true or not, but some directors believe in sex as the most essential human quality. So in order to look into the human problem they focus on human sexuality. Others are making this kind of film for a livelihood.

SIX

KON ICHIKAWA

INTRODUCTION

Kon Ichikawa, a generation younger than Kurosawa, is acknowledged in the United States as one of Japan's finest directors, one of the great craftsmen of the Japanese cinema. "As a stylist," Donald Richie has said, "Kon Ichikawa is one of Japan's most brilliant."

Ichikawa's first important film to gain foreign recognition was *The Harp of Burma* (1956), which portrays a Japanese soldier appalled by the scores of unburied bodies dotting the landscape of Burma at the end of the Second World War. Mizoshima is so stricken by the pathos of the mindless slaughter that he seeks a gesture—almost a ritual—that will enable him to redeem his own life and grant it some moral purpose. He resolves to remain behind and bury the dead. His fellow soldiers become haunted by his disappearance, knowing he is alive but not comprehending his mysterious absence. Nor does he wish to communicate with them; the emotion he feels is too profound to convey in words or explanation. He can only argue by example. His presence is thus felt even in his absence by his former comrades, who become obsessed with the meaning of his silence and solitude. Mizoshima becomes a Buddhist monk.

In a magnificent climactic sequence he plays his harp in unspoken communion with his former fellow soldiers. In this moving consummation, Mizoshima faces his friends from behind the fence of their prisoner-of-war camp. They are about to be repatriated and with tears in their eyes they plead with him to join them. But what he has to say can only be shown in the life he has chosen, a means of transcending the agony and moral shame of his war experience. Only as a monk, living for others, can he come to terms with the horror of his former existence and the social role he unwittingly played. It is the one way an individual caught up in the mesh of social barbarism can detach himself—short of transforming the world which so injured him.

The Harp of Burma has been lavishly praised both in Japan and the West. John Simon, focusing on the symbol of the Burmese harp alone, remarked in *The New Leader:* "The intimate role a musical instrument can play in the psychic development of a man, and how this can extend even to his fellow-soldiers, is delicately apprehended. If Ichikawa had done nothing more than capture this elusive theme with such lyrical finesse, he would already deserve our thanks."

Ichikawa's other great antiwar film, *Fires on the Plain* (1959), is also known in the United States. The absurd brutality of war is searingly depicted in the soldiers' elaborate descent to cannibalism during the last days of the Japanese occupation of the Philippines. Hopelessly outnumbered, surrounded and deprived of all food and supplies, the surviving remnant of the Japanese army strives to resist as long as possible and to die with dignity. It is the harshest irony that their determination leads them to do what is necessary to survive at all costs. Through this process they are led to feed on the bodies of their own fallen within moments of their deaths. And it is one short step to murdering other soldiers for the sake of "monkey flesh." Thus Ichikawa conveys how dedication and seeming selflessness on behalf of destructive goals turn men into beasts.

In the face of war, Ichikawa asks, what means have we of defining the human? He finds his answer in the decision of his hero, although close to death, *not* to eat human flesh. Pauline Kael in *I Lost It at the Movies* calls *Fires on the Plain* a "masterpiece," missing, however, Ichikawa's specific critique of imperial Japan with its code of unthinking fidelity to social codes no matter the human cost:

> We see no causes, no cures, no enemy; it goes beyond nationalism or patriotism. All men are enemies. It is a post-nuclear war film—a vision of the end, the final inferno. And oddly, when survival is the only driving force, when men live only to live, survival comes to seem irrelevant.*

---

* (New York: Bantam Books, 1966), p. 204.

Ichikawa is also valued outside Japan for his adaptation of Junichiro Tanizaki's novel *The Key* (1959), called *Odd Obsession* in the United States. The film reveals an ironic, bitter, and coolly detached side of Kon Ichikawa as he explores with microscopic objectivity the lives of four singularly repulsive people. A father during late middle age searches for a means of retaining vestiges of his potency; his wife is bored and frustrated by her older, unattractive husband; their daughter is the classic "modern girl" of the *gendaigeki* (film with a contemporary setting)—awkward and gauche in her assertion of freedom, and lacking the grace and beauty of her mother, who is played by Machiko Kyo. This trio is joined by an opportunistic young doctor (Tatsuya Nakadai) who decides to marry the daughter. However, he soon plans instead to seduce the mother, when this appears more pleasurable and likely to achieve the same end: appropriation of the family wealth. The husband is in effect "murdered" by his wife, who attempts to overtax him by inducing sexual frenzy in the hope that she will then be left a widow and free to pursue her relationship with the young doctor. Ironically, the husband had tried to invoke the doctor's lust in the hope of stimulating his own drives.

When the doctor discovers that their purported wealth is a sham and that they are in fact impoverished, he wishes to have nothing more to do with either woman. The maid, however, observes them all throughout the film. Serving as Ichikawa's surrogate, she poisons the three survivors. It is a a parable of the degeneration of relationships in contemporary Japan, with the older, formal values now replaced by cynical self-interest. Ichikawa punishes his selfish characters while taking a swipe at the press and the police who, despite the maid's confession, insist on viewing the deaths as suicides. More important than truth is retention of the traditional feudal view. Dignity demands that the woman left alone and penniless take her own life rather than live on in limited circumstances. Kael, again ignoring the social dimension, has nonetheless called the film in *I Lost It at the Movies* "perverse in the best sense of the word" and erotic in a subtle manner inaccessible to the American film:

> I don't think I've ever seen a movie that gave such a feeling of flesh. Machiko Kyo with her soft, sloping shoulders, her rhythmic little paddling walk, is like some ancient erotic fantasy that is more suggestive than anything Hollywood has ever thought up.*

* Kael, *I Lost It at the Movies*, p. 146.

Donald Richie's view in *Japanese Cinema* was similar:

Erotic obsession is presented with such near-claustrophobic intensity that one longs for outdoor scenes, anything to get away from that dark and keyholed and magnificently photographed house.*

Ichikawa's other fine films include his adaptation of Yukio Mishima's *Temple of the Golden Pavilion,* called *Conflagration* (1958). It is the story of a young novice appalled by corruption—his own and that of the world surrounding him. In a rite of purification he burns down one of the most famous and beautiful temples in Kyoto, the Kinkakuji. Ichikawa is also known abroad for *Tokyo Olympiad* (1965), severely cut in the versions shown both in Japan and the United States. He continued his interest in filming athletes under stress in his segment of the international production *Visions of Eight* (1972).

The issue remains of how to "place" Kon Ichikawa within the cosmos of the Japanese film. Richard N. Tucker in *Japan: Film Image* has said that, with Kobayashi, Ichikawa represents those "who have an abiding concern for the sanctity of the individual human being," a "champion of the ethical left." This designation, however, does not quite fit an often bitterly ironic Kon Ichikawa in whose films the Japanese critic Akira Iwasaki has found "a piercing and ironic view of humanity or a detached and satiric vision of society." Ichikawa could hardly be labeled a man of the left because he so often locates weakness and corruption in the heart of man rather than within the social structure which has nurtured us. His characters act out their conflicts on an internal battleground, rarely interacting with the environment at large. In this sense Ichikawa is diametrically opposed to a director like Mizoguchi, whose characters rebel within the framework of limitations imposed on them by an unjust and unfeeling world.

The films of Ichikawa tend to be reducible to their respective styles, finally concerned with no theme per se or cogent point of view. They all have something in common with *The Key.* Ultimately, Ichikawa is nihilistic in his pursuit for its own sake of the evil lurking in us all. "For me," Ichikawa has said, "the theme of a film is not so important," and indeed this insight helps us to understand the contradictions residing in his work.

---

* Donald Richie, *Japanese Cinema: Film Style and National Character* (Garden City, New York, 1971), p. 84.

A nihilistic discarding of the world as an irredeemable and un-
wholesome place is a theme to which Ichikawa persistently returns.
Tom Milne notes this in his *Sight and Sound* review of Ichikawa's
Matatabi (1973), in whose ending Milne hears "an echo of that
'filthy world' upon which the heroes of *Fires on the Plain* and
Conflagration tried to impose their own purity, and which finally
defeated them." This nihilism has led many critics to accuse Ichi-
kawa of an empty aestheticism—equating all things and reducing
everything to form alone, of a mentality dictated by an aesthetic in-
dependent of thematic or moral concerns. It is a point of view en-
couraged by Ichikawa himself, who has quoted his wife and co-
scriptwriter Natto Wada as saying that it is a "sense of beauty
which may be the motivation for my activities in film." Against
this charge of aestheticism Richie has valiantly defended Ichikawa:

> . . . this very interest in aesthetics is, after all, just what ac-
> counts for the extreme power of a Mizoguchi or an Ichikawa
> film. The latter's condemnation of the traditional is much more
> finished and much more subtle than that of Imai but it is just as
> strong.*

Our suspicion of aestheticism persists, partly because of the wide
variety of Ichikawa's styles and subjects—from his satire of the
matriarchal family in *Bonchi* (1960) to the endorsement of the fam-
ily in *Being Two Isn't Easy* (1962). Japanese critic and film pro-
ducer Kyushiro Kusakabe locates in Ichikawa's work three catego-
ries: films containing experimental techniques, which would
include *The Revenge of Yukinojo* (1963); films ironic in their obser-
vations of man, of which *Being Two Isn't Easy* would be an ex-
ample; and traditional dramas like *The Sin* (1962). Iwasaki locates
two streams: the comedy or comic thriller and the traditional
drama, where Ichikawa best exhibits his ability. Richie also, and
most eloquently, has pointed out the contradictions at the heart of
the Ichikawa *oeuvre:*

> Willing pupil of Disney, he is at the same time drawn to the
> dark matter of *Enjo* and *Bonchi*.† Maker of official documen-
> taries, he is also drawn to the most intimate of psychological
> revelations. A humanist, he is, almost consequently, drawn to

---

* Richie, *Japanese Cinema*, p. 196.

† *Enjo* is the Japanese title for *Conflagration*. *Bonchi* is an untranslatable Osaka
dialect word, as Richie points out, "used to affectionately designate the eldest son."

death and destruction. All of this is somehow redeemed through beauty.*

The frustration of the critic in locating the Weltanschauung of Ichikawa persists. Seemingly a man of the left and an impassioned opponent of the brutalities of war, he is also capable of praising the rigid Japanese family system. He assumes the posture of a detached observer of the actions of his characters. But he is not above a tritely pious ending, like that attached to *The Key,* wherein the press and police are rather didactically jeered at for their refusal to accept an obvious truth. In despair of locating schematically the identity of Ichikawa as cineaste, Akira Iwasaki, in the symposium with Ichikawa appearing in the May 1963 issue of *Chūō Kōron,* has well said,

> . . . the director Ichikawa must have thematic limits he can work on . . . the Ozu Tōfu † Restaurant can only sell *tōfu.* The Ichikawa Restaurant, however, can sell both *tōfu* and pork-cutlet, but not *tōfu,* pork-cutlet, beefsteak and *tempura.*

---

* Bean curd. Restaurants in Japan generally specialize in one dish for which they become known.

† Richie, *Japanese Cinema,* p. 196.

INTERVIEW WITH
KON ICHIKAWA

Mellen: Is the major theme in Japanese films still the struggle between one's duty and the individual desire to be independent and free of traditional values and ideas?

Ichikawa: That is a difficult question with which to begin. I don't know how to answer. Can't we work our way to that and start with the next question?

Mellen: Sure. The next is an easy one. What is your educational background? What did you study at school and what was the major influence which shaped your ideas?

Ichikawa: I didn't go to a university so I can't say in what I majored. After I left middle school [equivalent to American high school] I was always painting and drawing.

Mellen: Did you become a painter?

Ichikawa: No, later on, I switched to filmmaking.

Mellen: How did you start to make films?

Ichikawa: When I was a youth it was the time of the Western film world's so-called renaissance. There were so many great European and American films. They had a great impact on the Japanese. Japanese then began to pursue filmmaking seriously. This influenced me considerably.

Mellen: Which European and American films or directors most affected you?

Ichikawa: I should mention the names of filmmakers who moved me very much rather than individual titles. Among them in America Charlie Chaplin stands out, as does William Wellman. In France, René Clair. Nor can I forget Sternberg and Lubitsch.

Mellen: Why have Japanese filmmakers been so interested in historical themes and period films?

Ichikawa: I don't think Japanese films lean particularly toward the *jidai-geki*, or costume drama. Some people are interested in episodes of a certain era, but I would not want to make the distinction between *jidai-geki* and *gendai-geki* [contemporary drama or story]. To me they are the same. If I may add my opinion, films which have modern themes and modern implications should not be simply classified as *jidai-geki*, even if they are set before the Meiji era. They are indeed modern films although they may take the form of costume plays.

119

Mellen: You don't think there are more historical films made in Japan than in the United States, although we do have the "Western," which may be thought of as similar to the *jidai-geki?*

Ichikawa: We probably have a few more and it may have some significance, in my case for one. It is true of course that there are more *jidai-geki* made here than *gendai-geki.* You see, film is an art which involves the direct projection of the time in which we live. It is a difficult point to state clearly, but my general feeling is that Japanese filmmakers are somewhat unable to grasp contemporary society. In your country there seem to be many more dramatic current themes to portray. To render something into film art we really need to understand thoroughly what we want to describe. Unable to do this, many of us go back to history and try to elucidate certain themes which have implications for modern society.

Mellen: Is it because Japanese society is undergoing great political and social change at the present time?

Ichikawa: Yes, that is correct.

Mellen: Would you like to discuss problems of distribution, production, and financing of films in Japan in relation to your own experiences, for example with your *Tokyo Olympiad?*

Ichikawa? We are faced now with the most difficult time for all three problems. We have a very different system from yours. We used to have five major companies which monopolized all bookings. We never had a free booking system. Now the five companies have shrunk into three, Toho, Shochiku, and Toei, and these companies still follow the old system of distribution. They don't want to change with the times; they are anachronistic. So groups are forming individual production companies and trying to survive. Financially it is a cruel struggle.

Mellen: Have you personally formed your own company?

Ichikawa: At this moment it is an individual production, not yet a company. I am working right now to create a new company which I hope to start in November [1972]. This is my first independent attempt, and I have to raise the money by myself. Up till now I worked with large companies like Daiei and Toho. I am working on television productions at present to raise money to start my own company.

Mellen: Did you then make the *Monjiro Kogarashi* episodes to make money rather than as serious works of film art?

Ichikawa directing *Tokyo Olympiad* (*above*) and *The Sin* (*below*). "My general feeling is that Japanese filmmakers are somewhat unable to grasp contemporary society."

Ichikawa: I would say for both reasons. I should like to make some money on them, but I made them seriously as well. I could never proceed aimlessly.

Mellen: Are you interested in the theme of political apathy or indifference in the *Monjiro Kogarashi* stories?

Ichikawa: Yes, the protagonist is an outlaw and a loner, like an "isolated wolf." He is like the character in many Westerns. He is always antiestablishment.

Mellen: Do you suggest through this character that political action is fruitless, especially in the sense that an isolated individual attempting to do away with evil would find it impossible?

Ichikawa: You might say that in terms of the political implications, although the political element is not the main theme. I am much more interested in the search for what defines human nature.

Mellen: In general would you say that you are more interested in psychological aspects than in political?

Ichikawa: Yes, generally so.

Mellen: How do you account for the interest in pornography, or rather, the extreme desires of sexual life in Japanese films? I am speaking of the excessive sexual desire which appears even in the work of Imamura and in your own film *Odd Obsession.*

Ichikawa: I really don't know how to answer the question. I thought that in Japan sex was not given the prominence that the United States has given to it. In Japan, sex itself is not treated as a force able to change an entire aspect of social existence. I am referring to plays like *Cat on a Hot Tin Roof* or *A Streetcar Named Desire.* These works face up to the problem of sexuality in the human being. Well, in Japan we don't have such plays. Sex is not as important a problem in Japan as it is in the United States.

Mellen: Would you say that in *Odd Obsession* the sex was treated comically or satirically rather than seriously?

Ichikawa: I used it as a criticism of civilization, of our culture.

Mellen: In what way? Which aspect of civilization are you criticizing?

Ichikawa: The conflict between the soul or heart and desire.

Mellen: I find that a difficult idea to grasp.

Ichikawa: It is difficult to explain in words, but *Odd Obsession* is really not a movie about sex, at least not very much so. It is a story of human vanity and nothingness. It describes the humanness of the characters through the vantage of sex. I should say that the sex is deformed to impart the struggle of human beings. Sex connects to one's search for humanity, one's true thoughts and position in society.

Mellen: Then the true subject is not sexuality but the sex functions as a symbol?

Ichikawa: Yes, that is exactly it.

Mellen: Why does the servant poison the three surviving people at the end of the film? This aspect of the plot was not in the original novel by Tanizaki.

Ichikawa: I wonder if I can get this across to you in Japanese via an interpreter. I'll try. These three people are representatives of the human without possessing human souls. They are not really human beings. The servant is going to annihilate them because the servant represents the director. I wanted to deny them all.

Mellen: Then it is the moral judgment of the director on these three people?

Ichikawa: Yes.

Mellen: What aspect of the original novel, *The Temple of the Golden Pavilion,* were you interested in when you made *Conflagration?*

Ichikawa: In this film I wanted to show the poverty in Japan.

Mellen: Who wanted to show the poverty especially, you or Mishima?

Ichikawa: No, I.

Mellen: Is it a material or a spiritual poverty?

Ichikawa: I started from the economic and naturally pursued the spiritual also, because it is the story of man. The economic side represents 60 percent and the spiritual 40 percent.

Mellen: Doesn't this indicate a strong political element in your work?

Ichikawa: Only for this film in which spiritual poverty is caused by economic poverty. Usually I don't consider myself a politically minded director. When I am making a film, I don't think of the political side of the film very much; it is not the main thing.

Mellen: Maybe "political" is the wrong word. By "political" I mean social consciousness, the relationship between the individual and society, not in the sense of political parties.

Ichikawa: Then yes, that is important to my work. I am both aware of and concerned with social consciousness.

Mellen: Is there any similarity between your Private Mizushima in *The Harp of Burma* and Goichi of *Conflagration?*

Ichikawa: They represent the youth of Japan. In the case of Mizushima the time was the middle of the war, and with Goichi it was just after the war. In this sense both, whether a soldier or not, represent Japanese youth.

Mellen: What is the origin of their disillusionment with the world?

Are they each disillusioned about the same things and could we define exactly what they are disillusioned about in a general way? Although their behavior is, of course, different: one leaves the world to become a Buddhist monk and decides never to return to Japan and Goichi in *Conflagration* burns down one of the most famous shrines in Japan.

Ichikawa: Both are very young and both are in search of something. Neither knows exactly what he is after, as they are still young. Both thrust themselves against the thick wall of reality and disillusionment trying to find out what they desire.

Mellen: As in the burning of the temple. What do they desire?

Ichikawa: Truth.

Mellen: Is it the truth of themselves or of the world?

Ichikawa: The truth of their own lives.

Mellen: Is the meaning they seek in their lives similar to that of Watanabe in Kurosawa's *Ikiru?* Watanabe of course is an old man.

Ichikawa: Possibly so. I can say it is close. It depends on the viewer's interpretation.

Mellen: What is the statement about the nature of war that you are making in *Fires on the Plain?*

Ichikawa: War is an extreme situation which can change the nature of man. For this reason, I consider it to be the greatest sin.

Mellen: Do you use a social situation like war as a device to explore the human character? The social situation would be a means of showing what the human being is capable of—as in Tamura's cannibalism, homicide, or the massacre in the film—as opposed to showing what happens in a society that leads to war?

Ichikawa: I use the situation of war partly for this reason but also to show the limits within which a moral existence is possible.

Mellen: Why do you have Private Tamura die at the end?

Ichikawa: I let him die. In the original novel he survives to return to Japan, enters a mental institution, and lives there. I thought he should rest peacefully in the world of death. The death was my salvation for him.

Mellen: What he saw made him unable to continue to live in this world?

Above: Machiko Kyo, Tatsuya Nakadai, and Ganjiro Nakamura, *The Key.* "These three people are representatives of the human without possessing human souls. They are not really human beings. The servant is going to annihilate them because the servant represents the director."
Below: Tanie Kitabayashi and Machiko Kyo in Ichikawa's *The Key (Odd Obsession).*

Ichikawa: Yes, he couldn't live in this world any longer after that. This is my declaration of total denial of war, total negation of war.

Mellen: In *Alone on the Pacific* you seem to be saying that determination is important, not what you do, nor the nature of the act.

Ichikawa: Yes. That was my precise conception.

Mellen: Isn't *what* we do important? Wouldn't you say that there is some distinction between doing some useful thing and voyaging alone on the Pacific?

Ichikawa: No, no difference.

Mellen: In Japanese films and in yours in particular, much more so than in Western films, there seem to be mixtures of styles or rather varied methods of filmmaking which are combined sometimes even within a single film. Many of your films, and those of Oshima or Shindo for example, are so completely different from one work to the next. Is this a special characteristic of the Japanese film? I am thinking in particular of your segment of *A Woman's Testament*.

Ichikawa: [Laughs] Do you think so! Probably you are examining the films in great detail. We don't see this particularly. I believe that expression should be free, so this notion may affect the fact you have just described. But I am never conscious of differentiating my methods or that I have one single special style. All depends on the story or the drama on which I am working.

Mellen: This seems to be something unique about the Japanese film. In American films one director's works are generally similar, especially among the older directors.

Ichikawa: I think each should differ according to what is being expressed. As I am Ichikawa and no one else, even when I try to change the style according to the theme there is always some similarity from one film to the next. Right now I am working with an Italian director, Pasolini. I have really been influenced by him. I consider him one of the greatest filmmakers today. Do you know his work?

Mellen: Which films of Pasolini do you admire most?

Ichikawa: *Apollo's Hell, Medea, Decameron, The Gospel According to St. Matthew, Teorema.* I consider Pasolini the finest director making films today.

Among American directors I was impressed with Peter Fonda, not with his *Easy Rider,* but with *The Hired Hand.* He seems to be very young, yet he has a very good grasp of his subject. He understands love so beautifully. How old is he?

Mellen: He is about thirty-five. Whom do you admire among the younger Japanese directors?

Ichikawa: None among the young ones. I don't know any of their films.

Mellen: How about among the older ones?

Ichikawa: Mizoguchi, Kurosawa, of course.

Mellen: In connection with Mizoguchi's *Oharu* I visited the Rakan-ji [temple] in Tokyo. Didn't he film one of the main scenes there?

Ichikawa: But it could be that he made that movie in Kyoto. Is *Oharu* the American title? The title in Japanese is *Saikaru Ichidai Onna.* You know, there are several Rakanjis.

Mellen: Is there a contradiction in the fact that you seem to praise the family system in *Ototo* [*Younger Brother*] but attack it in *Bonchi?* Or were you criticizing the matriarchal family in particular in *Bonchi?*

Ichikawa: "Attack" is a strong word, but, yes, I have criticized the family system in *Ototo* and, yes, in *Bonchi* I attack the matriarchy. *Ototo* takes place in the Taisho era, before the war, about forty years ago, but today we still have much the same problem in our family system. I hold the opinion that each family should be accustomed to respecting the individuality of every member. This is what I wanted to say.

Mellen: What is your viewpoint in *Hakai* [*The Sin,* 1961]?

Ichikawa: The theme is racial discrimination. Japanese discriminate against *buraku-min.* Originally when the Koreans emigrated to Japan, they brought their slaves with them; these were segregated and called *buraku-min.**

Mellen: Were you then treating the great discrimination against the Koreans by the Japanese?

Ichikawa: I think all human beings should be equal.

Did you see Shinoda's *Sapporo Winter Olympics?* Did you like it?

Mellen: Yes, I liked it, but I thought that there might have been

---

* Originally these people came from Korea and settled around the Kyoto area, and for many centuries they were discriminated against by the Japanese. There is still very strong social discrimination against Koreans in Japan, and there has been since the Meiji era, but *buraku-min* were not identified as Koreans. This group of people were originally engaged in the trades of animal killing, footware making, and as executioners. Ordinary Japanese regarded them as morally unrespectable. They were outcasts, the untouchables of Japanese society for many centuries. They resided all over Japan, but lived separately from Japanese villagers. The name *buraku-min* means "people who live in the small village." Toson Shimazaki, author of the novel *Hakai,* was one of the first to cast light on the social plight of the *buraku-min* during the Meiji era. It is on this novel that Ichikawa based his film.

more insights into the psychology of the individuals competing. Visually it is extremely beautiful.

Could you say something about how you used the visual details of the architecture in *Conflagration* to reveal the psychology of the boy?

Ichikawa: Yes, I sought to do this. This beautiful structure was simply nothing but old decayed timber, no more than that. The boy didn't think so at first, but he gradually realized it.

Mellen: What is the relationship between his feeling about himself and his feeling about the building?

Ichikawa: Let me add this. It doesn't have to be the Golden Pavilion. It can be any one of the so-called great monuments in our history. They are so fine. Nobody questioned their greatness because many generations were taught to revere them. Well, in actuality some people think the particular monument, in this case the Golden Pavilion, is great, but some think it is not. Varying opinions should be accepted because excellence is solely dependent upon the viewer's conception.

Mellen: Does he hate the building and burn it down as an act of self-hatred?

Ichikawa: Yes, he hated himself and destroyed himself.

Mellen: The building represented everything which oppressed him?

Ichikawa: Yes, that expresses it.

Mellen: Is that why people are shown as very small and the building huge in some scenes? They are the individuals very vulnerable to and unable to control outside influences which dominate them, of which the Kinkakuji stands as a symbol.

Ichikawa: Yes, that's right. One further thing I wish to stress is that Goichi was handicapped. He stutters and cannot express himself well and in a sense he closes himself off from society. He has a sense of inferiority in relation to that magnificent building and he suffers from his isolation. I myself did not think the Golden Pavilion so great or beautiful a structure. I may be wrong, but my point here is that the presence of this great structure does not secure the well-being of human beings around it, or make them happy.

Mellen: Are you also thereby criticizing the feudal values associated with the Kinkakuji?

Ichikawa: Somewhat.

Mellen: Indirectly?

Ichikawa: Yes, not overtly. It is implicit.

Mellen: Then the temple itself would be a symbol of the feudal system?

Ichikawa: Yes, it is.

Mellen: Has there been any influence in your work, or in the Japanese film over all, of the impact of the women's liberation movement internationally and in Japan?

Ichikawa: I believe so. The consciousness of women is surfacing and it affects us all.

Mellen: There is of course a strong feminism in the work of Mizoguchi and Hani, perhaps Kurosawa too?

Ichikawa: Mizoguchi and Hani, yes, but Kurosawa hasn't been so influenced.

Mellen: Why in the recent Japanese film has the conflict between the "civilized" and the "primitive" been a prevalent theme?

Ichikawa: What do you mean by "primitive"?

Mellen: The "primitive" consists of people and society before industrial technology, unaffected by capitalism or competition, a society living by ancient patterns. I am thinking of Teshigahara's *Woman in the Dunes* and Imamura's *Insect Woman*.

Ichikawa: The question is very abstract, and I'm not sure I agree. In Japanese films the primary conflict between two antagonistic forces is the large theme. I am saying as well that Japan as a whole is a very poor society, an economically poor society.

Mellen: What did you mean when you said that your films were influenced in an important way by Walt Disney?

Ichikawa: At the time I was still painting and trying to be an artist I saw "Mickey Mouse" [probably *Steamboat Willie*]. It made the connection for me between picture drawing and filmmaking. I was very impressed by Disney's skills and methods. No doubt there were many who drew the pictures for him, but he organized the whole thing. Later came *Fantasia* and *Bambi* and so on. I entered the staff of a small cartoon-making film company around that time. The early works of Disney influenced me greatly.

Mellen: Do you consider the Disney films an example of abstract art?

Ichikawa: Not really; it's a little different from abstract art. The early Disney films were done authentically. Not in the same language as regular films. He had created his work in such a way that he could translate his material into the terms of the general public. Everyone understands him. I mean this favorably. Disney's innovations, his method of revolutionizing filmmaking, deserves a Nobel Peace Prize if we had such a prize for film.

Mellen: In his later films he turned to praising the American system and existing values, completely ignoring the suffering and despair in our society.

Ichikawa: Yes, I understand that. He became very conservative.

Especially in the eyes of younger people, he must have seemed very, very conservative. But you should not forget the fact that he, at one point of his career, provided dreams and hopes for children all over the world. He still should be remembered for his great contribution to the film industry.

Mellen: He was, of course, enormously popular when I was a child. But the dreams he offered were ones that could never be fulfilled.

Ichikawa: Yes, probably so. The times have changed. Today young people probably don't go for him anymore. However, in those days we received much from him.

Mellen: We can't deny him either because his world remains with us, in our minds. He is part of our childhood.

Can you tell me something of your future plans?

Ichikawa: After November, our production company and the Art Theatre Guild will start *Matatabi* [*The Wanderers,* 1973]. It is about the tragedy of a very young outlaw. Then I will go to Munich and film the Olympic Games [*Visions of Eight*]. The movie itself will be made in the United States, but eight directors all over the world were selected to shoot the formal version of the Olympic Games.

Mellen: Who are the others?

Ichikawa: Arthur Penn from the United States, Claude Lelouch from France, John Schlesinger from England, Franco Zeffirelli from Italy, and others. Each director can choose the event he wants to film. I chose the 100-meter dash.

SEVEN

MASAKI KOBAYASHI

INTRODUCTION

Masaki Kobayashi has attracted a following in the United States second, perhaps, only to that of Kurosawa and Ozu. His training at Waseda University was in philosophy, an interest which was to exercise considerable influence on his work as a director. In 1941 Kobayashi joined Shochiku Studios as an assistant director. Shortly thereafter he was drafted, and in 1942 he became a prisoner-of-war, an experience he would later depict in his films. When he returned to filmmaking in 1946, he worked as an assistant to the important Japanese director Keisuke Kinoshita.

In 1953 Kobayashi directed *The Thick-Walled Room,* which was based upon published abstracts from the diaries of men designated as "war criminals" at the end of the Second World War—a theme still so sensitive in Japan that it was not released until 1956. This should not have been surprising given Kobayashi's contention that the *real* criminals had escaped prosecution while those punished were their underlings. The screenplay was by Kobo Abé, who would later write films for Hiroshi Teshigahara.

Kobayashi soon established himself as one of the most trenchant social critics in the Japanese cinema. His *I'll Buy You* (1956) centered on the venality of the world of professional baseball, treating the fight between two teams for promising high-school prospects. Within the genre of the traditional socially innocuous sports-*mono* (film glorifying the prowess of athletes and/or the sport they play), it refused to insulate sports from its mercenary context. In 1957 Kobayashi made *Black River,* exposing the degeneracy surrounding

131

American bases in Japan, a corruption nurturing and creating whores and red-light districts, gangsters and petty crime. It has not been distributed abroad, although it is a film much admired by Anderson and Richie in their history of the Japanese film:

> . . . the picture was studiously just. The villain was not America for having camps in Japan but the Japanese social system, which permitted such lawless behavior to go unpunished.*

While this may indeed be true, the symbolic ending of the film underlines Kobayashi's sense of the destructive and oppressive quality of the American occupation of Japan. The young gangster-hero, played, as are many of Kobayashi's heroes, by Tatsuya Nakadai, is killed by an American truck in a convoy entering the camp.

Kobayashi's reputation in Japan was ensured with *The Human Condition* (1958–1961), a nine-hour and thirty-nine minute, three-part trilogy about the Second World War. The films were distributed separately as *No Greater Love, Road to Eternity,* and *A Soldier's Prayer.* Its theme was the corrosive effect of a cruel and unjust social structure expressed through Japanese behavior during the war. Its hero, Kaji, is an ambitious young man, appalled by the conditions he finds when he is stationed at a prisoner-of-war camp where Chinese are forced into slave labor and treated worse than animals.

Although Anderson and Richie allege "a tendency to melodrama," and Richie argues elsewhere that the work "slights character in favor of social comment," the films remain magnificent epics of the period. Kaji, seeking to help the Chinese prisoners, renders his own position tenuous. Finally, he is sent to the front. Captured by the Russians, he finds his socialist ideals shaken as he becomes, this time, the recipient of maltreatment as a prisoner-of-war. By the end of the film the world has proved itself too oppressive for him; socialism under Stalin has proved to be another variant of fascism. Having escaped from the Soviet camp in an effort to return to his wife, he is too weak to continue and dies covered by falling snow, his struggle over at last.

Richard N. Tucker in *Japan: Film Image* has called it a "revolutionary movie" which established Kobayashi as one of the leading radical spokesmen of the Japanese cinema:

---

* Joseph L. Anderson and Donald Richie, *The Japanese Film: Art and Industry* (New York: Grove Press, 1960), pp. 285–86.

Where Kurosawa sees the right of the individual as the right to adopt the values of those about him, to reassess them and to learn how to co-exist with other men, Kobayashi sees it as the right of the individual to act without the rigid strictures of an imposed order and if he finds the system wanting then to change it.*

Unfortunately, Kobayashi's trilogy has not been shown widely outside of Japan and, when it has, only in a severely cut version, a fact much lamented by critic Arne Svensson in his *Screen Series: Japan:*

> The sadly mutilated version generally shown in Europe can—with its insistence on violence and its exclusion of nuances in characterization—convey little of Kobayashi's rich original. The tragedy inherent in the crumbling of Kaji's pacifist and Socialist ideals exposes the Japanese militarism that made life so insupportable for the non-conformist.†

At the time of the release of *The Human Condition,* in 1960, Donald Richie summed up the importance Kobayashi had achieved in the Japanese film in an article entitled " *Vague Nouvelle* in Japanese Film," published in *Asia Scene:*

> In Kobayashi Japan has its first social critic since Kurosawa gave up contemporary life films for period drama (a stipulation in his Toho contract) and with the continuance of *The Human Condition* and its trenchant criticism of the Japanese army, and—by extension—the Japanese system of organization—one who it appears is just now reaching his full power.

Ironically, it is precisely through his own two *jidai-geki,* or period films, *Hara Kiri* (1962) and *Rebellion* (1967), that Kobayashi fully established his reputation as one of the greatest of Japanese directors.

His finest film is *Hara Kiri.* It is the story of a man who discovers that his son-in-law had been forced by a heartless clan superintendant to disembowel himself with a bamboo sword as a deterrent to future impoverished samurai who might seek mercy and alms from the clan. Out for revenge, the father-in-law returns to the scene, posing as another begging samurai. He is told the story of

---

* (London: Studio Vista, 1973), p. 98.
† (New York: A. S. Barnes & Co., 1971), pp. 77–78.

his daughter's husband to scare him off, and in return he informs the assembled clan that he has already destroyed three of their members who were responsible for the forced suicide. He fights both the clan system and the historical anomaly of a transitional era wherein masterless samurai outlive their feudal social function in a time of relative peace. The tragedy resides, finally, in the futility of a solitary individual seeking to defeat a social class as well as an entire era. Played by Nakadai in one of his finest performances, he can only attack in the end, hoping to kill as many of them as he can before he himself is destroyed. Tucker enters Kobayashi's mood:

> *Hara Kiri* is an angry and violent film calling for the serious questioning of all authoritarian systems, yet in the final moments his hero is cut down by the advances of technology. Being a product of that system he has no defences against the new muskets—and falling wounded he invokes the final irony of the film when he conforms to his samurai code by disembowelling himself with his own sword. Man may fight against a system but he cannot escape being part of it. The Japanese, he appears to be saying, must look to their own social structure yet they must at all times remember they are Japanese and carry with them the cultural history of their nation.*

Whether Kobayashi indeed confers a positive value on remembering Japanese feudal custom is open to serious doubt. The hero of this film in his protest has gone far beyond what it means to be a Japanese in this particular historical context. He has revolted against the entire system of authority, and if he has achieved little, it is because he acts alone. Beyond that, his own suicide is a defiant act, a refusal to live any longer in a corrupt, unjust, and cruel world. The suicide of his son-in-law was of course imposed on him by authority and performed in submission to that authority. The film is itself a celebration of the value and urgency of rebellion against injustice apart from the prospect of success. A more accurate reading of the film was expressed by Pierre Billard in an article entitled "Why Is Japanese Cinema a Major Art?":

> Fighting the weight of tradition that has left a code and ritual void of all meaning as its legacy, Kobayashi demands a return to the authenticity of a moral law.

Kobayashi's other important film of this period is *Rebellion,* or *Samurai Rebellion,* as it is sometimes called. Written, as was *Hara*

---

* Tucker, *Japan Film Image,* p. 100.

Kiri, by Shinobu Hashimoto, its subject was again, like that of *Hara Kiri,* the purpose and meaning of rebellion against arbitrary and unfeeling authority. It shares as well with the earlier film a hero of middle age whose revolt occurs after a lifetime of service to the feudal order. Defiance becomes psychologically possible in both films only after the hero's children are threatened by an injustice which denies their identity and dignity as human beings.

Kobayashi displays a subtle sense both of psychology and of the national character. The revenge of the hero of *Hara Kiri* occurred after his daughter and son-in-law had died as a result of feudal brutality. In *Rebellion,* the hero, played by Toshiro Mifune, has reached the age of retirement from active clan service when he is asked that his son accept a discarded concubine of the daimyo as his wife. Survival of the clan, and indeed of the clan system, decrees that obedience precede all other responses and the protagonist finally agrees. What results, unexpectedly, is great happiness. The woman is devoted and the son loves her deeply. They bear a daughter beloved by her grandfather as much as by the two young parents.

The turning point of the film occurs when the wife is abruptly called back by the whimsical daimyo. At this the strong patriarch played by Mifune finally revolts, prepared to do battle with the entire samurai corps, if need be, in protest against such inhuman treatment. He succeeds in defeating the clan only to be stopped at the border, again by the muskets that become symbolic in Kobayashi, as in Kurosawa, of the passing of the feudal Tokugawa period and the arrival of modern technological Japan.

As Donald Richie pointed out in his review in the *Japan Times,* Kobayashi's social critique is far too rich and historically rooted to be focused merely on the corruption of a single individual or group of individuals:

> It is the feudal concept which is at fault, and not the men who seemingly control but are actually controlled by it . . . such human qualities as love, dignity, self-realization are—as a matter of course—crushed beneath the weight of this terrifying, if man-made machine . . . the feudal philosophy (as lively as ever in Japan) is attacked head on and if the hero cannot win (Kobayashi is much too honest a director to let him) then he makes a grand display of his own immolation.

Howard Thompson in *The New York Times* was equally enthusiastic:

With crystal clarity and every word counting, it states a case
for human justice . . . when the murderous show-down
comes, and come it does, the slaughter not only underscores
the hero's bravery but also opens up the story on several philo-
sophical levels . . . it will haunt you.

Although the film is often remembered for its bloody swordplay (as
is *Hara Kiri*), critics have been aware that Kobayashi is not inter-
ested in spectacular combat for its own sake. John Simon, an ex-
ception, noted in *The New Leader* that "this is yet another movie in
which Toshiro Mifune pits his swordsmanship triumphantly against
more blades than there are blades of grass." Yet he does concede
an aesthetic point, granting that "the final mayhem, as in so many
Japanese films and so few westerns, is artistic as well as absurd."
Judith Crist called *Hara Kiri* "a stunningly beautiful and great
drama."

Other of Kobayashi's films known in the United States include
Kwaidan (1965), a four-part group of ghost stories based upon
works by Lafcadio Hearn. While *Kwaidan* lacks the powerful social
theme of Kobayashi's other films, its visual quality is superb as it
evokes the myths that have expressed the Japanese sensibility.
Pierre Billard awards this film his highest praise:

What he has done is to invite the hereafter to cooperate with
the visible and concrete world, to defend, exalt and sing of all
the ways of humanity, and to affirm that man in his wounds
and dreams remains that infinitely small residue that gives the
world its true meaning.

The most haunting of the four tales concerns a blind young
monk, a novice, compelled by the ghosts of a famous battle long
past to retell their story over and over again as they gather every
night in an abandoned graveyard. The head priest knows that to
break the spell the boy's body must be covered with sacred writ-
ings. And he is thus painted until every inch of him is covered. But
his ears are forgotten and these, lighting up in the dark for the
ghosts to identify (while the rest of him remains invisible and
beyond their power), are claimed in revenge.

In 1970 Kobayashi did another period film called *Inn of Evil*, a
work which pursues the themes of *Hara Kiri* and *Rebellion*. It
centers on a group of outlaws living at an inn, smugglers who have
created a sympathetic world of their own in defiance of authority.
For all their "crime" they retain more humanity than those

upholders of the law who ruthlessly pursue them. John Gillett in *Sight and Sound* argues that a certain lack of psychological credibility mars this film:

> . . . it is difficult fully to believe in the sentimental change of heart experienced by a wicked smuggler (Tatsuya Nakadai in his most pop-eyed mood) and his gang, who try to help a young man rescue his girl from a geisha house.

Gillett nonetheless admires the film for Kobayashi's characteristic visual magnificence:

> As in *Rebellion,* Kobayashi reserves his main action until the end: a fantastic ballet of black and white shapes as dozens of policemen carrying lanterns converge on the inn, chase the inmates across dark, menacing swamps, and finally trap them in nets and long, wispy ropes. If only European directors could shoot like this. . . .

Critical opinion is thus practically unanimous on one point. Kobayashi, like other great revolutionary artists from Eisenstein to Brecht, integrates his powerful social perception and radical passion with an abiding and inventive command of film as an art form.

INTERVIEW WITH
MASAKI KOBAYASHI

Mellen: How would you describe your own history as a filmmaker and the origins of your interest in the relationship between the individual and society which forms the central theme of so many of your films from *Hara Kiri* to *Rebellion* and *The Human Condition?*

Kobayashi: I was with Shochiku, one of the five major companies, for a very long time. [Laughs] I began as an assistant director under Keisuke Kinoshita and I was much influenced by his films. He specialized in lyrical, human, somewhat sweet dramas like *The Ballad of Narayama*. He had a reputation for being very good at them. I thought I really had to work on a different mode of drama. In fact I was much more interested in the social aspect of film, and gradually this interest deepened. If only to compete with Kinoshita-san I had to do it! Thus I made *The Thick-Walled Room* in 1953. This film dealt with the story of "B" and "C" rank, or second-level war criminals. It was my first attempt to confront a social problem in my work. Incidentally, this film was shelved for four years and I had to go back to making domestic dramas. After it was finally released, I was able to make *Seppuku* [*Hara Kiri*] and *Ningen no Joken* [*The Human Condition*]. Each of these films was a study of the individual against society.

Mellen: Perhaps the translation of my question was not entirely accurate. I was asking you not only about your relationship with Kinoshita, which interests me very much, but how you explore the relationship between the individual and society in your work.

Kobayashi: Naturally, I was very interested in the social aspects of the human drama from the beginning of my career. This was the very basis of my film art.

I should add that I was in the army for six years. This experience heightened my social consciousness. During those six years I never became an officer. In fact I withheld myself from becoming an officer. I was really a rank-and-file soldier. I had a strong conviction that I must resist authoritarian pressure. I was wholly against the power which bore down on us and I was against the war itself. I still think that I was able to make *Ningen no Joken* because I had voluntarily refused to become an officer. I was the protagonist and I felt this identification very strongly. The life the hero leads was much the same life I lived as a soldier.

138

Mellen: Are social issues and their impact on individuals the main theme in your films? Your people take on moral significance, indeed, self-awareness, to the extent that they confront the important social conflicts of their time.

Kobayashi: Yes. And I should like to add one more thing here. I am primarily concerned with history. I seek to discover the individual man in the historical setting surrounding him. In *Seppuku* this social background was feudalism and in *Ningen no Joken* it was the last war. These backgrounds provide individuals with true-to-life conditions. If my films have any meaning, I feel it lies in my depiction of human problems created by the powerful historical framework. Historical interpretation always plays a very fundamental, important part in my films. The relationship of an individual's consciousness to his setting is my main theme.

Many times I have discovered that my interest is not aroused unless I start locating a particular drama in its historical context. It is really essential to my filmmaking.

Mellen: Is there any special reason why you have used Tatsuya Nakadai, Japan's most glamorous male actor, in your films?

Kobayashi: He possesses a quality shared by both the pre- and the postwar generations. In *Ningen no Joken* I needed an actor capable of expressing the ideas and thoughts of both generations.

Mellen: Because of his age?

Kobayashi: Not so much because of his age. He had a quality, an ability to characterize the sensibilities of two strikingly different generations. When I made *Ningen no Joken* most actors at that time were either of the prewar or mid-war generations. I was looking for a person who could convey the feeling of the new generation. Nakadai was able to convey this new, strong, energetic side of postwar youth.

Mellen: His personality?

Kobayashi: This included his personality. But I must point out Nakadai's background as an actor. As you may know, he was educated with the Shingeki * group for a long time before coming to film. Shingeki's traditional training and atmosphere were unique among young film actresses and actors at that time. Nakadai had a solid theatrical background although he was very young. I still feel he was one of a small group of actors who combined the traditional

* Shingeki, literally "New Theater," contrasted with the old Japanese theaters, Kabuki, Noh, Bunraku, etc., the traditional theatrical modes. Shingeki was established after Meiji by young intellectuals who had put Western plays on the Japanese stage for the first time. There were a number of these groups performing Shingeki, and Nakadai was a member of Bungaku-za (Literature Company).

Shingeki background with the fresh innocence and energy of our postwar generation. He could thus effectively represent both pre- and postwar people.

Mellen: Would you say that in *Inn of Evil,* your most recent film, the police and the authorities are presented as worse than the criminals who are at the center of the film?

Kobayashi: Yes, that is part of my theme. The main subject is the beauty of the human deed performed without any expectation of reward. I wanted to delineate how this traditional appreciation of human generosity and dedication is still alive today.

Mellen: I feel how important this sense of affirmation is in your work. Would you like to expand on this?

Kobayashi: Those gangsters who died in the end were by no means related to the young couple for whom they died. Yet the gangsters gladly die for them without questioning why they must do this. I saw beauty in their actions.

Mellen: Another interesting thing is that the lovers are not particularly exceptional as people.

Kobayashi: I wanted to show them as random people who have no relation whatever to those gangsters. In other words, they could be anyone. In this setting I wanted to make a point of the particular actions human beings are still capable of.

Mellen: Have you ever experienced censorship by the big companies in Japan?

Kobayashi: Yes, I have. Some sequences had to be cut from *Ningen no Joken.* This was ordered by Eirin [Eiga Rinri Iinkai, the Movie Morality Committee]. Eirin was headed by Mr. Seiichiro Takahashi and it was a quasi-governmental committee to oversee so-called morality in films for public showings. We still have this committee today and I believe it is still run by the government.

Mellen: This is extremely interesting. Who makes up the body of this committee? Did this occur around 1959 and 1960? To whom is such a committee responsible?

Kobayashi: I have never really inquired into the details of this committee, but I am sure that the committee belongs to the Ministry of Education.

Mellen: Oh, to the government then. What is the basis of their censorship? What were they concerned to prevent?

Kobayashi is wearing the sailor hat and dark glasses. ''I seek to discover the individual man in the historical setting surrounding him.''

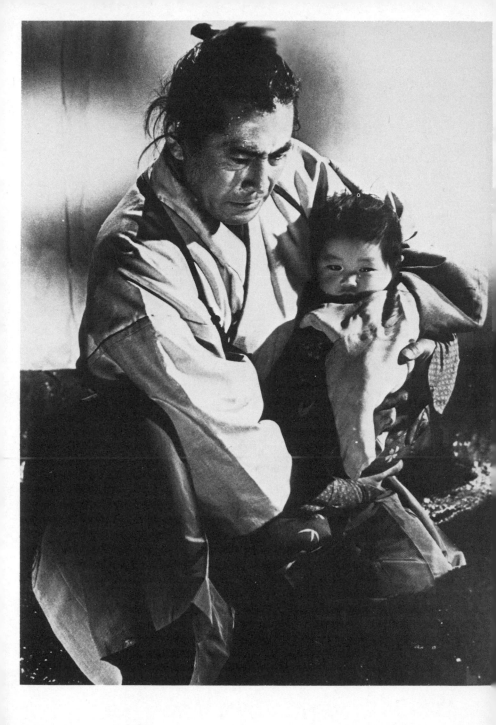

Kobayashi: It was about twelve or thirteen years ago. The nude scene was ordered cut in *Ningen no Joken*. The scene was the one in which the soldier-husband, knowing he would not be able to return to see his wife again, asked her to let him see her nude at the barracks where she was visiting him. It was an integral part of the drama and I felt strongly that this sequence was necessary. But it was not accepted. As I remember, this was the only time one of my films was censored. Let me see . . . Oh, I had one more experience with them. This was over *Kabe Atsuki Heya* [*The Thick-Walled Room*]. I never found out, though, that this film was ordered to be shelved or that the company was ordered to withhold the film "voluntarily" to avoid stirring up trouble with the United States occupation army. Anyway, I was ordered by the executives of Shochiku Films to cut and alter the film completely. I preferred to shelve it as long as there was some hope that it might eventually be shown. The film was released four years later.

Mellen: Was it censored for political reasons?

Kobayashi: Yes, I believe so. Around that time, just after the war, the film industry was extremely sensitive about bringing out anything which might result in criticism from the occupation army. After *Kabe Atsuki Heya* I made sweet domestic dramas and the company liked those all right!

Mellen: During which period in your career was this?

Kobayshi: From *Kabe Atsuki Heya* to *Ningen no Joken*.

Mellen: How would you sum up the ideological basis for these political criticisms?

Kobayashi: The film dealt with "B" and "C," or second- and third-rank war criminals. You should understand that during the end of the war, with such great confusion and all, there were many soldiers and low-ranking officers punished cruelly, although they were not directly responsible for particular crimes. I heard that many war-crimes trials were hastily arranged with only one or two native witnesses willing to point out a given Japanese soldier. The trials brought down severe verdicts on any Japanese who happened to be in the vicinity. Certainly I am not speaking of "A" rank war criminals such as those who were tried in the Tokyo trials. I am talking about small people, mostly conscripts—rank-and-file soldiers and low-ranking officers who were designated "B" and "C" war criminals.

Toshiro Mifune in *Samurai Rebellion.* "The relationship of an individual's consciousness to his setting is my main theme."

These war criminals were actually victims of the system itself, first because they had to obey the orders of their superiors while the war was going on, and second because they were punished after the war for performing their "duty." I must acknowledge, therefore, that on the surface you might perceive in my film certain criticisms against the American army, which was directly responsible for many of the war trials. But what I intended to portray in the film was a much deeper and more universal theme, namely the human dilemma, the human condition created by the particular setting of the last war. I couldn't persuade the company. They were afraid of such an explosive subject.

Mellen: What exactly is the definition of "B" and "C" ranking war criminals?

Kobayashi: All war criminals were classified into "A," "B," and "C" rankings. "A" criminals were those tried in the Tokyo trials and "B" and "C" were primarily ordinary soldiers and noncommissioned officers.

Mellen: Do you agree with the view that *Ningen no Joken* is a war-resistance film?

Kobayashi: Yes, it is. But the film's main theme simultaneously treats the fundamental evil nature in human beings. The war was the culmination of human evil. I wanted to explore this dark side of human nature.

Mellen: What precisely do you mean by "evil nature"? Do you mean something inherent, beyond redemption, like sin?

Kobayashi: Perhaps it is our "original sin." This has a relationship to the A-bomb also. I can understand all the circumstances that caused America to drop the bomb and finish the war, but to me it was an expression of human evil, our original sin, no matter who did it.

Mellen: In a Freudian sense? Do you refer to instinctive aggression?

Kobayashi: No, rather in a Christian sense. I expressed this sense of human evil throughout *Ningen no Joken* and also indicated the possibility of overcoming this evil at the end of the movie, when Kaji, the protagonist, dies. I wanted to negate the presence of evil.

Mellen: Is this conception of evil the inability of the human being to transcend a narrow self-interest and live for others, or at least sacrifice for them?

The Human Condition. "I can understand all the circumstances that caused America to drop the bomb and finish the war, but to me it was an expression of human evil, our original sin, no matter who did it."

Kobayashi: In Kaji's death there was hope that human beings could overcome this inherent evil. You can say that this is at once my desire and my personal tribute to Kaji.

Mellen: Is Kaji's view then the view of the director?

Kobayashi: Yes, I am Kaji in the film. Although Kaji dies, denying us the hope of overcoming evil, I fear the whole situation is not that simple. Probably many more wars will yet be waged in this world. But at the same time I don't believe that wishing, desiring, or hoping are totally useless.

I spent four years making *Ningen no Joken*. While making it, I received many letters from people requesting me not to let Kaji die in the end. I had considered that possibility, but to me his death was actually a resurrection. He had to die there. With his death he lives in the minds of people for a long time as a symbol of the hope that we can eradicate the human tragedy of war.

Mellen: Does Kaji's death imply any hope for the social condition?

Kobayashi: Since I am inclined to believe that wars will continue, you may say that I do not see much prospect for a changed society. However, we must live on, and to do this, we must have hope. I wanted to express this in the death of Kaji. Personally, I am not pessimistic, although it is very easy to become so after examining the history of humanity. You have to try hard to be optimistic.

In *Seppuku* the theme is similar. It ends as a tragedy. But my underlying theme transcends that. I try to express the possibility that human beings can overcome the tragic events of the world. I intend to be humanistic. In *Seppuku* the tragedy was triggered by authoritarian pressure which smothered individuals. In this film, human evil takes the form of an oppressive feudal power structure. I was fascinated by the tenacious human resilience which continued to defy this extreme pressure.

Mellen: Does your sense of inherent hostility and your feeling that change is possible reveal an influence of Freud and Marx?

Kobayashi: Oh, you are trying to start a large discussion [jokingly]. I never consciously try to describe in my films what these two great men said. I am not aware of them at all when working. I am primarily interested in history, and within a vision of man's past, I treat social consciousness, social conflict, and class struggle. In the end you may say that these problems are also the concerns of Marx and he did influence my work. However, I never consciously thought of being directly influenced by his ideas. When I was a student, I studied Asian art, particularly Buddhist sculpture. I spent

Toshiro Mifune and Tatsuya Nakadai in Kobayashi's *Samurai Rebellion*.

many hours looking at numerous statues and images in our ancient cities. While I was making *Seppuku,* I was very much aware of traditional Japanese aesthetics. *Seppuku* was my first costume film or *jidai-geki.* While making it I was keenly aware of, and attracted to, the stylized beauty of our traditional forms. Around that time I felt that I had come to the end of pursuing realism in film. This new approach delighted me. I had been searching for a meaningful mode of expression for some time and this stylized form of film-making provided me with the answer. I took *Seppuku* to the Cannes Film Festival and was granted the Special Critics' Award. At that time someone said the film reminded him of a Greek drama. The stylized beauty of the film was understood. I was very encouraged, rewarded, and flattered by this. I was already planning the second film in this style, *Kwaidan.* I intended to express in *Kwaidan* the ultimate in stylized film method. The main theme of the four fairy tales in the film was the right material for this attempt. I wanted to capture the spiritual importance of human life. *Kwaidan* was also my first color film. After *Seppuku* and *Kwaidan* the direction of my filmmaking has changed.

Mellen: How do you react to the view that *Kwaidan* was a horror movie, a series of ghost stories?

Kobayashi: As a sort of shorthand description one could say it was a horror film. My main intention in the film was to explore the juxtaposition between man's material nature and his spiritual nature, the realm of dream and aspiration. I wanted to create a drama which dealt directly with the spiritual importance of our lives. I also enjoyed conveying the sheer beauty of traditional Japan. Anyway, I am not really satisfied with the designation of "horror film." Its spiritual concerns are the center of the drama.

Mellen: One more question—relating both to *Ningen no Joken* and to *Seppuku.* Both of these films take place in the past, the former around the time of the Second World War, the latter pre-Meiji. Were you criticizing the social condition and state of mind in present-day Japan while you were speaking about the past?

Kobayashi: In any era, I am critical of authoritarian power. In *Ningen no Joken* it took the form of militaristic power; in *Seppuku* it was feudalism. They pose the same moral conflict in terms of the struggle of the individual against society. These struggles are the main drama of all my films.

Mellen: What is your view of Kurosawa's place in the Japanese film?

Kobayashi: Kurosawa-san's works have had a tremendous impact on Japanese filmmaking. We cannot think of or talk of Japanese film without him. I don't agree with those who say that his films have no direct connection with present-day Japan. They certainly have. I should say this, however. The present Japanese film industry placed him in a position where he could not create effectively. They ostracized him. I hold the opinion that Kurosawa-san is still capable of producing major films—now and in the future. He is indeed a great artist. Oshima has been mentioned by many as a new filmmaker who has a finger on the pulse of modern Japan; I myself consider him a political figure rather than an artist, a filmmaker. I think Oshima will have many future problems in his filmmaking.

Mellen: I found Oshima to be one of the most conservative men I have met in Japan.

Kobayashi: It is an interesting view. I understand the circumstances in which he works and I recognize what he has done. The more I get to know his work, the stronger I feel that he is not an artist.

Mellen: Going back to the interesting point you were making about Kurosawa, why is the Japanese filmmaking world preventing him from working?

Kobayashi: Kurosawa-san, Kinoshita-san, Ichikawa-san and I formed a group called Yonki-no-Kai [The Club of the Four Knights]. Our main purpose was to produce quality films. We were very much discouraged by the recent decline and degeneration of Japanese film as a whole.

Eventually we wanted to invite new directors into our club. At first we planned that each of the four original members would make one ambitious, serious film in the hope of rejuvenating the industry. Kurosawa-san was the first of the four to undertake this plan. He made *Dodes'ka-den.* Unfortunately, this turned out to be a box-office disappointment and it held up our future plans. Then came the tragic incident of Kurosawa's attempted suicide. All of us were terribly shocked. At present we are biding our time. In answer to your specific question, I should add that the movies which Kurosawa-san is interested in are so expensive to produce that none of the five major companies is, at present, willing to undertake the production. You cannot forget that the movie industry as a whole is fighting hard to survive. So today more than ever the companies are thinking in terms of how quickly they can earn back their investment. This sort of pressure makes filmmaking downright difficult, not only for Kurosawa-san but for me as well. It is a very difficult situation. [Laughter]

Mellen: Are you in sympathy with the sociological or artistic approaches to film of any of the younger directors?

Kobayashi: Let me see. I don't know them well. [Laughter] I can say the following, though. The current tendency among people is to communicate with images. This includes all sorts of media: film, photography, television, etc. I am sure this worldwide tendency is the result of the influence of television on our daily lives. So, I assume, and I am hoping, there will be young talents who will accomplish worthwhile and innovative work in this field. It is increasingly difficult now to draw a line between film and television or movies and photography. Now everybody can buy good cameras and film very inexpensively and increasing numbers of people are taking up these art forms. I should expect there will be many who will create something of interest.

Mellen: I was thinking more of the generation of Shinoda and Imamura.

Kobayashi: I know them very well, including Oshima-san. They came after us and we worked together at Shochiku. But I do not consider them of the younger generation, they are not "young." * [Laughter]

Mellen: Have there been many Western directors whom you admire or who have influenced you?

Kobayashi: So many of them. Too many. But I can say that while I was a university student, I saw many films of Renoir, Duvivier, René Clair, and the Americans Frank Capra and Wyler. This must have been around Showa 15 or 16 years [1940 or 1941 on our calendar]. So I can say that I must have been influenced by them. I still think of their work with a bit of nostalgia. But in the end an artist must rely on himself, you cannot depend on anybody. It is a very lonely, solitary existence. Last year I went to the Cannes Film Festival and met Charles Chaplin. They showed some of his works. I was deeply impressed by his greatness. His films, his methods and content, are modern and so contemporary; he is a great genius.

Mellen: Which of the Chaplin films is your favorite?

Kobayashi: I forget the title. It was the story of a poor blind flower-vending girl [*City Lights*].

Mellen: To express the nature of your visual style, could it be said that you consciously create and unfold geometric patterns within your shots and that you often contrast very static scenes with scenes involving many traveling shots?

---

* Shinoda, Oshima, and Imamura are in their forties, Kobayashi in his fifties.

Kobayashi: Probably this notion refers to the formal beauty I pursued in *Kwaidan.* In that film I modeled my shots on the stylized beauty of traditional Japan. I am very aware of the contrast between the static and the dynamic in my films. But I never plan on these shots beforehand. They are brought out by the particular demand of a shot which I execute in order to express a specific emotion or a particular scene of the drama. It is all an integral part of filmmaking.

Mellen: Does the contrast between the static scenes and those with traveling shots arise for you as a result of the emotional changes in the characters?

Kobayashi: You could say so, but these things never come out of intellectual analysis. Usually during the shooting I do not have more than one alternative. I *had* to do it this way. It is all a very emotional procedure. As the drama develops, I get a hunch that I should stop the camera or that I should move the camera rapidly.

Do you remember in *Seppuku* the sequence of the young man committing hara kiri? He was using the cut bamboo sword to stab himself. I still remember how I came to shoot these sequences. I was really struggling with the scene because I had tried several approaches and none was convincing. I drank sake and was thinking about it all night. At dawn it came to me suddenly that it is impossible for him to stab himself with the bamboo sword. There was only one way for him to kill himself—namely, if the sword were stuck into the tatami mat and the man threw himself over it. After this everything was easy. We finished shooting in a very short time. I was very satisfied with the result of this particular hara kiri scene and with its effect on the surrounding sequences.

This, as one example, explains how the artist's mind works. It is challenging to create something new, but it is a simple operation if it comes to the mind of the creator. If one flash of an idea shines, the whole is revealed as an epiphany. But, of course, this sort of revelation happens only after many days of struggling, checking every angle, and all possibilities.

The major points of making the film, such as the theme or the social aspect of the theme, must be worked out long before you start shooting. Once the camera starts rolling, I have to forget nearly everything. From then on the work is largely a projection of the director's mind. I have to depend on my mind to decide how to create the drama. I can say that in my own case I let my mind dictate what to do next to create each scene. My sensibility is then the sole guide to follow throughout the work. To the artist, this kind of dependence on his own sense (rather difficult to put into words) is, I feel, very important.

For instance, while the cameras were rolling someone asked me how I had decided the position of the camera. I didn't know. While working on the continuity of the film, I just knew that the camera should be at a certain height to shoot those scenes. If you are clouding your mind by thinking about the film's theme or its message, the film would be awfully dull. The audience would see nothing but the director's intention, not his execution of the theme. The artistic execution gives the film its flesh and blood. With this aesthetic effort of the director, the film becomes art. I myself become physically hot when I encounter this challenge. I get excited and emotionally involved. [Laughs]

Mellen: I have heard that you are a "method" director in relation to your actors. Would you agree?

Kobayashi: Perhaps. Naturally, I discuss the scenes thoroughly with the actors and perhaps this includes asking them to locate in their own lives feelings similar to what they are portraying in the film. Filmmaking is an art which integrates many different media. I talk fully, when it is necessary, to anybody—with the scenario writers, assistant directors, art directors, musicians, cameramen, and so on. I have to organize many people's endeavors into one. I get very demanding sometimes. I become very greedy. [Laughs]

Mellen: One last point. Do you write your scenarios yourself?

Kobayashi: I always bring in one professional scenario writer. I usually let him work first. After he has said he has put in everything he thinks appropriate, then I start to write the scenario myself.

EIGHT

SETSU ASAKURA

INTRODUCTION

Setsu Asakura is one of Japan's outstanding and innovative set de-
signers. The unusual calligraphic character for her first name,
Setsu, is derived from the combination used in "Prince Regent,"
as her birth coincided with the ascent to power of the present em-
peror. To have given this name to a girl expressed the advanced
views of her father, sculptor Fumio Asakura. Her development into
a woman of independent spirit and intellect in a culture which dis-
courages these qualities in women was aided by her father's en-
lightened attitudes.

   Working primarily in the theater, Asakura has done the scenogra-
phy for works as varied as the Japanese *Shingeki Chushingura,* a mod-
ern adaptation of the classical *Story of the Loyal Forty-seven
Rōnin,* Brecht's *Mother Courage* and *Arturo Ui,* Chekhov's *Uncle
Vanya,* John Arden's *Sergeant Musgrave's Dance,* and Dürren-
matt's *The Physicist.* Asakura has designed sets for films and her
credits include the expressionistic backgrounds for two of Toshio
Matsumoto's films, *Funeral Parade of Roses* and *Shura.* She has
also written a book about Picasso's *Guernica* and has illustrated
many children's books. In addition, Asakura is on the faculties
of the Tokyo School of Design and the Kuwazawa Design Studios.

   Her aim in her set designs is to return stage space to a primal
quality uncluttered by objects which have ceased effectively to con-
vey to audiences the values for which they originally stood. Her
vision is of a space disengaged from the trivia that serve only to
distance audiences from artistic events. For Asakura, only a space

153

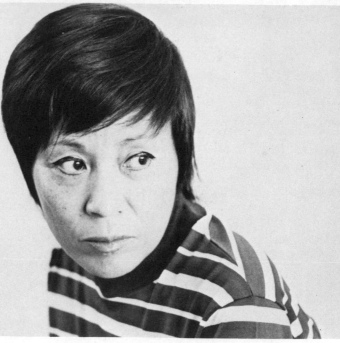

Setsu Asakura.

thus demystified can be returned to its original three-dimensionality. "It is in just such an uncluttered environment," she has said, "that the actor must undergo a qualitative transformation." Of late, Asakura has become interested in encompassing the fourth dimension, that of time, in her designs.

Critics in Japan have warmly praised her work. "There is an overwhelming quality in Setsu Asakura's settings," Shuji Ishizawa wrote of her work for a production of Arnold Wesker's *The Kitchen:* "The cold, hard wall makes one feel the cruelty of modern society." Of her sets for *Kamikakete Sangotaisetsu,* Koji Ozaki wrote: "Thanks to the work of Setsu Asakura's design the whole performance appeared as if some mirage were taking place in front of a black backdrop." Asakura's work has been praised in greater detail by Takashi Nomura in the *AKT* newsletter:

> Setsu Asakura began as an exponent of *nihonga* or Japanese style painting. She abandoned this genre when the Budo no kai (The Grape Society) asked her to undertake the artistic direction of one of their performances.
> Unlike European paintings which rely on a law of perspec-

tive that dictates that all lines should converge upon one focal point, *nihonga* is based on a representational method in which there are many, separate points of focus. This particular characteristic of *nihonga* was especially appropriate to Seigei's revolutionary fairy tale, *Hakamadare Wa Doko Da* (In Search of the Pretender). In Senda Koreya's *Kiiroi Nami* (Yellow Waves), her use of a projected backdrop served to bring out the scene of the colonial naval base much more effectively than any painted scenery.

If I remember correctly it was in Masumi Toshikyo's production of *Za Pairotto* (The Pilot) that this particular style reached its perfection. The settings captured the wasteland-like panorama of twenty post-war years through a clever juxtaposition of *nihonga* realism and theatrical fantasy.

But Setsu Asakura had already refused to confine her frame of reference to a simple flat stage. She began to think in terms of the theatre as a total unit. The inventiveness which she showed during her association with the drama group Henshin (The Metamorphosis), helped her to develop her own theories of set design. Durrenmatt's *The Physicist* was one of many peaks in her career. In it as in Satoshi Akiyama's *Anchigone Gokko,* she redesigned the theatre as she saw fit.

It was from this point on that Setsu Asakura began her revolution in stage materials. Be it Henshin, or Seihai, or Toen, or any other group of economically poorly endowed actors, she would nevertheless take on work for them. This was the time when new materials such as light alloys were being introduced in great quantity.

She was in character when she caused an uproar by making a forest scene out of suspended junk for Bungakuza's production of *Cyrano de Bergerac.* The material which she used for plants in the garden of the home of Baron Matsueda, part of a scene from the Toho geijutsuza production of *Haru no Yuki* (Spring Snow), was also the result of experimentation in this field.

Setsu Asakura is now concerning herself with the problem of whether an essentially space oriented art such as theatre can accommodate the additional factor of time. Her first step toward success in this regard was Matsuki Toshibumi's production of *Machi to Hikosen* (The Town and the Flying Boat). Her mind is taken up with thoughts of four dimensional settings which can lend time to the actor's motions.

Asakura is a rare woman for Japan—or any society. Over many years she has stood at the head of her profession, only mildly bothered by the efforts of men less talented than she and uncomfortable with her achievement to belittle her ideas as the work of a "mere woman." The following interview with Setsu Asakura was conducted at her home in Tokyo. It was an early Saturday morning. We sat in her large second-floor studio in which she both works and entertains. Bookshelves stretched to the ceiling; prints in progress were scattered everywhere. There were straw baskets full of purple flowers and a warm shaggy rug. The power with which she expressed her convictions made the choice of the name Setsu prophetic.

INTERVIEW WITH
SETSU ASAKURA

Mellen: How did your education and upbringing differ from that of other young girls of your time?

Asakura: As a young girl my friends were the boys at the university whom my father brought to the house. He was a sculptor and a professor of art at Tokyo University. He was against the educational system of the time and so I was educated at home by private tutors. As a result, there was little influence upon me of the values of the society as distinct from those of my own family. I had almost no women friends from outside; I had only boys as friends and these were usually painters.

Mellen: Who were the major artistic influences upon you?

Asakura: One was Käthe Kollwitz, the painter who was an antifascist fighter against Hitler. As a doctor's wife she was very poor and very oppressed by the Nazis. She painted her husband's patients—pregnant women, a woman with a dead child, women prisoners dancing around the guillotine in Germany. Her subject was woman; her major influence was Goya.

Mellen: Did you still plan to fulfill the traditional role expected of the Japanese woman and marry?

Asakura: Until the age of twenty-five I never thought about marriage. I had many boyfriends. This was during and right after the war. Girls were not allowed to go out with boys during this time. I was already painting and exhibiting by the time I was nineteen. I felt free of any comments people might make about my conduct.

Mellen: Did you have any political interests? Was there a woman's movement?

Asakura: At that time I was into Marxism. I was not a member of the Communist Party itself. I joined the Communist Party in 1952 and left in 1962. In 1960 I was involved in the big movement against the military treaty between the United States and Japan. But the Communist Party's position toward art was that of socialist realism. My work as an artist and my politics began to be incompatible. Finally the Communist Party and the Zengakuren movement,*

---

* A militant student organization, confrontationist in its tactics and frequently engaged in mass demonstrations and encounters with the police, it fought bitterly

157

composed mostly of students, split. For a year I had been going to demonstrations, but the bosses of the Japanese Communist Party never came to these demonstrations. They would sit and watch from a car parked in front of the Diet building. Through the bureaucratization of the Communist Party these leaders separated themselves from the people.

Mellen: Did you finally marry?

Asakura: Before I was twenty I thought I would not marry until I was thirty since before thirty we don't understand other human beings well enough. I also believed that a woman must have an economic base of her own. I was thirty-four when I married Mr. Tomizawa, my husband. He is three years younger than I. When I chose him I thought that the most important thing was that there should be political sympathy between us. He didn't have to be rich, and the most important thing would not be his personal tastes—he might even like golf! But being in political sympathy would ensure that we could discuss important things together. Other marriages in Japan, as elsewhere, are frequently characterized by fights over trivia—the husband asking the wife to "get me a coffee," and she protesting against being used. We don't have these kinds of fights. It was the student movement and politics that actually brought us together and the basis of our marriage was that we had similar views. He was a Communist since high school and, like me, he left the Communist Party in 1962. Spiritually we consider ourselves Marxists of the pro-Chinese variety, although I have many reservations about the Chinese Cultural Revolution. I have been to the Soviet Union and to East Germany but couldn't endorse either of these societies as models of socialism.

Mellen: How do you view the political situation in Japan?

Asakura: Japan is hazy, like today's weather. It is difficult here to determine what is good from what is bad. In New York I find it easier to decide about important questions.

Mellen: Has the women's liberation movement had any influence among Japanese women?

Asakura: No, the Japanese have not yet reached the level of the women's liberation movement. Japanese women still omit men from their own organizations. In the United States most of the women in the movement work at jobs and support themselves. Here the women who do something are not interested in the women's liberation movement at all. When a person with an international per-

---

against Japan's signing a military treaty with the United States. Zengakuren was similar in spirit and outlook to the Weatherman faction of the SDS in the United States.

spective thinks of the problem of women's liberation, she thinks as well of other questions, such as how we are to function in a community that men created and whether we want to do well in such a society. The Japanese women's liberation movement is more backward and is only interested in "women's problems." If women were to try for power, they would have to deal with men three-dimensionally. And as long as men don't see the problem as one shared by both men and women, the women's liberation movement won't grow. This is a problem for all of us.

Mellen: How do you see the life of an independent woman in terms of having children and raising a family?

Asakura: The first step must be that the woman have an economic base of her own. She should be able to hire help and use day-care centers. Washing diapers is a misuse of a woman's energies. A woman should also have the capacity to be a friend to her child. I have one daughter who is now thirteen.

Mellen: How did you get started as a set designer for theater and films?

Asakura: I taught at the School of Design for twenty years, although I believe that it is not good to remain in the same place for too long. While I was teaching, I studied. I don't consider designing to involve only one medium, but to encompass many of the arts in a synthesis: drawing, painting, illustrating are all part of doing stage settings for plays. I have worked on an animated film based upon a poem of Bertolt Brecht about a dead soldier, as well as on two Toshio Matsumoto films, *Shura,* a period film, and *Bara no Soretsu* [*Funeral Parade of Roses*], a story about homosexuals.

Mellen: In terms of your set designs do you consider yourself a member of the avant-garde as compared with other people working in the Japanese theater?

Asakura: I want and seek constantly to create that space which can include the spectator. Recently I became intrigued by theater enacted in an open, uncluttered space. When I work I do not feel or fully experience the weight of traditional European theater. Thus only direct, seemingly naïve, or transparent responses occur to me. I find it amazing that those sedate stone buildings have been playing Shakespeare since the sixteenth and seventeenth centuries. A natural counterpoint to these oversized houses can be found in the very small theaters of France and Germany.

Mellen: Do you see the traditional view of stage and film sets as detracting from the mood and content of a work?

Asakura: If there were a way, I would avoid setting and scenery at all. In that fashion, I would have a chance to move away from decorative scenography. I could then reassess the significance of the third dimension, that of space. I've long left behind any interest in merely delusionary or decorative stagecraft. The problem of advancing beyond mere decoration to an all-embracing space which integrates and assimilates the area of both stage and audience is a critical issue for scenography as it is for theater as a whole.

Mellen: In what sense are these ideas a break with your own past?

Asakura: More recently, having labored so long in halls which have come to be designated, I think arbitrarily, as "theaters," I have come to prefer a simple space with movable chairs to an auditorium. But even such elementary simple spaces are scarce. Were I to come upon one, I would begin work on the spot. The reason that I am so drawn to empty space is a persistent need with me, a feeling that I ought to start from the barest essentials, to launch work from nothing, from scratch.

Mellen: Have you been influenced in these conceptions by Western ideas?

Asakura: It would be easy, if quite erroneous, to perceive these ideas of mine as imitative of the small theater movements which have grown up over the years in the United States and Western Europe. I understand, however, that even in Japan's most ancient theatrical forms the concept of separating actor and audience is found along with notions of established dramatic styles. For my part, I strongly desire to start fresh from nothing, to begin cleanly with no more than empty space. This must be considered in terms of the visual nature of scenography. Nonetheless, it is essential to envisage theater as an entity and never as a number of discreet compartmentalized components like set design, lighting, props, costume, etc. In certain respects this involves a revamping of scenography as we have previously imagined it.

Mellen: Haven't you also been working with breaking down the traditional relationship between time and space in the theater?

Asakura: The failure until very recently to give proper weight to the relationship between space and time in the theater has been a source of puzzlement to me. Many different kinds of stage arrangements have been conceived and favored since the proscenium arch. We have had the arena, the stage, the thrust stage, tents, boxlike intimate theaters, huge theaters the size of gymnasia. All of these—including a theater like a warehouse—offer new space in which to work and in each instance there is sufficient space on hand to ponder the new element of time. By reducing the gap separating imagi-

nation and reality to the limit possible, we should be in a position
to create a theatrical space in which both time and space are al-
tered. In our age we have regarded spaciality in terms of genres like
sculpture, painting, films, tapestry, and so on. But our strictly
perspective-centered mode of thought has prevented us from ex-
plaining adequately the spacial relationships of traditional Italian
theater, to take one example. The work of Marcel Duchamp uses a
technique employing an electric eye. Duchamp arranged for light to
be projected on pictures exhibited by him for the length of time that
a spectator passed by to take a look. Robert Rauschenberg, through
the sense of touch in his studies of mundane stationary objects and
human beings in motion, sought to discover innovative space-time
relations for painters. If we are to examine the dilemma of time as
it affects the theater, I am convinced that we shall also have to
reassess the work of Moholy-Nagy and surrealist painting.

Mellen: Did you meet with many obstacles in your pursuit of a pro-
fessional career?

Asakura: Fortunately not many. I am constantly surrounded by men
since so much of theater design is men's work involving heavy
physical labor. But these men are my assistants. When we get
down to the nitty-gritty, they make me feel that I am a woman and
they are jealous of a woman who is a set designer and a successful
one. But I am established now. The men here are very conservative
artistically and are always trying to knock down new ideas in art.
Men have tried to stop me from executing my ideas as well. They
have felt that they had a right to do so because stage designing was
supposed to be man's work. If the same work were to be done by
two people, a man and a woman, only the man would be praised. If
a woman does it, they try to say in little ways that it's only a
woman's work and therefore not very important.

Mellen: Has this hampered you in terms of gaining recognition and
support for your ideas?

Asakura: It is certainly possible that I would be recognized more if
I were a man. Before I reached the age of twenty, I lamented that I
hadn't been born a boy. Now I don't think that way. It's pointless.

Mellen: What do you advise Japanese girls today in order to break
out of the old stereotypes and live independent and fulfilling lives?

Asakura: They should go abroad, perhaps to France. And they must
persevere. In this work, for the first two years girls are very good.
In their third and fourth years they seem to get worse and go
backward. Perhaps it's because they don't feel as if they need this
job to survive, to eat. But talent, true talent, doesn't really show up

in the first two years. And don't marry a Japanese man. In Japan, although there is now even a medical school especially for women, girls are still encouraged to be wives, and in the special design school where I teach most girls don't make it a profession.

Mellen: Have you been disappointed in the meager organization of the women's movement that has so far emerged in Japan?

Asakura: The problem is that there is no theory here. In the United States there are various tendencies and this encourages growth. Here in the offices the women still pour the tea and so the women's groups speak out against this. They concentrate on gaining certain rights, like not having to pour the tea, but they don't understand the structure of the society. You must remember that we never had a bourgeois revolution in Japan. This has retarded the growth of theoretical understanding of the structure of the society. So these women make an issue of such things as raising the price of public baths. They disperse their energies in quibbling over individual phenomena. In Japan the women's liberation movement would object to a woman's being friends with the new lover of a man whose wife left him or divorced him. The woman cannot be friends with the new couple because this would make you an enemy of the original wife. One might argue that a third party has no right to pass judgment, but there is the sense in Japan that the old friend of the couple would comprise a third person watching, a public eye. There is a word for this, *seken*.

Mellen: Is lesbianism popular in Japan? It has become an important tendency in the women's liberation movement in the United States.

Asakura: It is very popular, but then homosexuality is freer here. It has a tradition here and has never been associated with guilt. It is a question of fashion, although not perhaps "high fashion." In Kate Millett's case, her declaration of bisexuality was simultaneously a declaration of freedom. It would not necessarily be so here. Her book has been translated into Japanese, but it is popular so far only with students.

NINE

HIROSHI TESHIGAHARA

INTRODUCTION

Hiroshi Teshigahara is another director of the generation following Kobayashi and Shindo who has achieved an international reputation. Like Mizoguchi and Kurosawa before him, Teshigahara was trained as a painter. When he graduated from the Tokyo Art Institute, his primary interest was surrealism. Like Hani, Teshigahara began as a documentary filmmaker, working as an assistant to Fumio Kamei, the left-wing documentary director and socialist realist, who had made an antiwar short in the midst of the Chinese war. The film was finally banned by the Japanese army, which had put up the money for it. Teshigahara's own documentaries include a film about Hokusai, the most renowned of Japan's *ukiyo-e,* or woodblock, printmakers. Another of his documentaries concerned the American prizefighter José Torres. In 1967 Teshigahara made a car-racing film called *Bakuso.*

With the help of his father, who founded the most famous flower-arranging school in Japan, Teshigahara set up his own production company. In 1962 he completed his first commercial feature film called *Otoshiana* or *The Pitfall.* Like all of Teshigahara's subsequent films, with the exception of *Summer Soldiers,* it was scripted by the well-known Japanese novelist Kobo Abé. *Otoshiana* shares with the body of Teshigahara's work what Donald Richie has called the form of a "philosophical—or, better, metaphysical—adventure-story." It shares with his later films as well, as Richie puts it, a preoccupation with "the finding or losing of identity."

A quality, however, unique to *Otoshiana* were those scenes in which characters who have been murdered continue to walk the earth, hovering about their old hunting grounds, unobserved by anyone apart from other dead souls. At times they wish to speak to the living in order to warn them against impending disasters, but they are fated never to make contact with those who remain alive. Their existence in the world of the dead, moreover, duplicates the pains and suffering they endured while alive. A man who died hungry, for example, must wander in eternity forever famished.

Teshigahara has called *Otoshiana* a "documentary fantasy." Donald Richie considers that finally the film must be seen as a "moral failure." His objection lies with the Abé script, which attempts to integrate this metaphysical, if realistically depicted, allegory, with naturalistic scenes of strikers and of union activity and conflict in the mines of Japan. This pastiche of social commentary and allegory results, in Richie's judgment expressed in a 1962 letter to Teshigahara, in a confused film:

> . . . the leftist slant of the *Otoshiana* script is all right in itself but it militated against the allegory and made both unbelievable—it made the film a combination of Everyman plus protest plus metaphysics and nothing congealed: one was left with not one but a dozen different impressions.

Teshigahara's next film was his most successful: *The Woman in the Dunes*. It was rated number one in the *Kinema Jumpo* "best ten" for 1964, and received the Nihon Hoso Kyokai "best" award and the Tokyo Film Critics' Circle Blue Ribbon Award. It has been widely seen and approved abroad.

The Woman in the Dunes is based upon a novel by Kobo Abé about a schoolteacher and amateur entomologist who wanders to the dunes around the Japan Sea. Missing his bus, he decides to spend the night with the local villagers. The town elders deliver him to a tiny house down below the dunes where from this night on he is forced to live by the side of a recently widowed woman. Every night he must help her to shovel away the sand that by day threatens to engulf her little house.

The teacher uses every means at his disposal to escape. He even agrees to make love to the woman before the eyes of masked, reveling villagers who crave any distraction to relieve the endless monotony of their lives. All his efforts to flee are stymied. But by the end of the film the protagonist has discovered his identity through the necessity of commitment to this woman and to the village community.

The bane of their lives is the scarcity of water. The hero finds purpose through his discovery of a means of extracting water from the sand, thus rendering the difficult lives of these people perceptibly easier. Fulfilled by his contribution to the community, the hero is left at the end of the film in the little hut, with the ladder to the outside carelessly left at his disposal by the villagers. The woman, now pregnant, has been taken to the hospital. He refuses the opportunity to leave, having found a sense of self and of belonging—a true freedom born of commitment as compared with his previous random and unanchored existence.

The Woman in the Dunes is a lyrical film, beautifully photographed. An interesting aspect, which reveals the fineness of its camera work, is that viewers have been unable to perceive that, while all the exteriors had been shot on location, the interiors were filmed in the small Tokyo Eiga studios. Richie has said that in this film Teshigahara "achieved perfection." Bosley Crowther, writing in *The New York Times,* was intrigued by "a disturbing allegory of the fate of man in the world—a strong expression of the enslavement of the spirit by all the demands of environment." Judith Crist wrote of a "fascinating film, brilliant cinematically, completely absorbing in the allegorical tale it has to tell." Amos Vogel called the film "Kafkaesque."

At some showings, however, people found the situation of the film difficult to believe. In his remarks introducing the film before its showing at the New York Film Festival, Teshigahara acknowledged that such a deep pit could not be made in sand, and that it was always possible for a man to climb a dune. His idea that literal physical plausibility was of minor moment in comparison with the emotive world evoked in the film was perfectly logical, for the literal serves in *The Woman in the Dunes* only as an opening to the allegorical. Critic Gudrun Howarth described it in her review in "The Seventh Art: Commentary On Film" as "an extended metaphor for Teshigahara's conception of the modern human condition." Howarth also observes how the uniqueness of the textures photographed by Teshigahara adds an important dimension to the film:

> Everything is photographed with sensuality, each surface reacting off another—sand on skin, glass beads thrown into sand, the wood of the cistern barrel off the paper covering it

and off the sand in which both are buried. When the woman washing the man reacts to the touch of his skin and to the patterns of soap lather on his flesh, the sensual, almost tactile, participation of Teshigahara's camera creates one of the most erotic love scenes ever photographed.

Stanley Kauffmann in *The New Republic* compared Teshigahara's film version favorably with the original Kobo Abé novel:

> Abé's prose (at least in the English provided) does not equal Teshigahara's eye, and the novelist's structural sense—of sentence, paragraph, chapter—is inferior to the director's visual structures, his feeling for rhythm and montage. One of his potent devices is a counterpoint of extreme close-up—almost of pores—to convey the closeness of the pair and the inescapable grittiness of the sand . . . the erotic scenes are powerful, and in a relatively discreet way. There is much reason to hope for more fine films from Teshigahara after this fine debut.*

Richard N. Tucker, in his book *Japan: Film Image,* rightly notes a similarity between this film of Teshigahara's and those of his contemporaries: "Examination of the self as one looks at insects under a microscope has been a recurrent theme in recent Japanese films and literature." † Tucker's comment calls to mind the films of Shindo, and, more particularly, Shohei Imamura's superb *Insect Woman.*

Tucker, however, draws conclusions from *The Woman in the Dunes* that are unfounded. Because the woman in the film serves as a central element in the communal effort to preserve the village and prevent it from sinking or disappearing under the mounds of sand, Tucker concludes that "woman in Japanese cinema can therefore be seen as the presenter of a set of attitudes and responses which are in the main traditional and conservative, less often in a liberal central path and rarely of the ethical left." ‡

On the contrary, the woman in this film is the vehicle through which the young schoolteacher is taught by experience the relation between freedom and purpose. He comes to understand how aimless and illusory was the supposed freedom of his former life. She provides him with the opportunity to discover his maturity and

---

* *A World on Film: Criticism and Comment* (New York: A Delta Book, 1966), p. 388.

† (London: Studio Vista, 1973), p. 73.

‡ Ibid.

his identity. It is true that she does not seem to choose her own way of life; it is imposed upon her by a higher force, the community at large. But what counts for Teshigahara is how the individual functions and defines himself within limitations rooted in common necessity. The implication of the film is that all of us move in finite worlds within which we must find some means of defining who we are.

Immediately following *The Woman in the Dunes,* Teshigahara made two further films with Kobo Abé: *The Face of Another* (1966) and *The Man Without a Map* (1968). *The Face of Another* concerns a man who loses his face in an explosion and hires a plastic surgeon to make him a replacement. It is replete with surrealist images which intrigue Teshigahara independently of their service to the imagery or theme of the film. The film thus is finally more grotesque than emotionally compelling. But the sets of the plastic surgeon's office were again appropriately Kafkaesque—a perfect equivalent for the bizarre and unnerving quality of the surgeon's task, providing people not merely with new faces, but with new identities as well.

In 1972 Teshigahara made a film without Kobo Abé, using instead an American screenwriter. *Summer Soldiers* treats the difficulties facing American deserters from the Vietnam war who chose Japan as their place of refuge. The antiwar soldiers are confronted by Japanese modes of life which are too closed and insular to accommodate their needs or allow them psychological entry into the culture. They experience a frequent apathy on the part of the Japanese toward their plight.

Teshigahara used unknown semiprofessional American actors to play the deserters—with something less than full success. The plot, centering on the problem of communication between Japanese and Americans, between people of divergent cultures, was an interesting one, particularly as the Japanese who took in the soldiers were nominally well disposed. But the film is the least successful of all of Teshigahara's work, the most uneven, strained, and the least thematically sound.

Throughout *Summer Soldiers* the image of a deserter-cum-revolutionary appears. He tells us that he is in training for the future struggle. He is completely unreal and the result is didactic attitudinizing, even as the schoolteacher in *The Woman in the Dunes* is, in contrast, credible in his growth. Nevertheless, the film does treat a topic previously unexplored in the current cinema, as Paul D. Zimmerman observed in *Newsweek:*

Good movies about the Vietnam war, whether fictional or documentary, have been notably few. Just completed is a new film that sheds fascinating light on one of the least reported facets of the war.

And Zimmerman concluded that the film finally conveys a "well-balanced view of a delicate situation."

Summer Soldiers really fails because of an inherent lack of affinity for the political subject on the part of all concerned. Teshigahara's own forte has been the existential drama in which a character is viewed in the process of discovering himself. A political theme requiring perception of the dynamics of the American involvement in Vietnam is alien to his sensibility and knowledge. Teshigahara finally cares little for politics and thus shows little understanding in this film either of the nature of the relationship between the United States and Japan, its implied subject, or of the kind of political struggle needed to halt an imperial war. Donald Richie expressed this well in his definition of the particular quality of Teshigahara's moral sensibility written for the Museum of Modern Art archives:

> . . . the "humanism" which [has] animated all of his films [is] rendered all the more interesting because of its complete lack of political intention, its entire devotion to the aesthetics of cinema.

Teshigahara is at a point in his career which requires a new direction. Having accomplished much, working in the genre of the metaphysical allegory, but having discovered his limitations in *Summer Soldiers,* he would appear to be in search of a different cinematic voice, or, at least, new themes appropriate to the genre in which he has excelled. It remains without doubt that he possesses major talent. He has already made a distinct contribution to the Japanese cinema of his generation—one set in the present and focusing on the conflicts and dilemmas perplexing his peers.

INTERVIEW WITH HIROSHI TESHIGAHARA

Mellen: Do you have a special social or political purpose in making films, like so many Japanese directors?

Teshigahara: Yes, it is the undercurrent of my movies, but I do not intend pure political propaganda. In *Summer Soldiers* I had to include more about politics than I wished. It treats American deserters, and I could not avoid mentioning political issues explicitly. I wrote the scenario after interviewing many people who lived with real American deserters, so I had to be factual and adhere to the actual situation. Among my films the political overtones are strongest in *Summer Soldiers* and *Otoshiana* [*Pitfall,* 1962], which is an earlier work.

Mellen: What is the point of view of *Summer Soldiers* toward the American deserters? Is the perception that of the last character in the film who speaks of organizing a revolution?

Teshigahara: I sympathize with the deserters very strongly. But deserting itself doesn't equal opposing the war or the creation of a new, better society. But as a human being, I sympathize with them deeply.

Mellen: Does the director's view equal that of the character in the last shot who is in constant training so that he will be physically fit for the revolution to come?

Teshigahara: Yes, that soldier represents my political point of view more than any other character. But there are various types of deserters. I was most interested in the soldier who deserted for simple reasons at first and was only gradually awakened to political reality, thus becoming aware and sensitive. I made this type representative of all the deserters. I happened to meet such soldiers. They are the very ones who armed themselves with revolutionary theories and tried to bring about real change.

Mellen: Then is the thrust of the film a criticism of the existing social order which creates deserters rather than a psychological analysis of individual deserters?

Teshigahara: Yes, but more than that. I wanted to dwell upon the problem of communication between people—a very human problem.

Mellen: And between the two cultures?

Teshigahara: That is one of many factors.

Mellen: Were you conscious of mixing two styles in this film—the documentary * and a subjective approach? Sometimes the film looks at characters from the outside and at other moments from within.

Teshigahara: I was not that aware of mixing two different styles. However, let me give you one example. Suppose I am taking a shot of a physical scene, a landscape. I would not take the landscape as if you were looking at a single picture postcard. Like the actors, the landscape tells part of the story. The real meaning of documentary film is not the taking of objective shots, but that the film has to be interpreted by the director, who feels this way or that and draws some meaning from the subject. You have to add this human element; otherwise the film will not emerge as art. Documentary is the presentation of the subject which is construed and perceived through particular human eyes.

Mellen: In *Summer Soldiers* what story does the landscape itself tell?

Teshigahara: Take the city of Kyoto, since there is a scene set in Kyoto in this film. Kyoto is an attractive town for most foreign visitors as it is an ancient capital. Even among Japanese, Kyoto has been regarded as a traditional, beautiful city. This is the general conscious level at which Kyoto is viewed. However, one deserter was *forced* to live there and his personal, demythologized interpretation of the city began to emerge in the film. We get a contrast between his view of Kyoto and the typical or traditional view. He became extremely isolated and alienated in Kyoto. His concrete view, then, evokes his feelings about the people with whom he had contact and the city takes on his feelings of isolation and suffering.

Mellen: Is this why you include a scene in which he is unsuccessful with a prostitute? Does this scene express his alienation as well?

Teshigahara: By this time he has experienced many failures in communication. Through his experience with the prostitute his isolation and suffering reach a peak. I contrasted this misery, the reality of human alienation, with the quiet, serene, and beautiful Kyoto as it is viewed from the outside.

---

* Teshigahara began his career as a maker of documentary films and his style in general reveals a preoccupation with concrete physical detail.

Hiroshi Teshigahara (*above*) and on the set of *The Pitfall* (*below*). "People have to face a bottomless pit at the very moment when they have obtained the thing for which they have yearned for a long time."

Mellen: Is there any particular reason why you chose a truck driver as one of the few Japanese to show kindness to the deserter? Is there a social resonance in a member of his class being selected as the person to help him?

Teshigahara: It is not so much his particular class. The truck driver is the first Japanese he encounters who has had no prior knowledge of this American as a deserter. You see, up to then, all the Japanese he had met were those who maintained only an intellectual and political facade regarding lending a helping hand to the American deserters. The truck driver functions in the film as a completely new type of Japanese, one whom the deserter had not met until this moment.

Mellen: Were the families with whom he stayed sympathetic to the deserter?

Teshigahara: People affected a posture about helping the deserters at first. In the beginning people were quite willing to help; at least this was their initial premise when they agreed to associate with deserters and take them into their homes. However, in reality, as time passed and they had to live with these Americans, they found many difficulties which were intolerable to them. The egos of both appear and surpass the early goodwill and political sympathy. They quarrel. In return, the deserter began to feel the pressure and the need to escape. To maintain kindness intellectually or ideologically is not really enough to transcend the conflict between human egos.

Mellen: Is it human ego or anti-American feeling, latent among Japanese, which stands in the way?

Teshigahara: Very, very simple egoism which appears in our daily lives.

Mellen: Are you criticizing the Japanese families who took in the American deserters?

Teshigahara: Yes, to some extent. There are definitely elements of criticism.

Mellen: What kind of criticism do you make toward these families?

Teshigahara: The goodwill of the families toward the deserters is destroyed by the small things of everyday life. They fail for this reason to realize a common political aim. I wanted to show the ultimate difficulty in achieving a common goal among people because all of them still act and make decisions emotionally. It is not that I am criticizing anybody in particular. But I wanted to show the difficulty of uniting various ordinary people on a political issue.

Mellen: Is there any implication that they disagree on the political nature of the problem?

Teshigahara: No, they aim at the same thing, but their petty disagreements spoil everything.

Mellen: Why, in general, was the attempt of the deserters to remain in Japan so hopeless? Why was it futile, as the film implies, for them to try to integrate themselves into Japanese society?

Teshigahara: There are several reasons. First, Japan doesn't officially grant political asylum to foreigners. Second, therefore, deserters never can work effectively in the political field because they must remain nonpersons. Third, they even lost the means of getting out of Japan, since various devices to smuggle them out were eliminated by American espionage. The only thing left for them was to remain here. Japan completely disappointed the deserters. Being in Japan closed all their options.

Mellen: Is it true that Central Intelligence Agency agents appeared on the set of the film? How did they behave?

Teshigahara: While we were shooting at Iwakuni, near the big American base, several strange Americans were taking films of us and what we were doing. Also, at our hotel, a hotel where usually only soldiers stay, there were two American civilians who certainly didn't look like soldiers. It was very strange to see nonsoldiers at this hotel. After we finished our shooting schedule at Iwakuni, I was informed that two Japanese police detectives made many inquiries about us to the manager of the hotel. After putting these things together, I concluded that someone was watching us closely.

Mellen: Did they ask the names of the people who were involved in the film?

Teshigahara: I heard from the manager of the hotel that they didn't ask names, but they were very much interested in what we had been doing. They must have had the names of the people already.

Mellen: Were you satisfied with the use of nonprofessional actors in this film?

Teshigahara: In general I was satisfied with the result.

Mellen: Even with the main character?

Teshigahara: I am sure that there were areas in which I could improve, but generally I was satisfied with the result.

Mellen: Are there any particular problems in directing nonprofessionals? Other directors have spoken of the difficulties, for example, of directing uneducated people.

Teshigahara: Not so much regarding the acting. The most important point regarding work with nonprofessional actors is to choose the right kinds of people for particular roles. Since the movie is meant to be realistic, the choice of actors must reflect this realism. I usually choose people who are leading lives very close to those of the people in the film whom they represent. I hope they will compare their own lives to those of the characters in the drama. Then, if these people are capable of reproducing their actual lives in front of the camera, things go just fine. There are some who try to act according to their mental image of their roles; it usually means failure. If these people do not have the notion that they are "acting" and remain at a subconscious level with all their normal reactions I am usually satisfied with their performances. They should not be conscious that I am shooting. In other words, they are living in front of the camera as they live in their ordinary daily lives. Sometimes, nonprofessionals turn out to be finer performers than professionals.

Mellen: Are you speaking equally about the Japanese and the American characters in *Summer Soldiers?*

Teshigahara: I am speaking primarily about the Japanese nonprofessionals. For the Americans I went to New York to find suitable people to play the deserters. For the leading actor I chose a man who better reflected the mood of the film than a professional actor. I chose them according to my image of what it meant to be a deserter. Another important thing I would like to add is that we have to create a relaxed atmosphere in which nonprofessionals can work. When using professional actors, the more you demand, the finer the final performance will be. However, if you apply this to nonprofessionals, they usually end up not knowing what to do, because they have no prior knowledge on which to rely. So I usually let them do the scene as they feel it, after some preliminary discussion.

Mellen: What did you mean when you said that although *Summer Soldiers* is a very realistic film, you tried as well to extract metaphysical meanings from it? In what sense does the film have metaphysical overtones?

Teshigahara: Oh, that statement was the result of a mistake on the part of a *Newsweek* reporter. I have said that most of my work has a metaphysical element, but unlike my other films, *Summer Soldiers* is a realistic film. The backgrounds of all my previous films were rather metaphysical. This time I tried to approach human problems in a realistic setting.

Mellen: What is the major theme of *The Face of Another* [*Tanin no Kao*]? Is it the problem of personal identity in the crowded anonymity of Japanese society? Are you exploring how individuals find a means of distinguishing themselves from the group?

Teshigahara: No, I don't think so. This movie is about the breakdown of communication between people, not only in Japan, but universally. The protagonist loses his face once and finds a new face. It is a form of irony. He thought that his isolation was a result of not having a face, having to wear a mask. When he got the new face through plastic surgery, he thought this would mean that he could communicate with people once again. But he never recovers what he sought through this transformation. Not only couldn't he obtain what he wanted, but even worse, his alienation deepened. I sought to convey the magnitude of human isolation and loneliness. He believed at first that he could not relate to others and to the society in which he lives (he quits his job) because he has lost his face. Despite his successful metamorphosis, he still cannot unite himself to others. This is the bitter irony. As you see, I wanted to show a triumph which was really a failure. On many occasions people have to face a bottomless pit at the very moment when they have obtained the thing for which they have yearned for a long time. I would hate to say what the major theme of a film is. I usually deal with many human problems at once and pursue many different human conditions. All of these are interlocked within the man in *Face of Another*. It is hard to say which is the most or least important problem. I set this task for the audience. If the audience can relate its problems to the movie, that should be the most important consequence for the viewer. I am very satisfied with the varied reactions about my work. I do not look for a uniformity of response.

Mellen: Is the discontent of the protagonist at the end of *The Face of Another* why he kills the plastic surgeon?

Teshigahara: The doctor is but another part of himself. The surgeon is the man who is responsible for transforming him into a new person. After this transformation, he realizes that nobody recognizes him. He has lost his previous identity. The surgeon has thus denied him his entire past. Once he realizes this, he turns against the surgeon.

Mellen: Is there any special importance to the setting of the surgeon's office—its surreal austerity? It seems to be more than a mere doctor's office. It creates an environment unto itself.

Teshigahara: Not anything particular. I had the idea that the surgeon's room would involve a surrealistic use of space, the way space appears in one's dreams. It doesn't mean anything, but it had to be a place which set the mood and style of the film.

Mellen: Why does the man's wife abandon him so completely—is she meant to be vicious, cruel, self-protective, or what?

Teshigahara: She is a very smart woman. She foresaw that her husband would be undergoing a whole pattern of new behavior. As an ordinary, average human being, she couldn't follow him. It is not

that she abandoned him, but that she just couldn't stay with him.
Love is not such a phenomenon.

Mellen: What do you mean by "love is not such a phenomenon"?

Teshigahara: I mean that love is not a response to be gained by a
new face. Love could not be established on such a basis.

Mellen: Is it true that she recognized him as her husband all
along—even with the new face? To the Western audience, it is not
clear whether she is lying or not when she says this.

Teshigahara: Yes.

Mellen: Is there a relationship between your *Woman in the Dunes*
and the films of Shindo and Imamura which deal with a conflict be-
tween the civilized and the primitive in contemporary life?

Teshigahara: Imamura and Shindo have made very good films on
this subject. But *Woman in the Dunes* is not concerned with this
theme. The woman who lives in the dunes and the teacher who
visits her are not symbols of a backward element in society and an
advanced one. The story could take place in any corner of the
world. The sandpit is meant to have an international meaning, not
one particular to the Japanese. It symbolizes society itself. You
could find such a sandpit in New York or San Francisco, or any-
where in the world. Like society, it is ever shifting and continu-
ously moving. It doesn't rest a moment. It is relentless.

Mellen: What does the shoveling of the sand express?

Teshigahara: Protecting the house, which means protection of the
community. Each house was united around a mutual goal for the
continuation of one's life and the community's life as social exis-
tences. The shoveling represents survival.

Mellen: Is there a further metaphor in the shoveling of sand?
Against what element of society is the woman protecting her home?
And could she be protecting the society from the sand if the sand
symbolizes the society itself?

Teshigahara: In many cases living is comprised of continuing to do
things the way they have always been done. Digging the sand
reflects how people structure their lives according to custom. In this
sense it is a metaphor. The society is the whole assembled by the
small radius of each individual's activity. The woman is not pro-
tecting herself *against* society. Rather, she is performing her duty
as a member of society. You must remember that she is a very ordi-
nary woman. She behaves as her ancestors had behaved. It is a
simple primitive act. As a result, the young man joins in with her to
sustain the obligation. Do not think that she is fighting against or
protecting her life from something. The shoveling should be seen as

the theme of the film. The shoveling of the sand is the symbol of the duty itself which should be performed as one's function. I would offer you one more example. We have a fishing rights problem in the Northern Sea. These fishermen have to catch fish to live. Suppose a Russian vessel comes by and catches the boat and the fishermen. Their survival is threatened, so they try to manage somehow. The woman in the dunes is doing just that. She has to shovel sand; otherwise she would lose the house, and hence the village would eventually be destroyed. She has no choice but to do what she is supposed to do.

Mellen: Is there a contrast between the primitive responses of the woman and the more civilized responses of the man, who is a product of society as we know it. Is there a duality in the responses to life of the woman and the man?

Teshigahara: No, because the teacher is not a representative of civilized society at all. He is just an outsider, a stranger who was recruited from the outside world.

Mellen: What did you have in mind when you filmed that scene in which the villagers don masks and dance in frenzy demanding to watch the man and the woman in the act of sexual intercourse? It is one of the most dramatic moments in the film and seems to express a negative side of the villagers.

Teshigahara: Most of the time these people would reject an outsider. This time they are enjoying the whole process of an outsider becoming an insider. Through the sexual act the man is integrated with village life. They are very happy that he joins them.

Mellen: It seemed as if you were illustrating an animal-like quality in the villagers.

Teshigahara: Yes, and many human emotions. Naturally they want to watch it because they are ordinary human beings with their share of curiosity about sexual things.

Mellen: Is it something particular to this village or were you reflecting more general human emotions?

Teshigahara: Generally we have this curiosity in Japan. Because they are human instincts, however, I am sure that they are universal. While I was in the countryside during the war, I observed this open and uninhibited sexual curiosity. During the last war, many city dwellers were forced to take up temporary residence in the countryside in order to escape from the bombing in the cities. One day in broad daylight I witnessed an old country fellow peeking at two lovers through the hole in a shoji screen. [Laughter]

Mellen: Is the woman then a representative of the instinctive?

Teshigahara: Yes, she is very much so. She is so open, yet impenetrable at the same time. The man has to go round and round to approach her.

Mellen: How would you define the image of women in your films?

Teshigahara: [Laughter] That is a very difficult question. I would have to give it more thought. What I have done with women in my work reflects my own psyche more than a conscious attitude.

TEN

SUSUMU HANI

INTRODUCTION

Susumu Hani is acknowledged to be among the most talented of the younger generation of film directors in Japan. His work represents a clear break with the standards set for the Japanese cinema by older masters like Ozu, Mizoguchi, Naruse, and Kurosawa. All his films, like those of Oshima, occur in the present and examine what it means to be a young Japanese in postwar Japan. In "Masters of the Japanese Film" Donald Richie has succinctly drawn the distinction between Hani and Oshima in terms of their deepest concerns:

> If Oshima's films are often hidden allegories of Japan and its society, Hani's films are often disguised parables about the Japanese spirit, its insistence upon purity, its distrust of experience, and its willingness to compromise.

Searching for the essence of this "Japanese spirit," Hani has made several films in foreign countries. Two of the most acclaimed are *Bwana Toshi* (1965), with an East African location, and *Bride of the Andes* (1966) which takes place in Peru. By transporting Japanese characters to foreign environments, Hani has sought to place in relief what is distinctive about the Japanese sensibility and experience.

Hani was born into a famous liberal family in 1928. His father was a historian, his grandmother founded an acclaimed progressive school, and his mother was a distinguished educator. He remembers being joined by his sister during the Second World War in burying his father's books and papers in their backyard upon the ar-

179

rival of the military police. After the danger, he would rescue them. Hani's childhood was generally traumatic. At the age of six he was such a severe stutterer that his teachers thought him either retarded or mentally ill. It was a handicap he would partially retain into his adulthood.

At nineteen Hani worked for a Japanese news service, the Kyodo Press, and watched the execution of General Tojo and other war criminals. Shortly thereafter he joined a small film company called Iwanami Productions where he spent several years working in the field of still photography before raising enough money to make a movie.

His first films were documentaries, many about children, reflecting a preoccupation with the difficulties of his own childhood. In "Children in the Classroom" he shot with only one cameraman, and he refused to set up the camera in the center of the classroom because it might distract the children. He used a telephoto lens for close-ups, thus affording himself the opportunity to record the smallest changes of expression on their faces. In this way he evolved his semidocumentary, experimental technique of filmmaking. "Children Who Draw" was the first Japanese film to combine black and white and color. To complete this film Hani spent six months in a school. During his five years of making documentary films, four were about children.

In 1959 Hani made *Bad Boys,* his first feature film, costing the incredibly meager sum of $15,000. It was based upon a collection of papers called *Wings That Couldn't Fly,* written by boys in a reformatory. The film was shot in a real reformatory with ex-reform-school boys as the actors, reliving their own lives and speaking dialogue that was their own. Hani has defined the theme of the film as

. . . the spirit of totalitarianism, which is still deep rooted in modern Japanese behavior. What I found out was that even those delinquents who revolt against society behaved like their old feudalist fathers . . . the boys revolt against this society— but, within their group, they themselves are traditional and totalitarian.

In the reformatory environment Hani saw the persistent, old spirit of the Japanese army, with its cruel punishment of new recruits and demands of unquestioning loyalty. At the end of the film the hero, Asai, leaves the reform school and says, "Thank you" as the gates close behind him. For Hani the words were ironic, because Asai had earned less than one dollar for ten months of toil. But his thanks were literal as well because, as Hani has put it, "The prison treated him so badly that he resisted it and in his resistance he grows up." The film was shot almost entirely with a hand-held camera because Hani discovered that "a camera on a tripod is like an objective observer. I wanted the image to belong to the boys' feelings."

Bad Boys was greeted with almost unanimous praise by Japanese critics. Many were struck by what Hani had called his "spy camera," which allowed him to show an inside view of the boys. S. Iida said in the *Asahi Press:* "The creative volition established in their characters by Kinoshita and Kurosawa has always excited my admiration, but I confess that the film of this novice, Hani, has aroused me far more." It was extraordinary praise for Hani to be ranked with the leading figures of the Japanese cinema.

Toshio Oka saw *Bad Boys* as a portrayal of "a newly born human being as we have never been able to see in the Japanese film," a view echoed by the influential Kyushiro Kusakabe in the *Mainichi Press*. Kusakabe declared that Hani's film had rent asunder "the stagnation of the Japanese film" up to that time. Akira Iwasaki called *Bad Boys* "a daring experiment"; all praised Hani's use of amateur actors, the 16 mm telescopic lens, and an absence of artificial lighting. Iwasaki focused in particular on the social import of Hani's approach:

> He draws out their despair, moral starvation and fruitless self-consciousness. Therefore, this picture, without easy compassion or any ready-made tears for these boys, is opposed to any ordinary bad boy film.
>
> The house of correction, which is to redress them, serves in reality only to segregate them from society. It is dominated by a physical enforcement which reminds them of the ancient Imperial army with its violence, sadism and chicanery.

In another important review Fumio Etoh placed Hani not only in relation to other young Japanese experimental filmmakers like Oshima and Yoshida, but in the context of world cinema. Etoh saw *Bad Boys* as "almost homogeneous with the *nouvelle vague* of France," achieving a pure relation with films that would become characteristic of the French cinema of the early sixties. Hani thus anticipated and was the equal of Truffaut, Chabrol, and Godard. In 1970 in an article entitled "Susumu Hani: Film Craftsman; Moralist," printed in *The Human Voice,* Ronald H. Bayes compared

Hani with Fellini and, more to the point, with major young Japanese novelists like Kenzaburo Oë,

> . . . who completely forget the now old-hat battle about tradition and worry about people in the present's maw, and in the future, bringing to bear the deepest intelligent, visceral, and humanistic-spiritual concern.

It is a point about Hani also made by Donald Richie, who has described Hani's work as "a record of spiritual autobiography—complete with the sentimentality that only a true concern for innocence can bring."

One of the most important themes to emerge in Hani's work is his concern for the liberation of women, a commitment he inherits from the films of Kenji Mizoguchi. Hani proceeds to place the theme of the oppression of women in patriarchal Japan in its contemporary context. *She and He* (1963), which many have felt revealed the influence of Antonioni, examines the life of a middleclass Japanese housewife, played by Hani's wife, Sachiko Hidari. She becomes discontent with the empty life she leads with her husband, a typical white-collar or "salary man," and seeks to reach out to a world beyond, where she can express the deep feelings that find no outlet in her role as wife. Naoko finds a means of expressing her compassion in her friendship with a ragpicker (a former classmate of her husband) and with the blind girl he has adopted. Together, man and child reside in a vacant lot adjoining the housing project in which Naoko lives her routinized, gray life with her husband. The ragpicker is aided in his work solely by a huge black dog named Kuma who helps to pull his cart.

The contrast between the vulnerability of the poor and the egotism of the nouveau riche bourgeoisie is beautifully spelled out by Hani. But Naoko's efforts to help these people elicit only her husband's wrath and intolerance, and a jealousy born of his feeling toward her as a possession. The end of the film finds her still beside him in bed, seemingly reconciled, but with her eyes wide open and determined, a fact overlooked by Richard N. Tucker in *Japan: Film Image*. He wrongly designates the ending of this film as "close to *mono-no aware*," or resigned acceptance of the imperfection and transiency of life. There is a mood far from resignation in the expression of the wife who, as Tucker does admit, has achieved an individual identity through her struggle.

Hani's earlier film about the struggle of modern women in Japan for identity and purpose, *A Full Life* (1962), was less successful. It also posed the problem of how a conventional woman can locate a separate and fulfilling life. Its attempt, however, to interweave this theme with the issues of the student demonstrations of the early sixties is not fully realized.

While he was shooting *Bride of the Andes* Hani spent six months in a Peruvian village which is unrecorded on maps. The residents thought he had come to steal their land and were, in the initial period, less than sympathetic toward the project. Richie considers the film an example of "that peculiarly satisfying genre, the controlled documentary." Hidari's performance blends in so gracefully with those of the nonprofessional Peruvian actors that there is no disparity between the skilled and the unskilled performers.

Bwana Toshi was also much praised by critics, like the British writer John Gillett, who stated in the program for the 1966 London Film Festival that "Hani's response to the African scene is beautiful and complete; but although the tone is lighthearted, he is also concerned with his character's feelings, not *least* in the beautiful scene where Toshi bids farewell to his friends on the seashore."

The Inferno of First Love (1968), sometimes called *Nanami* and regarded by Richie as Hani's best film, concerns two seventeen-year-olds (played by nonprofessionals) attempting to resolve sexual anxiety by consummating their relationship. The actors were chosen by Hani after he had placed advertisements in news magazines and had sifted through six hundred applications. Most of the youths who applied said they did so because they were interested in the sexual problems dealt with in the film. Nanami is a young girl whose would-be lover, Shun, is impotent and dies just as they are on the verge of making love. As Gordon Hitchens has written in *Film Comment,* the film reflects "the Japanese irony—a nation in search of its own manhood and mission." Hani has himself explained that this quest unfolds "between two worlds of morality—the old traditional one, which is crumbling, and the new one, which is burgeoning. Living between both, we are confronted by both."

Hani remains unique for the Japanese cinema. A Japanese critic, whom Hani cites appreciatively regarding his work, has said that Hani, unlike most directors, is primarily concerned "with living persons." But what also distinguishes him is his strong interest in eliminating the multiple barriers between the director and his actors, the actors and their audience, and the director and his audience. Hani has found that the process of making the film invariably becomes the film itself. Hence the experience of working in one of his films becomes, for the participants, a progress toward understanding—and changing—their own lives. For Hani the making of a film is not only an artistic, but also a social act. Like all revolutionaries, he has found that it is not enough to understand or to represent the world. He has found through film his vehicle for changing it.

INTERVIEW WITH
SUSUMU HANI

Mellen: What have been your main concerns as a filmmaker?

Hani: From the start of my filmmaking I have been interested in working with nonprofessional people, people who have never been involved in film. Even in *Bwana Toshi* [1965] I worked with people who had never seen a movie before. When making such films I always think of how the actors can be made to forget the existence of the camera and the tape recorder because these mechanical devices involve professional techniques. I think my relationships with my cameramen and recording engineers have been extremely good.

I used to work with a very young cameraman and a very young recording engineer. I spent a few years with the Iwanami Film Production Company. The younger generation of that company and I grew up in our filmmaking together. Have you ever heard of a Japanese documentarist called Tsuchimoto? I think that the film *Minamata* [1971] by Tsuchimoto, about those who have suffered from *minamata,* a poisoning caused by the eating of fish polluted by mercury, is the best documentary made in postwar Japan. You should see it. He was my assistant director for *Bad Boys* [1961]. I persuaded many of my assistants to be cameramen; generally speaking, my relationships with those technicians went extremely well. But I was not completely satisfied with those technical machines, so I developed the idea of using 8 mm. In my film *Nanami* [1968] I shot high school students with 8 mm in one brief part. In the film a high school boy shows the hero and heroine a short 8 mm film called *First Love.* It was made by real high school students with our cooperation. Since that time I have been interested in using 8 mm to abolish the distinction between the people who play in a film and the people who watch it. In this film, of course, I made several technical experiments when I found out that 8 mm could be useful for theatrical showings. My new film is called *Timetable* or *Morning Schedule* [*Gozenchu no Jikanwari*]; it refers to a timetable in school. The subject is adolescent psychology in Japan. The main characters are two girls, both high school students. They agree to take a trip, a tour. I decided to use 8

mm and bought six or seven 8 mm cameras, one for each of the actors. I called in some other high school students and brought my own 8 mm camera as well so everybody shot and everybody played.

Mellen: The same people who are in the film are shooting the film?

Hani: Exactly. This is a quite important moment of the film. To make it in 8 mm is an important part of the story of the film itself. Several important characters make 8 mm films themselves. It gives a dimension of spontaneity and improvisation to the subject. I haven't decided the entire plot yet, but one of the girls will commit suicide or inflict harm on herself. But even in such situations, one always has to indicate in the movie who is shooting the film, because this question is always neglected. Of course it is covered in the part that is narrated. More than half of my fourth film was originally made in 8 mm. Even in 8 mm my situations and ideas are always explicit, and these always include who is taking the film. So the position of the camera is very important. By now this occurs in many new films. But in today's cinema when there is more action, when someone is always either speaking or fighting or making love, one must wonder if the actors don't unsuspectingly take on the coloring of the person who is taking the shot. It adds another distinct point of view which should be discerned. So in this film the 8 mm camera is another important personality or existence.

Mellen: I can't think of anyone else who is doing this—where the filming eye, the act of making the film, the eye that views the action, is contained within the film.

Do you agree with Gillo Pontecorvo when he says that most directors use the camera in a very passive way? He aspires to make it active. Do you agree that most people who make films use the camera passively, failing to use photography to its fullest potential?

Hani: Generally speaking it is true. Many (and it is the same in Japan) think that looking through the finder is not respectable for film directors. They pass the responsibility to the cameraman, the director of photography. But I don't include myself in this category because I'm particularly fascinated by the power and the unexplored potential of the camera. But I think Pontecorvo's assessment is largely correct.

Susumu Hani (with Sachiko Hidari) on the set of *She and He* (*above*) and *Morning Schedule* (*below*). "In my new film [*Morning Schedule*] I count on the performers not only to act, but also to observe, narrate, and express themselves with the camera."

Mellen: Has there been an evolution in your camera work from semidocumentaries like *Bad Boys* [1961] to the present?

Hani: I mentioned to you before that when I speak, I stutter. I have been a stutterer from the time I was very young. I can't speak the way you and Mr. Kusakabe * speak. I think that when I was young I must have been psychologically disturbed. Thus my own life experience has taught me to make documentaries about children; *Children in the Classroom* [1954], *Children Who Draw* [1956], and even my first feature film, *Bad Boys,* reflect my concern for people who have difficulty in communicating with others. In those films, documentaries, the camera is almost my own eye, my own consciousness. In *Children Who Draw* the boy who is the main character didn't draw anything, didn't paint anything the first time, but I was very interested in him. So every day I watched him, almost unconsciously. Probably this was his first experience of someone interested in him because he was so poor, etc. It allowed him to do something more expressive, or at least to feel happier than he had before. This idea already had its root and was developed by the time I made *Bad Boys,* suggesting to people who act in the film that the very process could help liberate them from psychological problems. During the first days of shooting Mr. Tsuchimoto, the assistant director, and I played all the parts ourselves. Then I asked the boys to criticize us. At first they hesitated greatly, but then they became very stringent critics, much more severe than Mr. Kusakabe. They criticized everything about our acting and felt that they could be far better actors than the director.

So they tried to start. At the beginning of the shooting day I went to a jewelry shop. One of the boys said, "I guarantee you, I can steal the things you want, but you must have the camera outside, you must be responsible for outside." I tried to explain to him that this was a movie and not a real robbery. But to him it did not make any difference. So I told him, "OK, the outside is OK." He stole three rings and did not come back.

We were waiting outside the shop. After an hour a friend of his came and called me and said he was waiting in a more secure place. I found out that to him, a nonprofessional actor, to play the part of a boy stealing rings was identical to his own way of life. Crime in his life was a way of getting money, but it was also a mode of psychological self-expression. I did that kind of shooting

---

* For many years the film critic for the *Mainichi Shimbun* newspaper, Kyushiro Kusakabe is now an independent film producer and one of the most respected film critics in Japan. My host during my stay in Japan, he accompanied me to the Hani household, where this interview took place.

for three or four days and then showed the boys the result. They enjoyed acting the parts so much that they said movies were far better than doing it in real life. This gave me the idea that acting is something derived from our life patterns. Of course in real life it is very difficult if we try to consider our own actions as experiments. But if I give people in my movies the chance, they can conduct an experiment with their own lives in my films.

In my new film I count on the performers not only to act, but also to observe, narrate, and express themselves with the camera. I don't know what I'll be doing, what I'll be trying to find out, for my next film, but what always interests me is people, the human being and his or her motivation. I'm much more concerned with what they want to do than in what they did. I started as a documentarist, but my documentaries do not record things that have already happened. I try to do something a little bit better, especially for children. The camera only follows my attempt to do something. It is not a record of the past. The camera is always pursuing the things happening now. Actually the people who appeal to me are living, growing people, not fixed people, but those who are changing, moving, and who want something. Those are the kind of people who are most interesting to me.

Mellen: So the process of being in your film may change the life of the "actor." He becomes conscious of his own life, of the acting that we all do in life, however unconsciously, and the film is a means to self-knowledge. The process of making the film for you is a social act, a revolutionary act in relation to the people in the film.

Hani: Yes, that expresses it. I am interested in two aspects of filmmaking. One side is shooting. This is a very rough process and it involves only the present actions of the people. I show the rushes of the film to the people who are in them, and I find another side to moviemaking. This aspect is more observing, more cool, more critical. So I am aware of two visions.

When you shoot, it represents the side of spectacle in film. Eisenstein says that cinema is spectacle; Bresson says that it is antispectacle. When we are shooting, it conveys spectacle. The camera is always following. You are moving, you are fighting, you are making love, and so on. But if you are in the film and you are also on the staff, you can see yourself on the screen. This self-conscious process represents the side of anti-spectacle. You can act, but can also judge yourself by seeing your rushes. So I'm interested now in trying to handle those two interesting aspects—and in how I can mix them together.

Even when I made *Children Who Draw* I took more than six

months, and after finishing it I showed the film to the children. At first they were very surprised and didn't recognize themselves on the screen. After five minutes they did and became very embarrassed. It was most interesting. By the end, at last, they became very happy. If you shoot and you show the results to the people themselves, it has to be more interesting. Now, in my new film, the actors also do the shooting. So they also want to see the film. It makes it much more complete and more fascinating. Of course we need to develop this, but if we can succeed, I think it can give a new dimension to our own lives and to our capacity for self-knowledge. I remember a Japanese novelist wrote that we should be very thankful that our eyes are not in our hands, because if our eyes were in our hands, we would always have to see our own faces. It would not be easy to live if our eyes always observed our faces. I think it is an interesting conception. Sometimes we can manage this in movies. Of course when you are acting, your "eye" should see your face, but when you view rushes, your eyes are constantly in your hands. I find it interesting to observe the relationship between cinema and the perception of our own image.

Mellen: As a director don't you live the life of the people with whom you work during the period of filming? Doesn't this change the relationship? Don't you become part of their world? For example, I read that when you made *Children Who Draw* you came to the school each day and the children said you must be stupid because you had to come back to school. They didn't believe that you were making a real film because you had only a small Arriflex with you. Was the experience the same for *Bride of the Andes* and *Bwana Toshi?*

Hani: Yes, Yes.

Mellen: How did you integrate yourself into the lives of the people in the Latin American film and in the African film? How did you manage to make yourself a part of the lives of the people?

Hani: It is hard to explain, but for me it was not very difficult. One of the most important phases of my life occurs while I'm making a film and the most significant part of my filmmaking is how I shoot the films. It is interesting that in my 8 mm film *Morning Schedule* one girl is the granddaughter of a very well known old Japanese novelist. It's a very strange relationship. She's quite poor and a

Akio Takahashi as Shun and Kuniko Ishii as Nanami in *The Inferno of First Love*. "It would not be easy to live if our eyes always observed our faces."

high school student, but doesn't go to school. After finishing the first part of the second level she spent only one day in school. The one day she went to school this year was for a special meeting for those who had to remain in the second level, an emergency discussion about the three or four girls in question. She was a very strange girl, but she had some very exciting characteristics. She was always smiling or crying or imitating something. At first I sensed that she was deeply insecure but tried to do everything to conceal her insecurity. When I gave her the 8 mm camera, I asked her to film something she liked. She went back to her home and made a short 8 mm film called "My Room." Actually it was not literally her room because they were living in a very small place, so it was a corner of a room. But she called it her room and she showed several lamps she had made, her dishes, a chair, and a record player. In the window she had made an arrangement of dry flowers; those flowers expressed her feelings about herself. Everything was so beautiful, entirely quiet, calm, and poetic. The film revealed a personality completely different from her surface appearance. I appreciated it very much. For her the quiet and peace conveyed the one thing she loved. So I understood. She looked like a very active personality, but she was so insecure that she could be calm only when she was in the familiar corner of her own room.

This gave me another dimension. I am so busy covering things, giving lectures, etc., that I forget that *my* room is a place where I can put my own heart, my soul. What that film tells you is that the room has meaning only when your heart is there, your spirit. It was a very interesting film. Those experiences encourage me, not so much about filmmaking, but for my own life.

Mellen: She expressed what she would like to be. She is not that way; in her own life she is in turmoil.

Hani: Yes. I think this actually reveals the miracle of filmmaking. In the beginning it was very difficult to work with her. Sometimes she came to our place and sometimes she ran away and we couldn't find her. Although during the shooting she said, "I can do anything," in fact she found it difficult to fix a face and stay with it a long time. Sometimes she couldn't sleep, talked the whole night, and asked me to stay with her. But I believe her experience with

Morning Schedule. "Sometimes she couldn't sleep, talked the whole night, and asked me to stay with her. . . . When she came to our film she was frequently thinking of when she would die. Now she is more confident about doing something with her life."

the film was a good one. When she came to our film she was frequently thinking of when she would die. Now she is more confident about doing something with her life.

Mellen: The experience of being valued gave her a reason to live?

Hani: Yes.

Mellen: I'm very interested in your having made a film in East Africa. How did you make contact with people? How did they respond to what you had in mind?

Hani: I must confess that I was not well prepared for that film [*Bwana Toshi*] because East Africa is so far from Japan. The only place I was able to reach from Tokyo was Nairobi. When I arrived in Nairobi, I tried to find out whether there was an amateur acting group. I finally discovered one or two groups, but they were composed solely of whites and East Indians. There was one black African who was thinking of creating an amateur acting group in Nairobi. I met him and talked with him. His ideas were most interesting but he gave us no concrete help because his plans were only in the talking stage. But he provided an incentive because he encouraged our notion that Africans could be very good actors.

Mellen: How many people from Japan went with you?

Hani: In the beginning I went with three. Then seven people came, including actors. The problem was that none of our people could speak either Swahili or English. When I was staying in Nairobi I met one African who could drive a car. At first I hired him as a driver. He was a very nice man and also had a winning personality, a nice facial quality, and was very clever. He played the role of the teacher in the film. He also taught us Swahili.

We spent one month in Nairobi. Then we traveled to the interior. We were looking for a good place to shoot. It had to be conducive to filmmaking in all respects. While I was traveling, I met the man who played Hamisi, the most important character among the Africans, while Toshi is the main character on the Japanese side. He came from a very weak, poor tribe. In the hinterland they have many oxen and cows. But that man had no oxen or cows so he was used to traveling and to working as an assistant for others. He was a very funny man and I asked him to come and join us.

As we were traveling, we picked up several other people. Of course we brought tents. Finally we got permission from the tribal leader and made the film. The interesting thing is that none of the Africans had ever seen a movie except for the driver. They could not grasp what a movie was. But I had brought a Polaroid camera and took a shot of each person whom I wanted for the film. Then I showed them the pictures. The interesting thing was that those Africans liked and enjoyed their own faces when I showed them the pictures. I think it is a more humanistic response than our self-consciousness. Sometimes people from industrial societies will say, "My face is awful," or something like that. But those people would say, "My face is very good-looking," or "very dignified." They enjoyed it.

Mellen: Self-accepting.

Hani: Very much so. I asked them if they were satisfied with the photographs, whether they considered them good. They said, "Yes, we enjoyed it very much." So I asked them to join our filmmaking. In that area there is not much circulation of money, but they know what money is. I said, we can pay you something, give you some goats or cows or other valued items. They accepted.

But the important thing was that I had forgotten I had started with a Polaroid camera. When I asked them to perform for the movie camera, they always made the action very short. If I asked them to smile or when I asked them to walk, they did it only for a few seconds. I explained it was not a short picture, that I was making a much longer picture. So I said, "Please do it long." They seemed to understand this quite well. The difficulty was that the next day they came and said, "You took a short picture. We liked it very much. Yesterday you took a long picture. Probably a long picture will take many hours to make. So we have waited until now. Can you show us that picture?" Of course it was impossible to develop motion picture film that fast. It was hard to explain. They thought that we Japanese were greedy—they give us the short pictures, but they won't give us the long pictures. We explained and they were intrigued.

Another interesting thing was that I had the rough story ready in advance. For a whole night I tried to explain it to them. They said they understood the entire story, but only wished to know what the subject for today was. I don't know why, but they were not very interested in what they had to do the next day or the day after that. Their concept was that only today is important. So they were not interested in listening to the entire story, but they listened most carefully to what we were doing today.

In the fictional part in which Toshi attacked them, they played very, very well. Sometimes I had to be quite careful because if I explained it and it became too vivid, they felt it as real. An example was the scene in which Hamisi is supposed to be wounded by an elephant and is lying on the ground. When we started shooting I saw that he was in too relaxed a mood. I told him, "You are seriously wounded, you might die tomorrow morning, so you can't act like that." But I overdid it a bit. He changed his entire attitude. He called one young Japanese boy whom he liked very much and confessed to him everything about his entire life. He tried to teach him not to repeat the errors he had made. He actually thought he was going to die. I rushed over to him and explained that it was only a movie, that he was not going to die, and in fact was never actually wounded. But he said, "You are very kind; I know you are trying to film me relaxed, but I know my fate." I think this is another piece of evidence that all human beings, even those tribal Africans, have a hidden but innate ability to act. This is not acting for theater or for movies, but the kind of acting that helps them in their own lives. Otherwise it would not be plausible that all people have acting talent, even in countries where there is no cinema or formal theater. I think it is essential for human beings to have this acting talent. Otherwise we couldn't change or educate ourselves. It was a valuable experience for me.

ELEVEN

SACHIKO HIDARI

INTRODUCTION

Sachiko Hidari was born in 1930 in Toyama, Japan. Before becoming a film star, she worked as a music and gymnastics teacher. In 1952 Hidari joined an independent film company called the Sogo Geijutsu Company. After doing nothing but bit parts, she received her first real chance in 1954 in two films, *An Inn at Osaka* and *The Cock Crows Again*. Each was by the old master of the *shōmin-geki*, or drama of the lower middle classes, Heinosuke Gosho. Anderson and Richie compare her in *The Japanese Film* with Jennifer Jones and praise her work unstintingly:

> Most Japanese actresses' performances are mutually identical, but Hidari's are always distinct and individual. With her appearance in Imai's *Darkness at Noon* both critics and public finally agreed that she had emerged as a real dramatic actress.*

Hidari's international reputation was assured when she received the award for best actress at the Cork Film Festival in Ireland for her role in *The Crime of Shiro Kamisaka* (1957). But her finest performances occurred during the 1960s, in Shohei Imamura's *The Insect Woman* (1963), and in *She and He* (1963) and *Bride of the Andes,* the two films she made with her husband, Susumu Hani. *She and He* won her the award for best actress at the Berlin Film Festival. For her role in *Bride of the Andes* she received the equivalent honor at the Chicago Film Festival.

---

* Joseph L. Anderson and Donald Richie, *The Japanese Film: Art and Industry* (New York: Grove Press, 1960), 400.

Hidari shares with Hani a major interest in the liberation of women as well as a distinctive and radical set of convictions. She is concerned particularly with the plight of women in contemporary Japan, a condition from which she herself has suffered. In the process of transcending the peculiar restrictions on her gender in Japan she has become an international woman of the world. She and Hani have a daughter, Miyo, who is the subject of one of his films.

INTERVIEW WITH
SACHIKO HIDARI

Mellen: I admired your role as the wife in Hani's *She and He* very much. I felt as if it were you, almost as if you were playing yourself.

Hani: But mama-san [Hidari] is more like the wife in *Bride of the Andes*. [Laughs]

Hidari: How wonderful to be identified as such. The bride was my favorite role and I am most honored to be identified with her. It is a proud moment when an actress or actor is identified with one of her favorite roles.

Mellen: Was it because it was a good part or that you wished to be that kind of person—warm, loving, and open with the ability to change your life and start again?

Hidari: It all has to come from within. The job of an actress or actor is not simply to present a likable figure because she is told to do so. You have to identify yourself with the personality of the role, you have to agree with her ways of thought and like the way she behaves. Many directors tend to think they are the sole creators of originality in film, but they are wrong. Actresses and actors can often contribute a great deal. They are always rethinking the best way to portray the character.

There are bound to be misunderstandings, discussing like this through an interpreter. I become very cautious because I don't know whether you are getting what I mean. From your vantage point, you must have many difficulties understanding people and things in Japan.

I have received awards in various film festivals such as Berlin, Ireland, etc., and I have visited countries where I met many filmmakers. But I found it very difficult to talk to them freely and openly.

Probably young people are changing, but nearly every Japanese who received his education before the war has this inhibition toward the Western world. I suppose this is due to the Japanese complex about the West ever since the Meiji restoration. Kurosawa's case is one example. I cannot express how impressed we are by his works, how we admire him. It is a deep emotional feeling because he is one of us. We criticize him, but I want to impress

upon you that this criticism is a small component of the great admiration we have for him. He has a great heart, and sometimes I feel sorry for him, not being understood fully. I really hope you won't misunderstand him, and not misunderstand the people who sometimes appear to be hostile to him. You should understand that young people want to live in their new world and are bent on destroying the old order, sometimes even a great institution. Don't get distracted because of this communication, or rather the difficulty of it.

Mellen: I understand you, although I was very surprised by the amount of criticism film people have directed toward Mr. Kurosawa. I am very glad to have met you and Mr. Hani because it has been a new experience for me.

Hidari: Another thing I want you to understand when you look into our society is Japanese women. Being a woman yourself, you understand that we have to insist sometimes on our voices being heard. We have heard of the women's movement recently, but Japanese women are about one hundred years behind Western women.

Mizoguchi has made some beautiful films about them, and some other great directors have done so, but not many have had their eyes on the real women of Japan. In my opinion, Japanese women are the actual foundation of Japanese society. Now that Japan is one of the economically great nations, some foreigners despise us as "economic animals," but if the Japanese have done anything great, this has been accomplished because of the quiet, suffering, yet diligent Japanese women. [Mr. Hani is about to interrupt and say something, but Hidari silences him] Papa, let me say what I want to say first and then we will listen to you.

Have you seen Imamura's *Insect Woman?*

Mellen: Yes, I think it is one of the best Japanese films of recent years.

Hidari: In my opinion, if you want to say something about Japan, you have to focus on women. Kurosawa did not do this. My greatest criticism of his work centers on this aspect. He is not very interested in women.

Mellen: But Mizoguchi was.

Hidari: He was interested in the women of earlier ages. His work doesn't provide us with much help in understanding modern women

Sachiko Hidari in Shohei Imamura's *The Insect Woman* (*above*) and as Hani's *Bride of the Andes* (*below*). "I feel angry about the injustice experienced by Japanese women."

in Japan. His films are artistically beautiful and they have a significant importance of their own. We acknowledge women's role in those films.

Mellen: You are interested in the psychology of women as in *She and He* and *A Full Life* rather than in the *Oharu*-style films of Mizoguchi? *

Hidari: Mr. Hani is working in the shadow of Mizoguchi's form of filmmaking about women, but he is trying to uncover new ideas and to reexamine the subject. We shall see how he will develop this theme. Viewing him as a film creator and not as my husband, I have much hope for him in the future. He belongs to the future.

Mellen: Definitely.

Hidari: You must have much difficulty in understanding the Japanese woman's place because you have developed your ability as you wished and flourished in your career. You have to look at the long history of Japanese women. Long ago, I am sure that many women realized a great number of things, but they were not permitted to live in a society which acknowledged a woman as a person. Only now are we beginning to have a society which is almost ready to accept women as complete human beings. You see what I mean when I say that Japan is one hundred years behind. And this is why I urge you to see *Under the Flag of the Rising Sun*. I fought with the director throughout while we were shooting the film. Later on I received a review from Russia; the critic pointed out all the things I insisted upon.

During the last ten to fifteen years Japanese society has undergone tremendous change. Japan is less provincial than before. You can read about and look at whatever is happening in the center of Tokyo no matter where you live. Everyone in this country has a high expectation of life. But do you know that an average worker who has served five years at a company after receiving his university diploma can earn only one hundred and fifty dollars a month? Do you think a family can live on that salary? Someone has to kill all his personal desires and manage the household. Japanese women have done this year after year. In the eyes of the outside world Japanese are rich. It is unfair. I lived in Europe for two years and I was constantly astounded by the amount of meat Europeans eat. Despite our situation, not many filmmakers are interested in the

---

* Mizoguchi's films which, like Hani's, center on the enslavement of women dramatize their oppression during feudal times and by specifically feudal norms. A typical example would be Mizoguchi's *The Life of Oharu* (1952).

woman's role in our society. I should say that there are only a few who have any interest at all. I feel angry about the injustice experienced by Japanese women.

We attempted to discuss the problem of the Japanese woman seven years ago in *She and He*. It was too early. Above all we are interested in contemporary problems facing Japan. Japanese filmmakers face a very difficult period right now, and it is almost impossible to predict where we are going. Right now it is safe to make a film which fits into the old world and which doesn't confront the problems of the present. I would say that Kurosawa and other masters are working in that vein. I have admiration for them, but we intend to look into current situations. We want to describe the suffering of the Japanese people today. I can say sincerely that the only director who is undertaking this honestly is Mr. Hani. He is the only one around.

Hani: You are relying too much on your own preferences. Your feelings are one thing, but look at the time when we went to Russia . . .

Hidari: Well, what I really want to say is that the ordinary people are the foundation of Japanese life, including the women who support our entire society. I went to talk at a retarded children's school today. I wondered why I should be asked to give a speech at the school because I am just an actress. It dawned on me that they are interested in my concern for other people and they are interested in my concern for women.

Mellen: How did you decide, how did you become what you are now? You are unique as a Japanese woman—independent, free. How did you accomplish this in your own life?

Hidari: Oh, well, if I started to talk about my life to you now, it would end tomorrow morning. Besides, I just gave a talk about it today at the school, so I can't face repeating it. But there is one vague worry I have about young women in Japan. Many of them do not know anything about the past history of women in Japan and their role in society. They don't have much experience of how to bear things when it is necessary. I have much admiration for women who have something to which they devote themselves. Of course, you are one of them. I am very, very glad to know, as a member of Japanese society, that you find Japanese films worth studying. I had much the same feeling about the works of Renoir. I liked his films, especially *The River,* so much that I couldn't describe my deep impression in words. I didn't understand a lot of the background, but I liked *Midnight Cowboy* recently. I wish that you

Sachiko Hidari in *Bride of the Andes*. "Many Japanese men don't like to have independent wives."

could find a new perspective on Japanese films which we Japanese have never realized. From a different background, you may find some works very impressive; those same works might not impress me. In American films we may find a similar situation. But it is all worthwhile if we can learn from each other and contribute some new facts.

Mellen: Yes, that is something I hope for too.

Hidari: You see, these differences are not due to technical aspects of filmmaking. I want you to understand that Japanese society has many injustices and inequalities. I want you to see the real condition of the Japanese people. I am telling you all this because I think that you are a person who came from the other side of the world and are interested enough to want to know about Japan through films. Through you we can make foreigners understand the better films of Japan.

Mellen: I have seen many of Mr. Hani's films and I am very interested in his treatment of women, but the most interesting thing is the picture of Mr. Hani clearing the dishes from the table. [He laughs] This is worth more than ten movies to me. [Everybody laughs]

Hidari: If he were not that kind of person, I would have divorced him long ago! Everybody should be equal. This is a very important principle. People should help each other, especially husband and wife. This is the only way to be happy together. But I have to say that our home is rather unique in Japanese society. It will take a long time for you to understand the Japanese. Many Japanese men don't like to have independent wives; you must realize that Japanese men are not yet ready to admit that men and women are equal. Probably Hani's family and Kusakabe's are exceptions.

Mellen: I am still most interested in how you became this way. In your youth, how did you free yourself to create a life like this?

Hidari: I started as an actress when I was already twenty-five years old and have been an actress for twenty-five years. I have performed many, many roles; some of them didn't contribute very much to my career. If you would see *Under the Flag of the Rising Sun,* which I finished a few months ago, you will find many of my answers.

Mellen: What did you do before you became an actress at twenty-five?

Hidari: I was a high school teacher then. I started very, very late for an actress. I am sure that you have never seen my earlier films. I played roles of women from fifteen to sixty years of age. I also played many roles of women who live at the very bottom of society. I always tried to bring out the earthiness of women, as in *The Grapes of Wrath.* It doesn't matter which country we're talking about; I tried my best to express the strength of women.

Mellen: Do you have any children?

Hidari: Yes [pointing to a huge poster on the wall of a little girl] this one, Miyo [also the title of Hani's recent film, *Miyo,* starring their daughter]. I am hoping that when the time comes for our child to be an adult, being a woman or a man won't make any difference as long as she is a whole person.

I also like Salinger very much. I am reading all of his works in translation. I liked *The Catcher in the Rye.* I also liked the recent American film *The Godfather.*

Mellen: Why *The Godfather?*

Hidari: There were many emotions expressed in this film which are well understood by the Japanese—such as the obligations to others and duty to the family.

Mellen: This is, of course, a different kind of family. They are a gathering of killers and gangsters who conveniently form a business clan structured like a family.

Hani: The ties between the political and other organizational groups in Japan are remarkably similar to the mobster family.

Hidari: No, that is not what I meant. Being in the film industry, I have experienced similar things myself. I have known at first hand how it feels to be threatened and blackmailed by underground organizations who have received orders from the film company and which resemble the Mafia. I wanted to leave Nikkatsu, which was one of the five major companies, and my life was threatened as a result of my "rebellion." With such an experience I can well understand the situations as they appeared in *The Godfather*.

Mellen: The current vogue for Marlon Brando expresses the fact that American women are still not liberated; they still enjoy seeing his masculine bravado in films.

Hidari: I prefer Christopher Jones. He was in *Ryan's Daughter*. I think younger people now like the type of man who has an air of homosexuality.

Hani: I don't think so.

Hidari: Yes, it is so. Many young Japanese girls nowadays like gentle men—the same type the homosexuals prefer. But it's interesting that *The Godfather* was so well received although it projects the opposite image.

The movie audience in Japan now is composed of women between seventeen and twenty years of age. I don't think Marlon Brando is the reason *The Godfather* was so popular here. The Japanese girls understood the feelings and moods of the characters in the drama. There is a certain Japanese-ness in that story. You can make an interesting study of the psychology of the Japanese people. I don't think any woman will throw herself at Marlon Brando if he visits Tokyo, although there are so many crazy things in Tokyo. I don't know how long you are going to stay in Japan, but I am certain that some places and people in Tokyo will really shock you. Tokyo is indeed a maniacal city.

I enjoy talking to you so much because you are interested in us and want to know about us. Don't think I talk like this to any foreigner. I am usually very, very quiet with them. Why should I talk to them unless someone like you wants to know about us? I want you to see the honest face of Japan, look at the good and the bad. I would really like to hear what you think about Japan.

Filmmaking in Japan is in a sad state now. Take us, Oshima-san, and others. We are all spending our own money to make films. It is pretty hard to get to the shooting stage.

Hani: I think that it is pretty much the same everywhere in the world.

Hidari: We all have to work hard outside to make money for production. Mr. Hani writes educational books.

Kusakabe: Yes, some of them are very good.

Mellen: Is that the reason Hani goes abroad to make films?

Hani and Hidari: No.

Hidari: It is one of the reasons, but never a major one. While we were in Europe, Hani was offered many filmmaking opportunities. We turned them all down because we feared that the person holding the pursestrings would try to influence us too much. This current film, *Miyo,* is the first one we cooperated with a French company to produce. It was shot in Italy. Moviemaking takes lots of capital. Thus it was encouraging to see that *The Godfather* was such a hit.

Mellen: I read in *Variety* that it has made at least fifty million dollars. This is the biggest box-office hit in American history. It will probably gross one hundred million.

Hidari: I don't know if it is popular in Europe or not, but certainly it is the hit of Japan. And as I mentioned, this fact interests me. There must be a connection between this film and the sensibility of the Japanese.

I wish I could speak English well. There are a lot of things I could share with you. The subject of Japanese women is but one example. There is a story called "Sandakan Hachi-ban Kan" which describes the suffering of lower-class Japanese women. It is about prostitutes sent to the South Sea regions during the Meiji era.

Well, in conclusion, if you have an opportunity, please see my *Under the Flag of the Rising Sun.* I made *The Insect Woman,* another important film about women, eight years ago. I want you to see the current state of women, which hasn't progressed much since *Under the Flag.*

Mellen: You don't see much progress in the status of women in Japan over the past ten years?

Kusakabe: No, not much change at all.

Hidari: It is so hard for me to answer that question. Please go and see the movie and you will learn my answer.

TWELVE

TOICHIRO NARUSHIMA

INTRODUCTION

Toichiro Narushima has enjoyed a long career in the Japanese film. He is not nearly as well known as Hani, Oshima, or Shinoda primarily because of the status granted the director in the film medium. Although Narushima worked with the great Kenji Mizoguchi and as an assistant director to Keisuke Kinoshita, also one of the masters of Japanese cinema, his reputation has been as one of Japan's finest cinematographers. It is a position of great artistic responsibility, but one seldom granting its practitioners a great deal of credit. Certainly Narushima deserves much of the praise for the magnificent shot compositions and textures of some of the finest films of the contemporary cinema—Nagisa Oshima's *The Ceremony* and *The Man Who Left His Will on Film,* and Masahiro Shinoda's *Double Suicide* and *The Scandalous Adventures of Buraikan.* He was director of photography for each.

In 1973 Narushima finally directed his first film, *Time Within Memory.* It is the story of a man approaching forty who returns to the primitive island where he spent his boyhood and where he lost his mother in a natural catastrophe. Her death had a traumatic effect on Minoru that has accompanied him into his manhood. They had wandered out together on corals extending into the sea when a flash tide came in. She was able to save her son, but not herself. The tragedy, which haunts him, accounts for his visit to the island after an absence of many years. Minoru returns in search not only of his past but also of his identity, and thus, indirectly, of his future. The search for identity is of course a theme which has preoccupied

208

younger directors in Japan, including Shinoda, Hani, Teshigahara, and Oshima, and poses the question of what it means to be Japanese.

Narushima believes that there is an endemic crisis within Japanese culture. One expression of it is the very fact that modern Japanese spend so much time and energy thinking about what culture *is*. Narushima's concern is to return the Japanese to the experiences which define them as a people. In *Time Within Memory* a major theme is the strong, traditional Japanese love for the natural order. Narushima equates the origins of human beings with the rhythms of nature. The cadence of island life provides the harmony from which people have lapsed, and the tribal customs of the island people are geared to this flow of existence. For Narushima, whatever people are, they receive from the natural order. As it is only from nature that we learn what is essential to human life, it is from these roots that we can rediscover a path of growth which will not do violence to our needs and possibilities. Narushima searches for the most primal and authentic human feelings, those which would still be part of us were we not victims of alienation and separated from our basic needs by a repressive civilization. One of the interactions closest to human need is the relation of son to mother, and this forms the subject of his film.

The original story by Jiro Ishiki, on which *Time Within Memory* was based, concerns a young man so obsessed by his love for his mother that he is unable to live his adult life in peace:

> My thirty-year absence from home has failed to dim the memories of my mother, who died young on Okinoerabu, her island home where the white reefs contrasted with the ultramarine subtropical sea. Back on the island, in her deserted weatherbeaten house with its ivy-covered walls, I see an old man who was once deeply in love with her. The music he played for her the night he proposed, and received her considerate refusal, is still sounding in his ears. I vividly remember those days; how young and beautiful my mother was. . . .

The mother, whose name was Sawa, had tuberculosis, and during her last days feared touching her son because he might contract the disease. As a man nearing forty he still recalls "long[ing] for her affectionate embrace." The intercut flashbacks work perfectly. To Minoru, as an adult, the night on which his mother danced at the annual August festival of the islanders remains with him as if it had occurred moments before. Their last day together reverberates too, as if it has just happened. The original Ishiki story relates this fatal incident simply:

> One serene winter day, she took me to the reef, played with grass boats, fished and missed the oncoming tide lapping the reef. That was the last of my mother; the incident was beyond my comprehension. On the seventh day after her death, I visited a medium named Yuta. And I heard my mother calling me; "Minoru! Minoru! How I wanted to hold you in my arms, even just once more."

Narushima's filming of the death of the mother is one of the most moving sequences in all of Japanese cinema. The cataclysmic day begins for Minoru in a mood of lyricism. Mother and son have gone fishing together, using a primitive method that links them with the traditions of the island. A poisonous herb is cast on the water, asphyxiating the fish, which float to the surface. A mass of beautiful multicolored fish lies beside them.

This graceful scene is broken by a change in weather. The sea, suddenly, like life, becomes stormy, ruthlessly washing away their fish. There is a faint intimation that the two islanders have become too uncaring of the delicate balance of their surrounding world, too preoccupied with themselves, taking more of the sea's bounty than they truly need or could use. Suddenly aware of the avenging tide surging around them as if on command, the mother attempts to escape the onrushing sea with her son. As they wade through the encroaching waves, she suffers a lung seizure.

Climbing up on a rock, she promises her son that she will wait there until the eight-year-old Minoru can bring help. She sternly makes him promise to seek the rocks and to climb from the sea without once turning around, a beautiful parallel to the myth of Orpheus and Eurydice. Her last view is of her vulnerable little boy intently stumbling through the water to safety. He turns, but, faithful to his promise, does not look back toward her until he has reached the security of the surrounding cliffs. Only when it is too late does he look back to discover that the sea has covered everything, including the rock to which his mother had been clinging.

Years later, out of a mixed grave in which the bones of three bodies were combined, Minoru, praying, lifts out first one, and then a second, and a third skull. He believes, mystically, that if he cuts a finger, his blood will stick to the skull belonging to his mother. He cups one skull and cries to it with feeling: "Mother!" Her image appears before his eyes, as she was the last moment he had seen her, lying on a stretcher as she was carried dead from the sea.

The adult Minoru cries. The old islander who had once proposed to her is with him and explains to Minoru that his mother's bones felt deserted by his departure. Thus she had called her son to her all the way from Tokyo. As Minoru cries, the sea washes over the coral and over the skull. Narushima cuts back to Sawa's body lying dead on the coral reef, her hair trailing in the water. Minoru has at last made contact with his past, with nature, and with his submerged but powerful feelings.

In *Time Within Memory* these three merge into one, even as the adult Minoru remains the boy he once was. To underline this, Narushima includes several times within the same shot both boy, in half flashback, and man in quest of a peace that will come only when the child's traumas have been rendered conscious, lived through, and accepted. As Minoru leaves, he carries the skull with him.

Sawa represents not only the prototype of woman as mother, but she embodies as well the physical beauty, grace, and enduring strength of the island culture. The moving and exquisite dance she performs at the time of the harvest moon festival is a magnetic event. The island population converges on a beautiful cliff overlooking the sea. Young and old are exultant, and Sawa's dance represents all that is redeeming and vital in their lives. Narushima thus conveys wordlessly how much more authentic and close the island society is to what it means to be truly human. It is pure and unsullied compared to the technologically advanced mainland with its merchant mentality.

Yet the islanders cast longing and envious eyes at this corrupted, commercial mainland. Already during Minoru's boyhood it had come to reflect a dehumanizing of the spirit that Narushima feels characterizes the culture of modern Japan. There is a suggestion that Sawa contracted her fatal illness as a consequence of living on the mainland. The widowed Sawa's cruel father-in-law, surrounded by a corrupt household presided over by a selfish mistress, had refused to give her a home.

It was among people who had lost the power to respond to others humanely that Sawa began the physical decline which led finally to her premature death. The sailor whom his mother had married in desperation refused to allow her to make a home for Minoru, and he was sent to live with his grandfather. The sailor too belonged to the neon corruption of mainland life. When Sawa fell ill he deserted her, and it was at this point that mother and son traveled to Okinoerabu, where Sawa would spend her last days.

Through the pain of these last moments, Narushima conveys his sense of the debilitating decadence of the new Japan. The folk customs of the island are symbolized by the song sung by Sawa as she sat at her spinning wheel, partaking of a way of life soon to be lost. The island people were linked to a living tradition. They knew who they were. And the few months left to mother and son were their happiest. In a voice-over Minoru hears his mother saying, "Without those months, my life would have been miserable."

Only by rediscovering their origins, however painful or naïve, can the Japanese recover what they once had as a nation and experience the solidarity and sense of community they shared as a people. There is, of course, an ambivalence among the islanders themselves which is expressed in the irony of the traditional dance performed on the night of the harvest moon. The song expresses the desire of the islanders to return to the mainland and to cease being cut off from the rest of Japan.

Time Within Memory was received very favorably at the Teheran Film Festival in 1973. *Variety* observed that although Narushima is perhaps too close to his subject, he escapes the danger of sentimentality:

> Skirting sentimentality, it avoids it, but is still too righteously searching for emotion rather than letting it develop. But a scene when the sick mother dances for a village suddenly crystalizes the film to show her nature, loveliness and strength, making it a pic that displays a budding directorial temperament when he can overcome his penchant for visuals for their own sake . . . not overcoming a certain pictorial prettiness and indulgence in nostalgia, pic still has enough good moments to have gotten it a nice reaction as a competer at the recent Teheran Film Fest.

In his review of the Museum of Modern Art "New Directors Series," Roger Greenspun in *The New York Times* was harder on the film, unwilling to respond in the slightest measure to the film's poignant power:

> I have seen half the films so far, and there is only one sappy movie among them. That is Toichiro Narushima's *Time Within Memory,* in which a middle-aged Japanese businessman revisits his childhood island home, remembers his last months

with his beautiful tubercular mother (30 years before), and puts together past and present in a succession of sticky images that all but beg for sentimental response. *Time Within Memory* fails utterly, but it looks like failed commerce rather than failed art.

It is odd and hardly to his credit that Greenspun is so unqualified, resorting to adjectives like "sappy" to dismiss a film that clearly raises important questions about our culture and its prospects. Narushima admits that the weakness of *Time Within Memory* may well be that "intelligence lost out to the senses," but the film remains a stunning document of a man's attempt to come to terms with his unresolved feelings. The emotion, moreover, if un-disguised, is patently sincere and deeply felt. Steeped in the writings of Freud, Narushima employs flashbacks in the conviction that only through a reexperiencing of childhood pain can we make contact with ourselves in the present.

Time Within Memory is a strikingly beautiful film of subtle visual texture and an impressive attempt by Narushima to encompass a complex theme. His aim is an integration of personal psychology with analysis of an entire society, moving at these two levels simultaneously to elucidate where our culture has been and what its future holds. If the film does not at all moments sustain its promise, its evocative power reverberates in the mind long after the experience of watching the film.

Unlike the other meetings, the interview with Narushima occurred in New York during the director's visit on the occasion of the film's American premiere at the Museum of Modern Art. Narushima spoke openly and with enthusiasm about his work and the discussion lasted long into the night.

INTERVIEW WITH
TOICHIRO NARUSHIMA

Mellen: Is there a disparity between what seems to be your exaltation of the primitive life and the desire of the island people to go to the mainland in *Time Within Memory?* Do you see a contradiction here? Life on the mainland is harsh, competitive, and destructive, yet one of the most beloved songs of the islanders describes the trip to the mainland with longing.

Narushima: The islanders live within two recurrent motifs. One is to remain on the island and lead a tranquil, familiar life; the other is to go to the mainland and to try one's fortune there. These two motifs are not felt by them to be contradictory. Naturally, everyone dreams of striking it rich on the fabled mainland, offsetting at least in their imaginations their miserable, impoverished lives. Nonetheless, each person's role is prescribed by the traditional family structure. The eldest son remains with his parents and continues the family line; the younger sons always leave to find prosperity on the mainland. In the film, however, Sawa wants to go to the mainland because she has left her child there.

Mellen: That emerges clearly in the film. Some felt during our discussion last Sunday that the film depicts life on the island as more moral, wholesome, and essentially decent than that of contemporary Japan as lived on the mainland. Do you agree?

Narushima: Yes, I do. Island people have very stringent moral codes, discipline, and a reverence for their own way of life. In many ways I felt they were too strict, even rigid.

Mellen: Yet there seems also to be a greater purity about them. Their lives have a rhythm symbolized by the unique musical instrument Sawa plays, and which is taken out for all solemn and emotional moments. Doesn't the film establish that "civilized" life in modern Japan is decadent, corrupt, and distractive? The contrast between the sense of self and purpose of the islanders and the frenzy and disorientation of the city dwellers is so marked.

Narushima: I didn't elaborate on this aspect in the film, but I intended to contrast the corrupt mainland with the relatively tranquil life of the island.

Mellen: But it is not that indirect. The people who go to the mainland contract diseases, become tubercular, and are very pale. The

Atsuko Kaku as Sawa. "I intended to contrast the corrupt mainland with the relatively tranquil life of the island."

people on the island, and here the use of color in the film is most spectacular, are healthy, dark, and resilient.

Narushima: There is one more thing I want to say regarding the contrast between the life and people of the island with that of the mainland. I haven't said this to anybody in New York. I wonder if you can understand this. At first, Japan herself was "the island." For good or bad, the Japanese people were shaped by this natural environment for many centuries. Islands have their own special characteristics. So what I have said about islanders in this film is a concentrated form of what we can say about Japan herself. This is the small play I intended within the movie. The islanders' ways recapitulate the Japanese experience in general.

Mellen: Finally, then, what it means to be a Japanese is to be an island person? The more you get back to your roots, the more you become an island person again?

Narushima: Yes, but there are both good and bad aspects to being an islander. Islanders can communicate and associate among themselves directly; they are emotionally involved with each other and can talk uninhibitedly. But their intimacy is insular. They are not

willing to accept outsiders. In fact, they have an egoistic, self-defensive fear of foreigners. I wanted to say something similar about the Japanese people through the example of these islanders. In such a community it is easy to maintain high standards of discipline, fixed mores, and general moral severity. If you interpret this concept of being an islander in the broad sense, you can well understand why Japanese feudalism lasted so very long.

Mellen: This is very important. In your film do you imply any solution to the problem of modern Japanese culture? Is it viable to return to more tribal or primitive thinking and ways of life?

Narushima: No, I am not hoping for that sort of solution. Since humankind is such that we all have to proceed, you must step forward. I don't think we are able to go backward. I wonder again if you will understand what I mean here, but Japanese culture is in a unique situation. What Westerners must recognize is that Japanese *culture,* not civilization (I think these two are very different things) is running ahead very, very fast. I think that the speed has accelerated so drastically in recent years that we now find ourselves in a messy state symbolized by the four huge pollutions confronting the Japanese. This acceleration intensified after the last war. Of course one can argue about the many interlocking reasons for our ending up in this state, but the fact is that here we are, whether we like it or not.

Mellen: What are these four big pollutions?

Narushima: I am referring to the four most famous trials for fatal pollution: the Minamata Case, the Yokkaichi Case, the Niigata Rice Field Case, and the Morinaga Milk Case. There were also a few other famous cases, such as that of Kanemi Oil in which many people ate the oil squeezed from rice hulls and the oil contained chemical poisons. In "Morinaga Milk" many died or were paralyzed from drinking powdered milk containing arsenic. Yokkaichi is the city in which the air is so heavily polluted that many residents suffer from asthma and grave respiratory diseases. I am sure that you have heard about the Minamata Case. Minamata was the most famous and earliest pollution trial. It attracted nationwide attention in Japan. A paper mill was located in Minamata City, near Shiranui Bay in Kyushu, and it was polluting the bay with waste containing large amounts of mercury. Large numbers of people were stricken

Toichiro Narushima on the set of *Time Within Memory*. "From our history I can almost conclude that the Japanese will never revolt. Revolution is not in our blood."

by mercury poisoning, particularly fishermen and their families since the fish in Shiranui Bay had been poisoned. Anyway, these are all examples of rushing technological advance, or "progress."

Mellen: What was the literal title in Japanese of the book from which the screenplay for *Time Within Memory* was adopted?

Narushima: Record of a Blue Illusion.

Mellen: Does the color blue have a special meaning for the struggle of Sawa to remain with the son who was taken from her?

Narushima: I like blue very much for one, but also childhood memory takes on a hue of blue in my mind. Blueness in the sky, blueness in the ocean which envelops dreamlike memories. These are sad but gentle, and seem to tell me much about illusion.

Mellen: In the film blue is the dominant tone in the photography.

Narushima: Yes, I also feel a modern quality in blue.

Mellen: So it expresses for you a highly personal feeling?

Narushima: As one matures from one stage to another, one's color preference changes. This has been my experience. Until *The Ceremony,* in which I fought with Oshima while making it, I leaned toward red and yellow in my cinematography—warm tones. Since then my predominant color has become blue.

Mellen: Did you enjoy working with Oshima in comparison to Shinoda?

Narushima: It really doesn't matter who the director is. Rather than being just a photographer, I consider myself a director of photography. As a result, I am quite stubborn and egotistic and stress my own view in every decision.

Mellen: But do you sympathize more with one or the other in terms of ideas or conception of film as a medium?

Narushima: It is not really a matter of one or the other because I am most concerned with what I can accomplish in the end. The film itself is the ultimate answer. As long as I am director of photography, it doesn't matter at all with whom I am working—Oshima, Shinoda, or even a young, new director.

Mellen: Returning to *Time Within Memory,* what were you trying to convey by repeatedly conjoining the adult hero and the hero as a child within the same shot—the past and the present simultaneously?

Narushima: That is a most important point. If someone matures

Hisano Yamaoko as the child Minoru (*above*); Takahiro Tamura as Minoru (*below*) in *Time Within Memory.* "If you interpret this concept of being an islander in the broad sense, you can well understand why Japanese feudalism lasted so very long."

happily and everything unfolds well, childhood is followed naturally by adulthood. However, if one matures unevenly or in conflict, hence inadequately, his adult self never outgrows the conflicts or sufferings of childhood. One is compelled to live in the shadow of that childhood for the rest of his life. Our lives move continuously from one stage to the next. As for the scene in the grave in which the hero addresses the skull of his dead mother, the bystander says to Takahiro Tamura, the actor who plays the hero, "You weren't very happy in Tokyo, were you? You must have many things you wanted to tell your mother." At this instant the forty intervening years vanish, and he is back in the past as a child. I wanted to express this idea with the double images. The old memory of his childhood, in which his mother was taken from him in that horrible accident when the sea engulfs her body with an unexpected high tide, has made him return to the island.

Mellen: In what artistic and personal ways have the ideas and perceptions of Freud shaped your own?

Narushima: Yes, Freud influenced me profoundly. Twenty years ago twenty-seven volumes of Freud were published in Japan. I read them all. After the war Freud was in vogue in Japan for approximately five years. Everyone was talking about him. Then the philosopher who wrote *Human Heart* replaced Freud. I am trying to recall his name; it is something like "Huberman." I still consider Freud to have opened up the problems of the human mind and laid the foundation for our understanding, but to me he seems to have provided a basic thesis on which we have yet to build. In our fast-moving modern culture, we seem to need more than Freud's foundation provides. For one, we have too many varieties of human psychological problems.

Mellen: What kind of problems have you in mind?

Narushima: Let me see. To give an example is rather difficult. How about dream analysis? No, that is not very good. Let me give the example of one's own complexes. Freud showed us that we all have neurotic complexes secreted in our minds, and he described many. But now, these models are not adequate to apply to our modern situation. Our consciousness of our complexes is sometimes not helped by his analysis. This could be something unique to the Japanese mind, but that is the way I feel about Freud now. Our peculiar expression, being Japanese, has to be interpreted by a Japanese model of understanding. I spoke of the variations in human psychological problems; there must be many which only Japanese minds can fully conceive and understand. From this point of view we need more than Freud in modern Japan. We really don't speak of Freud much now, and I understand that talking about him like this could be almost sacrilegious to some. If that is the case here, I am sorry. I am sure that I am not impartial either because I see the Japanese psychological structure as being particularly formed by the Japanese natural environment, shaped by its social aspect, and so on. I cannot detach myself and experience the Japanese psyche from an outsider's point of view.

Mellen: This is probably true for all of us.

Presumably your task is to locate and organize aesthetically the neuroses and experiences which are unique to Japanese culture and character.

Narushima: Yes, this is what I want to do. I believe that the Japanese character and experience possess a unique defining quality, although I am positive as well that there are many things one must explain as universal human experiences. This Japanese uniqueness is connected with the specific phenomenon of Japanese culture, always racing ahead so fast. I want to unfold the connections between the two. The problems of pollution, a too rapid growth of industry, the launching of the last war, the fact that Japanese are and have been since the Second World War called "economic animals," and so on—these are all connected in some way if you pursue it. Probably the suicide of Yukio Mishima is also connected to this. These are the preoccupations which led me to say in the beginning that I believe in Freudian concepts but for an analysis of modern society, certainly in Japan's case, they are no longer sufficient. The problems we face are so vast, enormous, that we really need further tools.

Mellen: Are there any other thinkers whose ideas are helpful to you concerning these current problems of pollution, war, etc.?

Narushima: That is the most important question. I can only speak from my experience of the situation in Japan, so I may be wrong. But in other countries if someone sounds a warning note loud enough, it can mobilize the masses. In this respect I am very pessimistic about the Japanese people. There were great philosophers and authors like Nyozekan Hasegawa, Noosei Abe, Yasunari Kawabata * . . . They all warned the Japanese people about

---

* Noosei Abe or Yoshishige Abe (1883–1966) was a philosopher, educator, and critic famous for his writings on the history of philosophy and for being an able university administrator. Yasunari Kawabata (1899–1972), author of *Snow Country, Sounds from the Mountains,* and *A Thousand Cranes,* was the first and only Japanese Nobel Prize winner for literature. Nyozekan Hasegawa (1875–1969) began as a journalist and fought for democratic freedom against the oppressive militaristic government. His writings were recognized and praised highly after the war.

unforeseen dangers. Well, the Japanese didn't change their ways at all. People in Japan are too busy pursuing their limited goals and so wrapped up in them. Let me give you an example in the United States which I thought wonderful—the meat boycott. Someone said that we must do this and enough people joined up to follow. In Japan such a thing is unthinkable.

Mellen: But the meat boycott was minor in itself because it couldn't be sustained.

Narushima: Oh, I see. I understood that the meat boycott didn't work. But still, what I saw was a unity in people. I see a quality which can be expanded into more powerful action in the future. In contrast to this, Japanese food prices have been going up exorbitantly for many years; we have a consumer group called Shufu Rengoo Kai [United Housewives' Organization]. People have been crying over food prices for many, many years, but not once did the Japanese people, in mass, protest them.

Mellen: Do you think it requires revolutionary action to effect serious change?

Narushima: No, the Japanese are incapable of being revolutionary. In several thousand years of Japanese history we have had only one full-scale revolution. To be more exact, there was one quieter example, so we had two revolutions, and that is all. There was the Taika reform * in A.D. 645 and the other was the Meiji restoration † of 1868. The former was bloody and the latter bloodless.

---

* In 593 Shotoku Taishi (573–621) was appointed to the regency. He was a philosopher-statesman deeply devoted to the spirit of Buddhism. He had the dream of making Japan a spiritual, orderly nation under strong imperial rule. His practical politics were drawn up in the Constitution of Seventeen Articles. His face still appears on most denominations of Japanese currency.

The political thought of Shotoku Taishi was translated into action in 645 by Prince Naka-no-Oe (later the Tenchi Emperor) with the assistance of a high court official named Fujiwara-no Kamatari. In that year a court coup d'état was effected killing scores of old rulers, and the reality of reform was soon achieved. Although the head of the old rulers murdered by the Prince was the lover of his mother, the event had a strong political quality as well as the overtones of a family struggle. The reform revoked the hereditary privileges of the local chieftains. All land and people, except the slaves, were placed under the direct control of the central government. All subjects were granted a uniform lot of land fixed by law and were obliged to pay the same share of tax.

The reform of Taika was not without opposition, but was achieved smoothly with no bloodshed on a national level.

† For 260 years the Tokugawa Bakufu (literally "temporary government, not by rule of the emperor") enjoyed peace, troubled neither by internal strife nor by foreign invasion. But there were forces at work bringing about social change at

From our history I can almost conclude that the Japanese will never revolt. Revolution is not in our blood. When I went to Israel, I really couldn't understand why two groups of people, for the sole reason of believing in different religions, were actually killing each other. That was the riddle which hit me first when I was standing in the border regions. I have the same feeling over the split between Pakistan and India.

Mellen: People are also trying to recover their lands, so religion is not the sole issue.

Narushima: I understand that these conflicts are not simple, but they still have strong religious overtones.

Mellen: Why do you consider the Japanese *character* as incapable of revolution? Is there something about the inherent character of the Japanese that accounts for this particular social history? The English are also an island people and they too did not have a true bourgeois revolution. The passage from feudal to capitalist transformation was through amalgamation rather than revolutionary change. And the English are also said to be incapable of revolutionary change. Is not the question ultimately whether Japanese feudal or capitalist institutions can solve the problems of the people of Japan?

Narushima: No, I don't think so. In the case of other countries, in order to solve social problems, many took the road of revolution. Well, in Japan people didn't turn to this solution. Being a rather

---

home and abroad. In 1853 the American government sent Commodore Perry to Japan to open Japan once and for all as a market for foreign trade. The Black Ships, as Perry's frigates were called by the Tokyo inhabitants, with all their modern armaments, were enough to make Japan change her old idea of closing the country. Threatened by force, the Japanese acceded to the American demands. After the Bakufu, or Tokugawa shogun, was forced to open the country to foreign powers his prestige was lowered in the eyes of most Japanese people. As a result, antiforeign movements were launched and eventually came to be a means of attacking the Bakufu. Many noblemen close to the emperor, who had long remained silent in Kyoto, responded to the movement among lower samurai to destroy the shogunate. Eventually the Bakufu could no longer afford to disregard the opinion of the court, as his predecessors had done for centuries. Patriots began to be active, creating anti-Bakufu factions, and the emperor came once more to form a bond of national unity; Kyoto became a political center once again in rivalry with Edo (Tokyo). Soon such calls as "Down with the Bakufu," "Restore Imperial rule, expel the foreign devils," became overwhelming. In 1867 the Bakufu returned the reins of government to the emperor and ended warrior rule, which had lasted almost uninterruptedly for nearly seven hundred years, since the establishment of the Kamakura Bakufu in the Kamakura Era (1192–1333). Some remnants of the Tokugawa Bakufu offered resistance, but were subdued by 1869.

unique society capable of cutting off any outside contact for three hundred years, I understand why the Japanese people didn't take up revolution. Let me try to explain a little more. If we compare the histories of Japan and China, we can see this better. Anyway, that is how I have arrived at this view.

For several thousand years the Chinese changed their dynasties by revolutions. They have done this all the time. However, in Japan once the *Tenno* system of imperial order was firmly established at Jinshin-no-ran in the small court struggle of A.D. 672, after the Taika reform, little happened. The Japanese have since respected the lineage in the *Tenno* or emperor system and there has not been much argument once the matter comes to the blood of the *Tenno*. For the first time in our history young Japanese feel somewhat differently about this.

So the Japanese have always respected the emperor, because one is born to a family line and thus accepted as the ruler. They have never challenged this. I am sure that the Japanese educational system has had something to do with this too. It is hard to believe this now, but no Japanese scholars were permitted to study about Jinshin-no-ran.* The Japanese people are traditionally obedient toward authority. The long years of feudalism were the result of this character and the Japanese frame of mind is still, in many respects, feudal. The Japanese had a very long rule by the warrior class. These warrior rulers slipped into the position of the old imperial family and once their rule was established, people accepted it and moreover respected their families, as in the case of the last warrior family who ruled Japan for nearly three hundred years until 1868, the Tokugawas.

In contrast to this Japanese experience, China has had real struggles from one dynasty to the next. They do not respect the blood and lineage of rulers.

Mellen: Was Chinese feudalism truly different?

Narushima: China, being the central flower of the world, regarded every country around her as barbarian. But if someone like Genghis Khan appeared in the west and was capable of taking over central China, he became the ruler. Whoever took over the main part of

---

* Jinshin-no-ran (Struggle of Jinshin) 672: Right after the death of the Tenchi Emperor (he was the former Naka-no-Oe), there was a power struggle among the successors in the court. Tenmu, who was the brother of Tenchi, was soon placed at the head of the nation and the struggle ended. He was a peaceful man of common sense who believed deeply in Buddhism. He was considered one of the emperors who actually devoted himself to governing the nation and thus succeeded in establishing a strong imperial rule.

China was respected as the ruler. It didn't matter much which family he came from.

I'd like to get back to *Time Within Memory* to elucidate this. [Narushima makes a drawing.] This is the island; this is Kagoshima, the southernmost prefecture of Kyushu which, to the islanders, is part of the mainland. Japan consists of four large islands: Honshu, Shikoku, Kyushu, and Hokkaido. These are Okinawa; two islands make up Okinawa. There is the island of the movie. These six islands were called Amami Oshima. From these islands people would all go to Kagoshima. Okinawans also went to Kagoshima. The trip was called "going to the mainland." In the past, long ago, Okinawa belonged to China and it is very close to Korea.

The rest of the small islanders could go only to another island which they thought was part of the mainland of Japan. The people who originally came from these six islands, the Amami Oshima, were called *jiki-jin,* or beggars, by the inhabitants of Kagoshima. They were treated very badly in Kagoshima, but were extremely patient and forbearing. In my film there was a scene in which people are making sugar from sugar cane, in which people were going round and round with their horses trampling the cane. The sugar-making industry was strictly controlled by the Lord of Kagoshima. Every ounce of sugar was appropriated by the Kagoshimans. The rulers had so strict a control over sugar making that they knew exactly how much sugar was produced in every acre. Anyone who stole the slightest amount of sugar was severely punished.

Mellen: It was a true exploitation of the islands.

Narushima: Right. The interesting thing is that this mentality still exists among the islanders. There are a few people who came from these islands originally and who became very successful—company presidents and very rich—but if they are asked about their home country, they still answer, "I am from Kagoshima." They are too ashamed to acknowledge that they came from these islands.

Mellen: Is there a racial aspect to this?

Narushima: Possibly. But the main thing is that these people have been so conditioned to hide their original identity that they cannot change, even after they have become successful in Tokyo. Almost all of them who have made it in big cities like Tokyo or Osaka are professional people or officials, such as lawyers, college professors, police officials, and so on. This is but one example of how completely we are intimidated by the old ways of thought.

Mellen: What does the catching of fish with poisonous leaves symbolize in the film?

Narushima: This technique was one of the oldest methods of catching fish in Japan. I wanted to show our continuity and the persistence of the primitive. There were not many written records, but these customs were handed down from generation to generation, and I was interested in showing a very old primitive mode still existent in Japan. Incidentally, these fishing techniques were completely banned in Japan about fifty years ago. There were four or five kinds of plants used for poison, but after these plants were completely eradicated, people began to forget the method.

Mellen: I thought that the poison leaves foreshadowed the death of Sawa at the end of the film.

Narushima: I had thought about this and in the original film I had additional short sequences to prepare for this point of view, but in the end I cut them. I had two small sequences which intimate the coming death of Sawa but I thought those scenes were too obvious. In one scene she feels pain in her chest as a large ship passes by; in the other Sawa exclaims "How pitiful!" when she views all the floating poisoned fish.

Mellen: Sawa was native to this island and presumably she was very familiar from childhood with the sudden tides and patterns of the sea. Why did she go onto the reefs with her child to fish when the tides were about to come in? She must have known of the danger. This suggests that she, in some sense, has been corrupted by life in the mainland and has been cut off from her own intimate knowledge of nature.

Narushima: I have been asked this in Japan by many friends and critics. She had lived on the island until she got married on the mainland at the age of seventeen or eighteen. Naturally, she knew the island well. But it is very common for people to forget their fear of nature. I have heard of many fishermen trapped by the unpredictable tides and drowned. The power of the tides, which I explained to you, is so strong and unpredictable at times that it overwhelms us. You understand that this is the area where the Pacific Ocean and the East China Sea meet. Around the islands there are many coral formations and reefs. In some areas they are still growing, creating extremely uneven depths in the ocean. When the tides come up, you can never tell just how they are going to move. In fact, while we were staying on the island for location shooting, we were warned many times about the danger of the tides. Nevertheless, Takahiro Tamura, the principal male actor in the film, was trapped by the tide one day while he was fishing. He was soaked to the neck and lucky to get back. It is natural to assume that Sawa knew of the dangers of the tides when she returned to the island, but she was completely absorbed by her fishing. When the warning sound of the tides came, it was already too late. I am still afraid of the sea around there. Usually the weather doesn't help much as a guide. The tide can change by itself. I don't know of many islands like this one which are surrounded by such treacherous seas.

First of all, my assistant director had to spend a week finding a location with a large hole in the rock within two hundred meters from the shore. We knew the trick tide would emerge from such a spot. We had to spend six days shooting the scene in which Sawa is trapped by the high tide. If we missed the sunset, we had to wait for the next day.

Mellen: It keeps returning to my mind. The scene was very beautiful; the child acted so well.

Narushima: I took the sequences in which the tide was coming in minute by minute, but I cut some of this footage. The boy was separated from his mother and he tumbled down many times. He had to walk only on the black rocks, but the black rocks were actually dead coral and their surface is extremely rough. It was a pitiful sight; the boy started to cry and his body was covered with sores. We had to urge and coax him to finish that shooting. We said to him, "If you are a man, you can do it! Be man enough!" and so on. On top of all this the water was very cold. I wanted to cry. I had to pat him for encouragement. I couldn't quit while all of our crew were lined up behind us.

Mellen: How old was the boy?

Narushima: Eight years old.

Mellen: Do you plan to work with the composer of *Time Within Memory* again?

Narushima: I have made about twenty-five films as the director of photography, including *The Ceremony*. Among them, I have worked with Toru Takemitsu in about ten films. We have different directors from time to time, but Takemitsu and I usually work together. He considers every sound, even the human voice, to be part of the music. When you mentioned how closely the shots and the music match, this is because we try to find the identical rhythm in photography and in music. Photography has its own rhythms such as the long shots, close-ups, and so on.

Mellen: Who have been the important influences on your work?

Narushima: Among Western directors I would mention John Ford and David Lean for their camera work, for the camera which travels directly to the object. Among Japanese my favorite director was Mizoguchi, with whom I worked on *The Life of Oharu* and *A*

Story from Chikamatsu. I was also an assistant director under Kinoshita and worked on such films as *Twenty-four Eyes, Broken Drum,* and *She Was Like a Wild Chrysanthemum*. I have also been influenced by the French post-impressionist painters and by the Japanese ukiyoe [woodblock prints, au.].

Mizoguchi was a perfectionist. At one point during the shooting of *A Story from Chikamatsu* the lights went out. He demanded that we hold the fuse by hand so that the shooting could go on. He brought his own lunch to the set and didn't leave the studio the way everyone else did. He didn't even go the the bathroom, but brought a bedpan, wrapped it up and emptied it later. He was completely obsessed with a movie once it started.

Kinoshita would shout *"baka"* ["fool"] at me and say, "There's no bigger idiot than you." During the making of *Time Within Memory,* I often thought of what Kinoshita would have done in a given situation. When it is hard to direct, I escape into the camera.

Mellen: Can you tell me something of your future plans?

Narushima: I wish to continue to talk about the Japanese and Japanese culture in all my future works. I would like to make a film of the opera *Yuzuru* [*Sunset Crane*] based on a Japanese fairy tale about a woman who is transformed into a crane and goes to heaven. I would like to make it in 70 mm widescreen as a spectacular. I would also like to make an epic film set in a small village in North Japan which suffers extremely severe winters. I also have a project on the kamikaze pilots of the Second World War. By the end of the war they had to follow orders although they no longer wanted to. And only at the beginning were they treated as heroes. At the end their existence was like a living death. They wouldn't wash or clean their uniforms. They were full of lice, lice which cling to the body just before death. I myself worked as a technician fixing bombs during the war, having given up literature and photography earlier. This film would be set at the base at Kagoshima where sexual mores were completely upset and the militarization of the people made them hard. One character would be a man who rejects his girl friend after which she goes mad. I can never forget the people who died in this way. Wars express how history repeats itself. This film would portray the whole thing from the woman's point of view and would be made for the thirtieth anniversary of the war. It is only one of the tragedies of Japan that I wish to depict.

THIRTEEN
MASAHIRO SHINODA
INTRODUCTION

Masahiro Shinoda is one of the most brilliant directors of his generation. In his forties, Shinoda is well known in his own country (he has made thirteen films since 1960), but only now has he begun to be appreciated outside Japan, alongside the "classical" directors— Ozu, Mizoguchi, and Kurosawa. The range of his films is as wide as Japanese history itself. *Assassination* and *The Scandalous Adventures of Buraikan,* his two finest works, located distinct moments in the fall of the Tokugawa shogunate during the middle of the nineteenth century.

Buraikan captures the shogunate's decadence through the irrelevant and ineffectual reforms of 1842 which Lord Mizuno was incapable of imposing upon a recalcitrant population. *Assassination* moves us closer to the Meiji restoration of 1868. As the film opens, we are informed of the arrival in 1853 of Commodore Perry and his warships. Their demand of the right to enter Japan was followed, we learn in titles, by the assassination of Premier Ii, who had acquiesced, intending to open Japan to the West.

Silence defines Japanese culture through the impact of the Spanish and Portuguese missionaries who, doggedly and with breathtaking futility, sought to add Christianity to the long-assimilated Shinto and Buddhism. The film is set in the beginning of the seventeenth century when the first Tokugawa shogun, Ieyasu, decreed irrevocably that the practice of Christianity was a crime punishable by torture until the Christian apostatized and trampled underfoot a picture of either Christ or the Virgin Mary. It is the period of Namban art, in which foreigners are portrayed grotesquely with long pendulous noses and spiny hairs protruding from their heads, reflected in Shinoda's casting of the foreign priests. It was also a time at which there were 300,000 Japanese converts to Christianity.

Clouds at Sunset and *Punishment Island* take place in the twentieth century which, for Shinoda, is overshadowed in Japanese history by the Second World War. The setting in both films includes the late 1930s with intimations of Japan's aggression upon Manchuria and the repression of liberal opposition at home. Through depiction of the subjectivity of written mythological history Shinoda's *Himiko* explores the beginnings of Japanese nationhood and identity. Like *Assassination,* which offers the interaction of perceptions about the positive and negative consequences of Western intrusion for Japan, *Himiko* perceives the world of the second century dialectically, through a confluence of interpretations advanced by peoples of the fourth, eighth, and twentieth centuries.

The fluidity of points of view in Shinoda's films permits the director to affect a facade of objectivity; his own particular choice among the critical decisions facing his people is barely discernible. In *Punishment Island* we remain unsure of Shinoda's attitude toward the obsessed man, who lives only for the moment when he can avenge the unspeakably cruel death of his parents. In *Silence* Shinoda offers no moral judgment of the stalwart priest, Rodrigues, who, facing the silence of God, apostatizes while Christians are tortured before his eyes. The objectivity of Shinoda's camera expresses his sense that an era can be properly felt and understood only by those who experience its conflicts. "On one level it is impossible," Shinoda says in reference to *Himiko,* "for those who believe that the gods did not exist to tell about the people who believed in the gods."

In all of Shinoda's films, violence appears as an inevitable, even pedestrian aspect of everyday life. It is through the extremes of violence that Shinoda denotes the nature of an epoch, and consequently his films often skirt the melodramatic. "Culture is nothing but the expression of violence," he says, "human tenderness is unthinkable without violence." Shinoda's violence thus carries within it Freud's sense of ambivalence; it is expressed explicitly in the eternal conflict between Naojiro and his possessive mother in *Buraikan.* Violence, however, is also the central means through which men test their convictions. In Shinoda's films the trauma consequent upon extreme emotion and action often leads his characters to doubt, as with the Portuguese priests. Both Ferreira and

Rodrigues at the end of *Silence* question the absoluteness of their belief.

Silence is as much a study of the nature of Japan on the basis of its response to the invasion by the Christians as it is a portrayal of the psychology and fate of two priests in a hostile land. Shinoda has said that "the Japanese came to understand Western culture not through Christianity, but by the guns Christianity brought with it." Even in his documentary *Sapporo Winter Olympics* the most interesting moments occur when violence is incipient, and an athlete is observed responding to his own inadequacy, to the disparity between will or desire, and its execution.

Shinoda's sweeping camera style and sharp cutting provide a precise formal counterpart to his central concern: the pursuit of the meaning of an epoch through the violence of people trapped within a cultural and individual destiny. There are long, frequent, rhythmic tilts, often matched with a fast pan. These serve, virtually in themselves, to move the action toward defining moments. More than most directors, Shinoda makes artistic use of the wide screen. It becomes, in his hands, not only a perfect vehicle for photographing the long, low houses of Edo, as in *Double Suicide, Assassination* and *Buraikan,* but also a means of filling the screen with a variety of action, plots, and counterplots. What assumes real importance in his films, which are frequently episodic in structure, is not their plots or the nature of each individual conspiracy (in *Assassination* we soon lose count). Rather, it is the world view derived from the totality of the film's images which evokes an era in Japanese culture.

There is enormous variety in Shinoda's camera style. A striking example is his use of the hand-held camera in the last scene of *Assassination;* as if from the eyes of his assassin, we view the narrow alley along which the hero, Kiyokawa, will be murdered. By camera movement alone we perceive the assassin's fear, weakness, and uncertainty, and the power of these emotions, at this instant, associates them with the director. He, like us, ultimately remains unsure of the value of the dissident samurai Kiyokawa, "the mysterious Hachiro," whose motives never become explicit, even by the end of the film when his rejection of the shogunate has become clear.

Shinoda's frequent use of the freeze frame allows him to raise the transitory to a defining moment of permanence. The freeze of the beheaded man "splashed" with blood, Kiyokawa's first victim, is appropriate because it foreshadows the destiny of Kiyokawa himself. At the moment of his own murder, Kiyokawa's blood is splashed over the face of his assassin, as an endless cycle of incoherent violence makes a sham of the idea that the Meiji restoration offered a moment of significant reform or meaning to Japanese culture.

The "blood splash" is a frequent image in Shinoda's films. Nowhere does it occur more strikingly than in the repeated flashback in *Punishment Island* in which an MP slays a bespectacled man in a library while blood splashes upon his books and a child huddles under a piece of furniture. Only very near the end do we realize that this is the primal scene of the film, and an actual occurrence in the life of the now adult avenger, Saburo.

Tradition itself becomes part of Shinoda's imagery. *Double Suicide* opens with the actual presence of the Bunraku puppets for whom the story was written. People and puppets are interchangeable, an expression of Shinoda's sense of the powerlessness of ordinary men like Jihei, their defeat inevitable in the conflict between duty and inclination (*giri-ninjo*).

In *Double Suicide* the violent passion between the paper merchant, Jihei, and the prostitute, Koharu, propels Jihei's wife, Osan, to self-fulfillment. In triumph, Osan sets out to pawn her wedding clothes and the kimonos of her children to buy Koharu out of bondage. Koharu and Osan are both played by the same actress, Shinoda's wife, Shima Iwashita. The film explores the dual nature of a woman, and in so doing unfolds the life choices possible for women during the era of Chikamatsu, one of whose plays was the source of this film.

After he kills Koharu, Jihei is aided in carrying out the double suicide by Kabuki stagehands (*kuroko*) dressed in traditional black. They represent the hands of fate and the wills of both director and author. Their presence is a further symbol of what Donald Richie has called the fatalism in Shinoda's depiction of the conflict between character and tradition. (The same point is made in the opening tilt from pagoda to lovers in *Punishment Island*.) In addition, both the Bunraku puppets and the *kuroko* remind us that we are in the presence of fiction or artifice, that truth is to be found somewhere between fiction and life, illusion and reality.

The pervading mood of Shinoda's films is one of nihilism, a mood especially appropriate to the last days of the Tokugawa shogunate. This epoch has been described in *The Western World and Japan* by the scholar G. B. Sansom in two sentences which could serve as a plot summary for Shinoda's *Assassination:* "The throne rebukes great officers for doing what it knows they have already approved, or enjoins them not to do what it knows they have already done . . . patriots assassinate other patriots for views they have never held or professed, and statesmen declare intentions that everybody knows to be contrary to their real purpose.'' *

Shinoda's nihilism allows him to look beyond official versions of history, to show the hero Ryōma Sakamoto, who wrote many of the Meiji reforms (before his own assassination), as a man in need of a bath. The Meiji leadership is symbolized at the end of the film by the vainglorious leader who dons the gift of a Western military costume, perfectly reflecting his betrayal of sincere followers of the emperor like Kiyokawa, who fight for the imperial side believing, unwittingly, that, unlike the shogunate, it is prepared to repel the foreign invaders.

Buraikan, as Amos Vogel has aptly stated in his *Village Voice* review, is ''a sophisticated equivalent of an exorbitant, cartoon strip serial, its studied 'vulgarity' married to a profoundly modern ironic pessimism.'' In this film Shinoda bathes the screen in reds, yellows, and blues to reflect the unreality of the last days of Edo in which leaders remained stubbornly blind to their failure to meet the needs of the people. It is the vision of a nihilist because it describes a culture hollow at its core with nothing to hold it together. Shinoda and playwright Shuji Terayama, who did the script, have Lord Mizuno, in the midst of a revolution, refuse to admit that his day is done. One character, Kochiyama, opens the door so that Mizuno can see the fireworks. Despite the evidence before his eyes—the red burning sky of Edo—Mizuno denies what is: ''It can't be fireworks because I banned fireworks!''

The vision of *Buraikan* is nihilist as well because the end of the cruel social order, symbolized by Mizuno, does not mean that it will be replaced by anything better. ''Power will never perish,'' yells Mizuno, ''it'll be replaced by another.'' Naojiro, who has tried to drown his jealous mother, emerges from his house carrying her on his back, ready to re-attempt getting rid of her. ''Wherever you desert me,'' she chortles, ''I'll be back again.'' ''Then I'll desert you again,'' is his reply. Nothing changes. Man, for Shinoda, will always be as perverse, destructive, and sadistic as the character in *Buraikan* who proclaims with relish, ''I've always wanted to cut virgin skin.'' And as an expression of man's enslavement to his nature, Shinoda frequently shoots through barred windows and gates.

* (New York: Alfred A. Knopf, 1963), p. 281.

Thus the quest of Saburo in *Punishment Island* to destroy his old enemy, Otake, is destined to be as futile as the final punishment he inflicts, forcing Otake to cut off his thumb. There will, as well, always be men like the converted Christian, Kichijiro, in *Silence* who betray the priests for a handful of silver. All of Shinoda's characters inhabit a world like that surreal, Kabuki-esque, *ukiyo-e* (wood block print)-come-to-life, *Buraikan,* in which ''all the devil masks are sold out.''

There is, despite all, some hope in Shinoda's universe because, although as a character in *Buraikan* declares, ''it is hard to change the world,'' society is always undergoing transformation. Saburo at the end of *Punishment Island,* although he has sacrificed the present, his affection for Aya, daughter of Otake, has at least freed himself from Otake's obsessive hold on his life. This is indicated by the final unfreezing of a frame which Shinoda had repeatedly depicted throughout the film as static and unchanging. It is the scene of Otake with the bloody, unconscious body of the boy, Saburo, as he is about to fling it into the sea. At the end, in the final flashback to this image, the action is completed. The body descends and Saburo is at least partially freed of the nightmare in which a man beat him senseless and left him for dead, the very man who had earlier murdered his parents.

For Shinoda injustice appears endemic to the human condition. Searching in an impressionist manner for the true nature of his characters, the director discovers who they were only through the injustices which befell them. Psychology is minimized in Shinoda's films because there is so little about others that we can ever really know. Other than his despair over the murder of his mistress, Oren, we are given no overt explanation of why Kiyokawa, suddenly, inexplicably, changes sides, allying himself with emperor rather than shogun. The only clue we are given about the ''mysterious Hachiro'' is that he was a man bitter about the fact that his low social origins made it impossible for him to rise above the lower rungs of the samurai hierarchy, despite his being the brightest student in the academy. That infamous figure in Western garb at the end of the film remarks that Kiyokawa will always be a ''common samurai even if he did receive an imperial order.''

The destiny of Jihei to commit double suicide with Koharu is linked to his low social status as a merchant; in one scene he is beaten by a rich man who is determined to buy Koharu. Nothing will change, says Shinoda, as long as there are men like the cowardly schoolteacher, Mr. Kuroki, in *Punishment Island* who was afraid to defend the boy Saburo from Otake. "I don't want to be involved," he had said, sitting ironically before a photograph of Abraham Lincoln. The universe itself is amoral and seems even to conspire perversely against the good. Mr. Kuroki enters old age in good health while his kindly wife, who wished to help Saburo, lies shaking with palsy. All remain enclosed, like Yamaoka's goldfish in *Assassination,* by the glass bowl of their epoch.

The extraordinary achievement of Shinoda consists in the complexity and power with which he evokes those chaotic moments of turmoil accompanying the close of one historical epoch and the birth of another, a theme he shares with Kurosawa. *Buraikan,* in fact, could stand as a companion piece to *Yojimbo.* But Shinoda's characters, his revolutionaries like Rodrigues in *Silence* or the mysterious Hachiro in *Assassination,* are finally as defeated as are his ordinary men, like Jihei in *Double Suicide.* In Mizoguchi we sense that the weight of history will ultimately turn in man's direction. In Shinoda, as in Ozu, universes apart in theme and style, there is a shared sense that the turn of events will only confirm our helplessness. Life itself reduces our strength and misinterprets our motives, like Paul Akamatsu's *Meiji 1868,* a recent history of the Meiji restoration, which dismisses Shinoda's Hachiro Kiyokawa in one sentence as a "xenophobe *rōnin.*" *

---

* *Meiji 1868: Revolution and Counter-Revolution in Japan* (New York, Harper and Row, 1972), p. 158.

INTERVIEW WITH
MASAHIRO SHINODA

Mellen: Could you tell me how or why, as a filmmaker, you became interested in incorporating elements of the Kabuki theater in your films? I am thinking particularly of the Kabuki atmosphere and conventions which pervade *The Scandalous Adventures of Buraikan*.

Shinoda: The characteristics of of the Kabuki theater reveal a cultural conception peculiar to the Japanese at the time of the Edo period, in which this film is set. At this time Western influences were insignificant in Japanese culture. The civilization of this period is therefore unique to the Japanese people and this is why it interests me. My purpose was to adapt a play of Toshi Shige Kawatake, the son-in-law of Mokuani Kawatake, who wrote the story of Kochiyama, Kanekochi, and the other characters who appear in the film.

Mellen: How did your education prepare you for this particular approach to filmmaking?

Shinoda: I went to Waseda University to study the history of the Japanese theater, especially that of the Middle Period or the Middle Ages of Japan because there were so many things still unknown about this epoch. Take the Noh masks, for instance. It is clear that Indian and Chinese influence is very strong in the introduction of these masks to Japan. However, it is still impossible to trace their origin, which has been lost in the darkness of the Middle Ages.

There is no doubt that the Kabuki theater developed from the Noh theater, but the link between these two theatrical traditions, Kabuki and Noh, is still unknown. This, I think, is because Kabuki was not the theater guided by the ruling class of the country, but was a theater fostered at the base of the society by the masses. Therefore, all the aesthetics seen in *Buraikan* have been almost ignored or never noticed in the history of Japanese arts.

Kabuki theater, cosmopolitan in its origins, went through a process of purification when the country closed its doors to the West, and certain fundamental characteristics of the Japanese people clearly appeared in this theater. And there I found that violence is at the root of all human passion, the fundamental enthusiasm of the human being.

236

A characteristic element of Kabuki is that violence was not presented realistically on the stage, but was done in a stylized or formalist manner—which reveals another characteristic of the Japanese people.

Mellen: Are you referring to the tendency to repress their feelings of violence?

Shinoda: Yes, this too. For example, Peckinpah's film *Straw Dogs,* where the action is expressed realistically, would be impossible in Japan. Of course in this film the violence is also expressed stupidly because all the enemies are defeated at the end.

Mellen: It is not meant to be realistic in that sense. It is meant, I think, to express a basic experience of human beings. When someone comes and attacks you and everything that belongs to you, and attacks even what you are inside, what do you do about it? The important thing in this film is that the hero holds onto his human dignity. It is unrealistic that he should win, but it is also an affirmation of the human being. You root for him to win at the end, although you may hate violence. You walk out of the theater feeling uplifted.

Shinoda: I feel that Peckinpah's way may be good and even his conception of violence right for him, but the Japanese think another way.

Mellen: Of course, *Straw Dogs* is also reactionary, saying "every man for himself," and "kill whomever gets in your way."

Shinoda: The violence of the people who act in the movie and that of the audience which watches it is connected by fictional time. Fiction is closer to truth. I hate documentary presentations.

Mellen: How do these ideas relate to your new project of making a film about the birth of Japan—that is, will you be dealing again with the failure to discover such a moment as that when the Noh and Kabuki came together, these moments in Japanese history that still remain undiscovered?

Shinoda: The time of the film is around the second or third century. The history at this time was recorded by the Japanese as being that of the gods, not of human beings. The second and third centuries of Japanese history, as written by the Chinese, however, were very different. The Chinese version was factual and has a tremendous impact as opposed to that recorded by the Japanese, which was mythological. However, I think that the Japanese version conveys some elements of truth. In this history the gods and the people are mentioned as being half-castes, of mixed blood, which indicates how the imaginations of the Japanese people of the time operated.

Masahiro Shinoda directing
Kichiemon Nakamura as Jihei;
Shima Iwashita as Koharu (*above*),
as Osan (*below*) in *Double Suicide*.
"What characterizes Japan is the
imposition upon the people of
absolute power and authority
without the right to question and
debate. . . . I am against Japanese
capitalism and foresee its demise
in pollution."

In this film I would like to represent in one shot the world of the second century seen through the eyes of the people of the fourth, eighth, and twentieth centuries. We, as people of the twentieth century, have a realistic way of observing the world which might be identified with the camera eye. The people of the eighth century misconstrued history and mythology, mixing the two up. In the fourth century, when there were *kataribe*, families of professional narrators who orally passed down history, the sense of history must have been much more mystic or mysterious. The eighth-century historians wrote their works half believing the words of the *kataribe* and half doubting them. *Katare* means "talking."

Mellen: Will the film come out with a particular point of view toward this history? Is it content to give objectively each of these points of view, those of the fourth, eighth, and twentieth centuries? Will it suggest that the twentieth-century view of Japanese history is the most accurate?

Shinoda: I think the camera eye, the perception of the twentieth century, is the most doubtful. I would like to show that it is impossible for those who believe that the gods did not exist to tell about the people who believed in the gods.

Mellen: Or to judge them?

Shinoda: But I have to judge. To tell about them doesn't mean that I cannot judge them as well. As projections from two points may cross at a certain point, a film which has more than two points of view can focus on an image, or allow an image to come into focus. There must have been a will to create a mythology. I am sure that political motives are basically involved. Not only in Japan, but in all countries, mythology is a political record.

Mellen: In what way?

Shinoda: The world was something very fearful to the prehistoric or ancient people and so they had to think in terms of gods. Gradually they came to realize that the world was composed of the people themselves, not of gods, and the first to realize this were those in power. Then, in order to protect their authority, which was absolute, they thought of making use of the power of the gods by deifying their authority and granting it the power of the gods. We Japanese contended with America in the 1940s. In those days we fought believing that Japan was a country of gods. Our gods were crushed with the atomic bombs and democracy, but they survived as well. The emperor, whose ancestors are gods, remains an object of worship for the Japanese people. The symbol of these gods is a copper mirror. Archaeologically, the copper mirror was produced in the second or third century. The world connected with the sun reflected in this mirror has been sacred for the Japanese people ever since the creation of the earth.

Mellen: What is your point of view toward this mythology?

Shinoda: My point of view is to throw out a question: Can we die for these gods as Mishima did?

Mellen: "Can" or "should"?

Shinoda: That is a very good question. I would like to ask again whether we should die or whether we are able to die for the gods. These are two questions which we must ask ourselves: Can we die? and should we die or is it our duty to die? The question of whether we should die for the gods, that it is our duty, is related to a third question: In what form does Japanese culture or civilization continue? The question of whether we are able to die for the gods is related to this question: If we abandon the gods, what must take their place in order to support the center of the culture? My film will eventually face these questions. It is difficult to decide what will take the place of the gods. I have never believed that culture is something one can "make." The tree whose flowers bloom in Japan never grows in any place but Japan.

Mellen: What will this film be called? Has it a title yet?

Shinoda: Perhaps *Himiko,* the name of a queen who was really both a shaman and a queen. At her left hand was God, at her right hand policy. Maybe her right hand, power politics, killed Him.

Mellen: What is the attitude in *Silence* toward the two Jesuit priests? What is the point of view of the film toward the mission of these two men, and what is your point of view toward the capitulation of Rodrigues at the end when he steps on the idol and renounces his faith?

Shinoda: The first problem is what sort of reaction was caused by the transplantation of the Western profile onto the Japanese landscape.

Mellen: Is the film critical of the very fact of the Catholics coming to Japan and imposing an alien culture on the Japanese?

Shinoda: Japan is an island surrounded by the sea. Many cultures from outside have come here. Japan could not refuse them. The sea current itself conveyed these foreigners to Japan's southern shores. Japan's culture thus consists of many, many foreign cultures in a

Masao Kusakari and Shima Iwashita in *Himiko.* "I would like to show that it is impossible for those who believe that the gods did not exist to tell about the people who believed in the gods."

mixture. Sometimes it caused us to lose our essential Japanese culture. I'm not even sure sometimes what Japanese culture is. In the sixteenth century Christianity and the gun were introduced into Japan. The introduction of the gun was a traumatic event and had a much deeper impact than did Christianity. The Japanese people were perplexed, but they are a realistic people and they made their choices pragmatically, giving up the metaphysical. We are empiricists, materialists.

Mellen: If I had made that movie, I would have questioned the right of the Jesuit priests to come to Japan and impose their ideas on the Japanese.

Shinoda: No, it was impossible for the Jesuits to impose their religion on the Japanese because of the animism believed in by this insular, island people. It was not to be destroyed by so severe a religion as Christianity. Christianity destroyed the Roman gods, but the Japanese gods were protected by the softness of Buddhism. Buddhism is so soft that it was absorbed into the Japanese culture of the time. The Japanese people believed that Buddhism could easily marry with Shinto, and thus Japanese culture is a mixed breed of both religions. Then Christianity came, but by this time the native animism of Shinto and Buddhism were already coexisting in harmony. I think that there was no room for an additional religion. All Eastern religions are in accordance with a belief in the oneness of man and nature, whereas Christianity deals with the relationship between one man and another. When movies, or film culture, were introduced into Japan they were already based on modern Western thought. But Japanese culture influenced the kind of films that would be made here, despite the Western origins of the cinema. I must categorize the films of the world into three distinct types. European films are based upon human psychology, American films upon action and the struggles of human beings, and Japanese films upon *circumstance*. Japanese films are interested in what surrounds the human being. This is their basic subject; the Ozu films would be a prime example. And neither are my films an exception. In the case of *Buraikan* my focus is on the circumstances which caused the revolution.

Mellen: Buraikan is very pessimistic toward the revolution, isn't it?

Shinoda: Yes, to the Western viewer the film may seem to be very pessimistic.

Mellen: At the end, Lord Mizuno says that as long as there are human beings, there will be someone ready to take power over others. The film seems to support his point of view that there will always be an authority and people subservient to it no matter how many revolutions occur.

Shinoda: These insular people, the Japanese, at the beginnings of their history, already had the insight that they would face a great danger once they themselves got power. They always felt uneasy in the presence of authority and thought that it would be much easier to be in a place where gods' eyes could reach. The Japanese despair of politics, which they think is unchangeable in substance. For example, Mao and his nation, which many students here thought was a paradise of the revolution, recently made a deal with the United States. This caused a great disappointment among young Japanese students.

Mellen: I hope they didn't attempt to justify this deal.

Shinoda: It was the extreme leftist students who were most moved by the death of Mishima. It is because Mishima's death was on behalf of the invisible gods; in other words, it was nonworldly and nonpolitically or purely motivated.

Mellen: As if he were trying to make the gods real at a time in Japanese culture when they no longer seem real by sacrificing himself to them?

Shinoda: The Japanese have a belief that it is purer to sacrifice themselves for things invisible than to do so for a political cause.

Mellen: Why was Mishima's suicide an act of desperation? Was he trying to give the old culture of Japan a validity that it was losing?

Shinoda: That's exactly right. It was that kind of desperation. As for Mishima, he wrote his novels based upon Western methods because they were extremely functional. His literary world was realistic and surrounded with Western rhetoric. However, he never believed that his Japanese blood could run with any meaning or freshness through his literary works. For example, were a Western writer or poet to describe a flower using mere words, Mishima would have considered this to be only playing with words. For Mishima, being a living thing, a flower must cease to exist. He thought that in order to obtain an eternal flower it is best to make it an artificial or "Hong Kong" flower. This is how he thought of Western culture. But at the same time he never believed that this flower was a real one. Therefore, he had to shed his own blood to make it real. I wonder then why Mishima so ardently needed to make a plastic flower into a real flower and then into an eternal one. I think he must have been interested in the question of eternal revival or the eternal return.

Therefore, a revolution to the Japanese does not have such a temporary, "up to date," object as the overthrow of a political system. It must concern the achievement of some everlasting, unchangeable ideal. For example, some Americans might have considered it a revolution had McGovern defeated Nixon. But to us Japanese it would not have brought about an ideal world at all. For the Japanese a revolution must create the eternal and the unchanging, a kind of utopia.

Mellen: In this world?

Shinoda: But this world is so changing. When a revolutionary seeks an eternal world, he is no longer in the dimension of political revolution.

Mellen: Is it then an eternal world of truth? The problem may be also that we can't find any country in the world today that could qualify as "revolutionary." Where are the revolutionary values you speak of to come from?

Shinoda: For the Japanese to achieve a true revolution would be a mere reflection of the desire for an absolute God. He departs from Marxism. I think it is a religious reflection. For the Japanese, Christianity and Buddhism are of the distant world, far from the Japanese people and powerless in the contemporary world. Yet people today cannot find any new religion either.

Mellen: In *Buraikan* there is a strong Marxist vitality shown among the people, a feeling of restlessness, struggle, and unwillingness to accept their condition. It is a very revolutionary movie in the traditional sense of the term even if it doesn't end with the creation of a revolutionary utopia.

Shinoda: I think that it was only in the twentieth century that this vitality came to be called Marxism. To me, however, this vitality originated in what I call violence, which is a basic human passion. For example, take salaried men who are shut up and being gradually killed, surrounded with concrete walls like those of a modern building such as this [the Imperial Hotel], and those who are killed in struggle because one hates another. There isn't any difference to me between these two murders. I think that instead of greeting someone with "Good morning," it is quite all right to stab someone to death, saying, "I hate you." And I certainly know that by contrast there is undoubtedly also a place for the contradictory emotion of love as expressed in the words "I love you." It is possible to hear these two different expressions from the same person.

Mellen: There is a great deal of this type of psychology, this notion of ambivalence, in both *Buraikan* and *Double Suicide.* Are you interested in the ideas of Freud?

Shinoda: Yes, very much.

Mellen: In *Buraikan* an important theme is the idea of being an actor. Naojiro, the hero, wants to be in the theater. When he is refused, he decides to become an actor in real life. They are interchangeable—you are an actor in the theater or an actor in real life.

Shinoda: I think that the wisdom of the common people is seen in Naojiro's mistake. He sees no difference between acting for the theater and acting in real life, which is a substitute for living his life.

Mellen: The film makes it seem as if Naojiro is right, although this may be the influence of the scriptwriter Terayama.

Shinoda: To me, in considering how to control the violence which lurks in the human body, the answer is not to live in moral restraint; it is to express one's violence as if acting a theatrical role. It is the best way to communicate with other human beings. For example, I like the expression of Jesus Christ which says, "I have come to this world not to bring peace, but to struggle." Culture is nothing but the expression of violence. Also, human tenderness is unthinkable without violence.

Mellen: Do you think this is a particularly Japanese idea? In Japan I have found the attitude toward me as a foreigner to be that of violence rather than gentleness.

Shinoda: It is probably so. However, I think it is very violent to assimilate man with nature as the Japanese have done. In a certain sense, it means a denial of society. And if there is a foreign society corresponding to Japanese society, the Japanese will not admit it. They see themselves as distinctly separate from all foreigners.

Mellen: I have found considerable dislike of foreigners here in Japan. It is bewildering and I can't really understand it.

Shinoda: Did you write about this in your article?

Mellen: I've just written a new article on this theme ["Games Japanese Play"].

Shinoda: I think it is because we Japanese do not really understand the violence within foreigners. In other words, it is impossible to understand another culture without going to war with it. A war is the best way to understand one's enemy. If we had not gone to war against the United States, we would never have understood the country called America or the American people. We came to know American culture by seeing American battleships and American strategy. In the case of *Silence* the Japanese came to understand Western culture not through Christianity, but by the guns Christianity brought with it. Jean-Paul Sartre's existentialism, for example, has been introduced into Japan as one type of culture. I suppose the Japanese understand Sartre's ideas only as written words in a book. I am sure it is not so in Europe. If we struggle with Sartre or spend a week or a month with him in a room, we may be able to discover a human being named Sartre. After that his character would become more important than his philosophy.

If we Japanese meet today with a foreigner without any prior knowledge of his character, we find ourselves at a loss, being unable to understand his character as a foreigner, unless he resembles or is someone like Lincoln or Eleanor Roosevelt. I think the *Mainichi* people's understanding of Joan Mellen is only through the paper you wrote. I do not believe that they have had a chance to understand you as a person.

Mellen: They believe I think Kurosawa is the only filmmaker in Japan simply because he is the one I wrote about—which is ridiculous.

Shinoda: Yes, that is ridiculous.

Mellen: Was there anything in your education or experience that contributed to the strong visual quality of your films? One of the most outstanding aspects of your work is the strong use of the camera. Did you have a previous interest in art that encouraged you to develop this talent?

Shinoda: The influence I received from the old Japanese paintings is immeasurable. They are paintings which have no sense of distance or perspective as Western painting has. The most recent period would be that of the *ukiyo-e*—of Hokusai [1760–1849]. And then, the paintings of the Middle Period [the Kamakura period, 1185–1333]; in these paintings you can depict the entire world. This is impossible to do in Western paintings, but Japanese paintings are not done in perspective.

When I was a boy, next door to me was a Protestant church, and an American missionary family lived there. The father was Jewish and I became acquainted with their daughter. It was a chance I had to get myself my first cosmopolitan training.

Mellen: Were they Jewish or Protestant?

Shinoda: Their name was MacAlpin. I heard they were Jewish, but I could be wrong. Do you think MacAlpin is a Jewish name? It may be my mistake, but I was told that they were Protestant and Jewish. The father and daughter talked to me often and their lifestyle came as quite a surprise to me. I was able to realize when I was still very young that there were other cultures and ways of life besides the Japanese. This experience may have been the first cause of my interest in the visual arts and in filmmaking. It stirred my curiosity toward the visual world.

Mellen: Are there any filmmakers, Japanese or foreign, whose use of the camera influenced you in your own techniques?

Shinoda: Ozu and Mizoguchi provided the strongest influence.

Mellen: Your films are much more sensual than theirs.

Shinoda: Yes, I am looking for eroticism in my films.

Let me see—among foreign filmmakers who have influenced me. I try to see almost all American films because I have always thought that Americans are geniuses at filmmaking. The films I saw during my high school days left a strong impression on me—the films of Robert Wise and Fred Zinnemann I remember well.

Mellen: Technically these people are very good, but as for the content of their films, many Americans find them superficial. Although he is a great director, what John Ford *says* in his films is often unacceptable.

What was your point of view in *Assassination,* which deals with the time of Ryōma Sakamoto, toward the Meiji restoration and that moment in Japanese history?

Shinoda: The reestablishment of imperial rule was the central theme of the restoration. The justification of the revolution was the return of Japanese imperial rule. During the Meiji restoration the Tokugawa shogunate fell, but the powerful samurai of the Meiji restoration kept the emperor as a ruler. The Tokugawa shogunate had kept the emperor too. There was actually no change.

Mellen: Let's speak for a moment about *Double Suicide.* Why did you use the *kuroko,* those stagehands in black who change the sets in the Kabuki theater, as part of the action of an otherwise realistic film? Why are they mixed into the action?

Shinoda: One of the reasons is that I believe that truth can be obtained somewhere between fiction and reality. The use of *kuroko* is also one way of expressing the author's will; the author is both Chikamatsu and myself, the director.

Mellen: Do the *kuroko,* like Chikamatsu, help the characters to fulfill their destiny?

Shinoda: Right. And the director's willingness keeps the *kuroko* on the scene. The *kuroko* then become fate itself. They become the hands of the authors.

Mellen: The film is in many ways very pessimistic. You, Chikamatsu, and the *kuroko* force the characters to live out the old story. You refuse to change the story and they are forced to relive the old experience again. It all seems predestined.

Shinoda: Let me tell you something about the world Chikamatsu

Kichiemon Nakamura and Shima Iwashita in *Double Suicide*. Chikamatsu "wanted to show the enormous power of human sensuality over a very ordinary man. . . ."

Shinoda's *Double Suicide*. "The director's willingness keeps the *kuroko* on the scene. . . . They become the hands of the authors."

worked in. Around this time in Europe Napoleon was at the height of his power. The Western world was well into the age of industrial progress. In comparison to this technological advancement, Japan was in the midst of feudalism, under the rule of the Tokugawas. Chikamatsu was born into a samurai family, but he abandoned his background, gave up his samurai status, and escaped into the city. He hoped that he would find a new sense of morality there, but he found nothing but the worship of money. The merchants in the towns had no morality, and Chikamatsu foresaw that the merchant class would eventually control the country. The samurai class at least had the moral code known as *bushido;* the merchants' only morality was that of money. Chikamatsu, having been displaced from the samurai world, now found himself alienated from that of the merchants.

Mellen: And so he was left with nothing?

Shinoda: Right.

Mellen: In *Double Suicide* are you saying something about human nature in general in your treatment of the husband who is a weak character and has no self-control. He desires the prostitute and will give up everything for her, although she does not appear to be worthy of all the destruction this man causes to possess her.

Shinoda: I agree with you. It is very hard to understand why Chikamatsu selected Jihei as the hero. However, he did. He wanted to show the enormous power of human sensuality over a very ordinary man and how this kind of love could destroy the small, solid world of ordinary people. Love destroyed the established world of this man, a world which he had constructed so carefully. To Chikamatsu, love always took the shape of sensual passion; it was never platonic. This is pure conjecture, but I believe that Chikamatsu also had a burning hatred of the merchant class and had a desire to victimize them. The reason for this lies in his once having been a samurai. He hated the merchants as economic animals. However, he could not become a samurai again, although he was a samurai by nature.

Mellen: Are you producing all your own films now outside the big companies?

Shinoda: Yes.

Mellen: How do you finance your films? Where does the money come from?

Shinoda: First I make a distribution contract for my film. Some are made with the major companies and some are with small independents. Based upon this contract, they supply me with roughly half of the total cost of the film. This gives me my start. Then I call upon my staff, including the actors and actresses, and I show them the contract. I usually make individual contracts with the actors and actresses for one third of the amount they usually get as their guarantee. When I receive more payments from the distributors later on from ticket sales, I pay the balance of their fees to the cast.

Mellen: Have you ever experienced censorship in your work as a film director?

Shinoda: Do you recall the scene in *Pale Flower* [*Kawaita Hana* 1964] where the young gangster cuts off his finger, signifying that he will never again be accepted in normal society? He was ordered to do this by the boss. Well, the original of the film showed a scene where the finger seemed to be actually cut off. This was censored in Japan; the court didn't want me to say that violence, or murder, as I show later in the film, can involve an ecstatic moment.

Mellen: The gambling scenes in *Pale Flower* seemed terribly complicated. Could you enlighten me about the game that was being played at such breakneck speed?

Shinoda: I should add that in preparation for this film I went to real gambling places to get the feel of the gambler's life. The game is called Tehonbiki and it is played with flower cards, one for each of the twelve months. The cards are hidden, and the player must guess what they are. If there is a "match," their winnings go up to six times the amount they are playing for. There was a strong influence on me of Baudelaire's *Fleurs du Mal* throughout this film. When I finished shooting it, I realized that my youth was over. The film is about two characters who cannot live in established society: this is what the man and the girl who gamble together have in common.

Mellen: Did your choice of the gambling motif have any symbolic resonance?

Shinoda: I wanted to locate this film at the point at which Japan was just getting ready to compete industrially with the West. Thus there is a mood of uneasiness in the film. I added heavy breathing on the sound track to reflect a certain breathing among human beings going on at this time, a tension in the air.

Mellen: The film seems somehow autobiographical. How does the hero of *Pale Flower* reflect your own consciousness?

Shinoda: Once I started making this film, I realized that I could no longer pursue naïveté as my subject. I decided to pursue my own evil through the film. The heroes would be people who do evil deeds. In this sense the film stands as my protest against established society and the characters could be called brothers of the Elvis Presley generation.

Mellen: I was disturbed by the sinister character named Yoh, the

Chinese who tried to kill the hero and who isn't permitted to say a single word throughout the film. Why is he made Chinese?

Shinoda: He is Chinese because I wanted to reflect the violence of Chinese culture. He is also a Hong Kong Chinese and is therefore associated automatically with the underworld and the black market.

Mellen: I found the dream sequence interesting, but too brief and therefore an abrupt intrusion into the film.

Shinoda: My original plan was to make the entire film with the feeling of the dream sequence. Perhaps the threats of danger in the dream reflect paranoid feelings in the director while he was making the film.

Mellen: Let's speak again for a moment about *Assassination,* one of your finest films. Your Kiyokawa, the hero, must be one of the most fascinating characters in the history of the Japanese cinema.

Shinoda: I think the scene best reflecting the personality of Kiyokawa must be that occurring after his victory and alignment on the side of the emperor. He writes a haiku and then stares out the window. It is at this moment that his despair begins. Power has brought him no satisfaction, no fulfillment. His drinking and whoring begin at this point, foreshadowing the end of his life when the ground beneath which he has been assassinated smells of sake. Kiyokawa was interesting to me because he raised the question of utilizing the emperor. And for me the dissipation of Kiyokawa leads directly to my later film, *Buraikan.*

Mellen: How do you view your own work in relation to that of the great masters of the Japanese cinema?

Shinoda: My real teacher at Shochiku, where I began, was Ozu. I considered Kobayashi my elder there, and I respected him very much. Once he saw me wearing a red shirt and in an army haircut and he said that I would never make a film.

Mellen: How do you view the works of Kurosawa?

Shinoda: My generation has reacted against the simplistic humanism of Kurosawa in, for example, *Rashomon, The Bad Sleep Well,* and *Redbeard.* Kurosawa has also been resented by the younger people not only because they were looking for a new metaphysic, but also because he had the advantage of large sums of money to spend on his films and they did not. You know he has been called "the Tenno of Toho" [the Emperor of Toho]. We of the younger generation have been in search of a Japanese Ingmar Bergman. I, of course, am looking for my own distinct camera style, something that would be for me what Ozu's static camera style was for him. I prefer Ozu's subtlety through simplicity to Kurosawa's camera, which travels with his characters. Kurosawa has exhausted himself pursuing the traveling camera.

Mellen: What do you see in contemporary Japan as the greatest threat to individual expression and the freedom of people to choose their own destinies?

Shinoda: In my films I have tried to show the present through the past and history, coming around to the truth that all Japanese culture flows from imperialism and the emperor system. What characterizes Japan is the imposition upon the people of absolute power and authority without the right to question and debate. The United States, despite its injustices, has seemed to the Japanese a fresh force, an inspiration for those burdened with the weight of authoritarianism. But there is a problem in communication between the United States and Japan because the United States has never been bombed or suffered a major defeat in a war, as Japan has. I am against Japanese capitalism and foresee its demise in pollution. I also see a need among the Japanese people for personal dignity despite the absence of space and the lack of privacy which characterize the lives of all Japanese, rich and poor. I find, however, that politics lead to nothing, and that power politics remain empty.

FOURTEEN

NAGISA OSHIMA

INTRODUCTION

The films of Nagisa Oshima represent a full and complete break with those of the acknowledged masters of the Japanese film—Ozu, Mizoguchi, and Kurosawa. More insistently than any of the younger generation of Japanese filmmakers, Oshima has pursued a revolt against the artifact of the Japanese film, mired in conventions fixed during the 1940s and 1950s.

For Oshima, the work of the two decades preceding his own treats problems of being Japanese at this moment in history only indirectly. Donald Richie has said that Oshima is the director most critical of the new Japan, and Oshima himself has reiterated that he could not, like his contemporary Susumu Hani, make films abroad:

Completely involved as I am with being a Japanese, I have no way to make films except by examining the Japanese and endeavoring to discover what they are.

Nowhere is this theme better developed than in Oshima's finest film, *Ceremony* (1971), in which, as Richard N. Tucker points out in *Japan: Film Image:*

. . . Oshima sees a society which has lost its sense of direction and looks backwards to the signposts that are to be found in tradition. What he also sees is that many of these rituals are empty, they have no real link with the past and therefore cannot provide any basis for the future.*

---

* (London: Studio Vista, 1973), p. 142.

254

In this film Oshima treats the family as an institution, as did Ozu and Mizoguchi before him, but as Philip Strick wittily declared in *Sight and Sound,* "Ozu could have supplied the devoted members of the family. Mizoguchi could have supplied the elegant camera movement. Only Oshima could have added the blood."

Unlike Kurosawa and Mizoguchi, and even younger directors like Shinoda, Oshima rejects the genre of the period film, the *jidaigeki* or historical film which attempts to make its points about the inadequacies of the present through the guise usually of a Tokugawa (1608–1868) setting. More bold, Oshima sets his films in the present, unmindful of offending. Like most of the younger directors, Oshima, having begun at Shochiku Films, now works independently, financing his own films and personally arranging for their distribution. This is in contrast to his predecessors who worked at the height of their careers for one of the big companies.

Oshima makes each of his films in a different style, which also distinguishes him from such older directors as Kobayashi, Imai, and Shindo, as well as Kurosawa and Mizoguchi. Only Oshima has so frequently rejected the mode of the narrative film and has been, like Hani, directly influenced by the French New Wave—particularly by Jean-Luc Godard and by the recent work of the Yugoslav director Dusan Makavejev. Yet Oshima has also made films which follow a strict narrative plot, like *Boy* (1969), which marked his debut in the United States at the Lincoln Center Film Festival in New York.

Boy was inspired by a newspaper story Oshima had read. A couple had taught their child how to run in front of moving automobiles skillfully enough to suffer only minor injuries. They would then collect damages and conscience money and repeat the trick. The plot proved successful for some time before they were caught. Oshima, as Richie has noted, "refuses himself any emotional, let alone sentimental gestures" toward the boy. The film is spare and convincing in the detachment with which Oshima impassively records the lives of the parents and child.

Oshima's earlier *Death by Hanging* (1968) was also suggested by a news story. It had taken place in 1958 and concerned a Korean jailed for a crime he hadn't committed. Oshima's attraction to the project was derived from his general interest in the relationship of Japan to Korea, his feeling that "what Japan did to Korea was the biggest crime it ever committed." * He treats Japan's relation to

---

* Japanese expansionism into Korea dates from A.D. 369 when the rulers of the Yamato region, one of the original tribes of Japan, invaded Korea and established a

Okinawa in a similar spirit (if in an entirely different style) in *Dear Summer Sister* (1972).*

In the plot of *Death by Hanging* the police attempt to reenact the crime, even pantomiming the earlier life of the youth in an effort to justify his execution. As Donald Richie has observed, ''There is an unassailable logic in the condemned Korean's observation, upon being warmly assured that it is indeed very bad to kill, that 'then it is bad to kill me.' '' †

Far different in style, and much closer to the Godard and Chabrol of the early days of the *nouvelle vague* in France, was Oshima's *Diary of a Shinjuku Burglar* (1968), a film with no plot at all. It proceeds with a beginning, middle, and end—but, as Godard put it, ''not necessarily in that order.'' *Shinjuku Burglar* contains, rather, a collage of the feelings and experiences of a young couple at the time of the great Zengakuren demonstrations during the sixties against American bases and influence in Japan. In the manner of Makavejev and Bertolucci, if more elliptically, Oshima tries to fuse the dynamics of sexuality and politics. Like Godard, Oshima inserts quotations from his favorite authors into the fabric of his film. We are read the words of Genet during scenes in the famous Kinokuniya Bookstore in Shinjuku where Oshima shot many of the film's sequences.

The Man Who Left His Will on Film (1970) was an even more

---

foothold in its southern coast. With Korea under the control of China from the latter part of the seventh century, Japan had to adopt a defensive posture. But the history of Japanese relations with Korea has been one of continual invasion and exploitation. At the end of the sixteenth century Hideyoshi, as one of his last acts as shogun, led an expedition against Korea. Certainly from the beginning of the Meiji era Japan even more actively pursued its imperialist aims in Korea. In 1895 Korea was seized as a colony, its inhabitants treated with extreme cruelty, both in Korea and in Japan, where Koreans were reduced to slave labor, particularly in the mines. Military rule was imposed on Korea in 1910 with the Koreans being deprived of all political rights. Today in Japan there remains considerable racial prejudice by Japanese against the Korean residents, who continue as clearly second-class citizens with little hope of obtaining jobs of substance in the big corporations—or of being treated fairly by trade unions.

* The Okinawans have also suffered at the hands of the Japanese, beginning with the decision to punish the islands, then independent, after their less than enthusiastic response to a Japanese request for troops to join Hideyoshi's expedition against Korea in the late sixteenth century. The return of Okinawa to Japan from the United States has meant only a turnover of economic exploitation from the Americans to the Japanese. It is in this context that Oshima made *Dear Summer Sister*—to call attention to the plight of Okinawa, which has now become only another area of investment for big business from the Japanese mainland.

† *Japanese Cinema* (Garden City, New York, Anchor Books, 1971), p. 138.

personal statement by Oshima. It depicts a student making a film who commits suicide at the end. His film turns out to be the one we have been watching, Oshima's own. *Ceremony,* mentioned earlier, was more ambitious, tracing the history of the Sakurada family over twenty-five years. The film thus becomes a history of modern Japan, beginning just prior to World War II.

Unlike Kurosawa, whose films focus on the individual and a search for redemption, Oshima more ambitiously seeks to explore "how and to what extent the Japanese people have or have not changed over the course of (their) history, and how they will make the transition into the future." Kurosawa has lamented our particular transition into the present as a descent into the world of the *Yakuza,* the gangster who flourishes under capitalism; hence he has returned again and again to the salutary efforts of the ennobled individual. Oshima continues his struggle against Japan's tendency to walk the "same road that led her to invade Korea and Manchuria before the war."

Through his elaborately self-referential films, Oshima sets up a hostile relation between himself and his audience, a quality which has induced many critics, like Vincent Canby in his review of *Death by Hanging,* to dismiss his work as obscure. Ozu gently draws the spectator into his world, bent on a subtle conversion of his viewer to his sense of the sweetness and value of the old Japanese ways. He counterposes this perception to the harsh vulgarity of modern industrial Japan which has worn away the fabric of delicate family feeling which displayed the Japanese at their best.

Mizoguchi's social protest, particularly in response to the brutal and demeaning treatment of women in feudal Japan, was softened by the exquisite beauty of his shot compositions. His many-layered shots, each of which exposes a microcosm, a full world containing all of life in its richness, work in subtle opposition to his depiction of the maltreatment of particular individuals and groups. It is as if his panorama, which embraces suffering, is almost a natural order, for although Mizoguchi might not have intended it, his breadth unwittingly suggests resignation. Kurosawa's flamboyant camera style whets our appetite for his cinema; his elaborate traveling shots envelop us in his world so that we are rendered participants in the action. We join Mifune in his swordplay, confident of victory, and we wish Kurosawa's protagonists well.

With Oshima we feel assailed, as if the director were blaming his audience for the moral failures of Japan. As Hideo Osabe has said, the films of Oshima are "provocations directed at the spectators.

His extremely intellectual and hermetic films refuse every indulgence.''

Some of the harshest of Oshima's critics have been his fellow Japanese film directors, particularly those of the generation immediately preceding his own. For example, Kobayashi has said that while Oshima's films have a certain political interest, he is clearly not an artist who loves the craft of film for itself. And Daisuke Ito, representing the first generation of Japanese filmmakers, who began their work with silent films in the twenties, has spoken of Oshima's lack of artistic quality. Overtly political filmmakers, however, like Kaneto Shindo, have found no difficulty in praising Oshima's work, perceiving him as a fresh and vital force in the contemporary Japanese film.

It remains true that Oshima is one of the foremost innovators among Japanese filmmakers today. To Imai's Galsworthy, he would be a Japanese Joyce. Rare among filmmakers of any country, Oshima remains a revolutionary both in his subject matter and in his struggle to make films within new forms. If, as in *Death by Hanging,* he can be one of the most inaccessible of Japanese directors, a film like *Ceremony* reveals him to be one of the most rewarding as well.

INTERVIEW WITH
NAGISA OSHIMA

Mellen: I didn't fully understand the role of the odd-looking girl named Lily in your new film, *Dear Summer Sister*. The film seemed to be an allegory, not only about the characters, but about something beyond them.

Oshima: I don't understand the question.

Mellen: She is very different looking from the other characters. She doesn't look Japanese. I thought she was meant to be different from the others, and in this way illuminate the American presence in Okinawa—a form of distortion of the Japanese essence or identity as a result of the American occupation.

Oshima: Yes, she is different. She is not completely Japanese. The actress who played the role was of mixed blood. But I don't think she is odd-looking. She is rather pretty, if judged by general Japanese standards of beauty.

Mellen: Is there any relationship between her role in the family and the political theme of the film which explores the relations of Japan and Okinawa, Okinawa and the United States, and Japan and the United States? More generally, is there any relationship between the family relationships and these political themes?

Oshima: Yes, there is. The story begins like this. The man from Okinawa is looking for his real sister in Tokyo, and he mistakes Lily for his real sister. Simultaneously, his real sister goes to Okinawa searching for *her* real brother. She meets him, but neither can recognize the other. This is an allegory about Japan and Okinawa today. Between them there exists a misunderstanding—each is unable to recognize the true self of the other. We think about Okinawa differently from the way it really is, and Okinawans think about Japan differently from the way Japan really is.

Mellen: What is the basis for this inability to understand?

Ohima: Japan always felt that Okinawa was a part of Japan. Okinawans thought so as well to some extent. The Okinawans thought all their problems would be solved when they were returned to Japan.

Mellen: Do you feel that the critics who say that you are strongly influenced by Godard are correct?

Oshima: Oh, we happen to live in the same epoch, and we are concerned with the same subjects.

Nagisa Oshima directing *Boy*. "I am proud of the fact that I have never at-
tached myself to any formal party line."

Mellen: Which are the subjects you have in common with Godard?

Oshima: One is politics and the other is cinema.

Mellen: I noticed in *Dear Summer Sister* several techniques also used by Godard: the flat background and absence of depth of field, the use of close-ups, the talking of characters directly into the camera, and the frequent use of the hand-held camera. Do you agree with Godard that a causally determined narrative structure or a film having a beginning, middle, and end is uncinematic?

Oshima: It depends on the story or the subject of the film. I use both. Some narration doesn't necessarily require a logical sequence. In some the material obligates you to follow it.

Mellen: It seemed to me that in *Dear Summer Sister* the scenes were symbolically connected rather than based on causal connections.

Oshima: I don't understand why you say that *Dear Summer Sister* is not in a narrative mode. It has a very simple narrative style and construction, and is not one of the films in which I elaborate upon this film technique.

Mellen: With which of Godard's political views or aspirations do you agree?

Oshima: I don't agree specifically with any of his positions, but I happen to agree with his general attitude in confronting political themes seriously in film and with the way he immerses himself in politics.

Mellen: Do you agree with the way he approaches the subject matter, with his manner of exposition.

Oshima: No, not with the way he expounds it.

Mellen: Could you speak a little about your background and education. How did you come to make films?

Oshima: As a student at Kyoto University I studied law. I was active in drama groups and in the student movement.

Mellen: What were the issues of the student movement then?

Oshima: In brief, it was generally a political theme not only for the student movement, but for the political life in Japan as well. There was anti-American xenophobia, a certain patriotism, and an inclination toward the ideas of official Marxism.

Mellen: Were you involved in any political party?

Oshima: I never joined any political party. I am proud of it. I am proud of the fact that I never attached myself to any formal party line.

Mellen: Did you find it difficult to work politically without joining any party? You said you were studying law at the university. Did you become a lawyer or was law merely an academic subject for you?

Oshima: No, I did not become a lawyer. I was interested in political issues, law included.*

Mellen: How did you start in film?

Oshima: I started as a simple laborer at Shochiku at first. I became an assistant director and worked under various directors.

Mellen: On which movies and with which directors?

Oshima: I don't think you could have seen any of them. They were not of a very high quality and were not released overseas.

Mellen: How did you get your chance to direct?

Oshima: I first did all sorts of things—scriptwriting, editing, many aspects of the craft. Finally I was recognized as a director.

Mellen: Did you have many difficulties working for a big company like Shochiku?

Oshima: In those days, some years ago, the film industry was well off financially, so the company and the filmmakers could work out terms and make compromises. However, recently, the situation has become such that neither side can any longer produce a compromise or work with the other. This is apparently an external problem. There is also a more concealed difficulty in my personal case. For some time, the company and directors had tacit agreements, never openly acknowledged, about the quality of film to be released for the Japanese audience. There were general standards for a film. I was dissatisfied with these "average" movies. I and other young people wanted to do something more and cease being handcuffed by the so-called common-sense agreements prevalent in the film industry. Breaking this unwritten law made it difficult for me to stay at Shochiku. At that time they were releasing two films a week, like a factory. The audiences expected films at this low level and the companies catered to this expectation.

Mellen: What types of film do you have in mind when you speak of "average" movies?

Oshima: So-called artistic films of a high standard made by well-known masters such as Ozu and Kurosawa as well as films of a much lower level—program pictures or pure entertainment films and melodramas, silly sentimental films, and so-called political films sponsored by official Communist Party dogmatists. Fun-

---

* In Japan many law graduates do not take up law as their careers. Law graduates of the universities of Tokyo and Kyoto are notoriously to be found among high governmental officials and executives of giant corporations.

The Ceremony. "Our generation cannot rely on the congeniality of our all being Japanese in order to communicate. . . . I try to start out with the problems of the individual, and these problems should be meaningful to anybody in the world. It shouldn't stop at the Japanese experience."

damentally all three groups fall into the same category. Their structure is the same—very conventional and acceptable to the audience.

Mellen: Would you elaborate on these political films sponsored by the Communist Party?

Oshima: Between 1948 and 1950, Showa 23 to 25, we had severe labor disputes. When the Korean War started, the film industry experienced a "red purge." Many directors and technicians were chased out of the industry. They formed their own group and started to make two or three films a year. These films were mainly sponsored and financed by the Communist Party. If I am to mention names, among them would be Satsuo Yamamoto and Tadashi Imai. They were the main directors.

Mellen: Do you still distribute your films through a big company?

Oshima: Oh, me? No, I have no intention of working again for a big company.

Mellen: So, you work with your own production company. How do you finance it?

Oshima: It is financed by my friends and people I know. In Japan people outside the film industry rarely invest in film. We don't use such methods.

Mellen: Have there been any directors in the history of the Japanese film whose work has been meaningful to you?

Oshima: I am sure that there are many worth mentioning, but the directors of the older generation and my generation have different points of view and different approaches. These are the differences between those who produce "standard" films within a conventional framework and those who try to go beyond this.

Mellen: I'm not sure I understand what you mean by "standard" here. I don't believe that Ozu, Mizoguchi, and others are just standard directors. Are you speaking of "standard" or "average" as a description of the intellectual or artistic level of these directors?

Oshima: Let me see. This is not a question or discussion of bad or good. My point is that their films were made to be acceptable to the Japanese because they were based upon a familiarity with general concepts readily understandable by the Japanese; they used a narrative style or convention long established and understood. We are attempting not to remain within the congenial, older mode. Our films are absolutely different from theirs. Our generation cannot rely on the congeniality of our all being Japanese in order to communicate.

Mellen: Then what you are actually trying to do is to go beyond the standard, the conventional, the familiar or accepted in film regarding the aesthetic handling of problems?

Oshima: I don't know if I am trying to go beyond or surpass. I try to start out with the problems of the individual, and these problems should be meaningful to anybody in the world. It shouldn't stop at the Japanese experience. All the old masters began with the assumption that their work should be readily understood by the Japanese audience. It is the way of thinking that is different. They start from the audience's level.

Tetsu Abe in *Boy*. "We are attempting not to remain within the congenial, older mode. Our films are absolutely different from theirs."

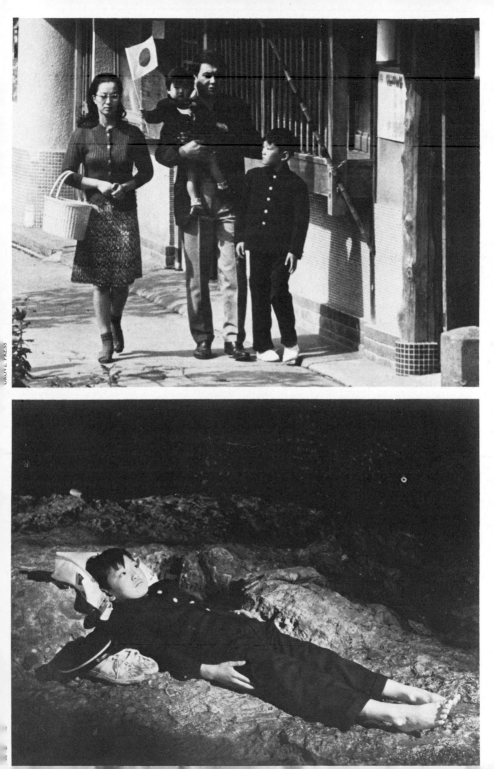

Mellen: Of course, some old filmmakers certainly had an ability to go beyond the Japanese setting and implied a more universal social and political dimension in their imagery and film metaphors. In some works of Imamura, Shindo, and Kurosawa dealing with the continuation of past consciousness, this is evident. They deal with themes that would apply to any society during a period of rapid industrialization. How would you relate to these political films and directors who seem to go far beyond the specifics of Japan?

Oshima: If you speak only of being accessible internationally, probably Hollywood had more international impact than all of them combined. [Laughs]

Mellen: Of course, if we mean "international" in that sense, Hollywood is it. A film like *The Godfather* invokes cheap sentiments for any audience while it obscures the cultural drama involved. But in this sense it is not universal at all, but very specific. But in a film like *Kuroneko,* Shindo treats class issues, the conflict between present consciousness and older loyalty—a problem which has a universal reference. I don't quite see how we can talk about those two films in the same way.

Oshima: That is a beautiful example. To me, *The Godfather* and *Kuroneko* are not really so different. To me, *Kuroneko* is an example of a Hollywood movie.

Mellen: In the sense of being dishonest?

Oshima: Yes, indeed. Although it has the surface theme you mention, *Kuroneko* has nothing to do with anything serious.

Mellen: How do you define your own political preoccupations and interests? Which are the questions that interest you and how do they go beyond Japan?

Oshima: I am not interested in the surface of politics or in how political issues appear to our society. I try to look into political perception *in the minds* of the Japanese, not as an element which you can see, but rather as interior feelings.

Mellen: What are these political assumptions in the interior of the Japanese mind?

Oshima: They are things Japanese have nurtured for a long time. It is difficult to set out in brief because these patterns of thinking have been created in the long history of Japan, but an example would be the *Tenno* or emperor system, the imperial order.

Mellen: How does the internalization of the emperor system in the consciousness of the Japanese manifest itself in films like *The Ceremony* or *Dear Summer Sister?*

Oshima: In brief, in the consciousness of the ruler and those who

Akiko Koyama as Setsuko Sakurada in *The Ceremony*. "In the consciousness of the ruler and those who are ruled is this ingrained idea of the emperor system. My characters reveal that in fact no one can escape this mentality in Japan."

are ruled is this ingrained idea of the emperor system. My characters reveal that in fact no one can escape this mentality in Japan. I am pursuing how we can break away from it.

Mellen: Could you sum up what effect the existence of the emperor system has had on the mentality of the ruled?

Oshima: It created a mentality in the population that they allowed, even wished to have, such a system in Japan, and allowed that such a person as the emperor should exist.

Mellen: Does this have a relation to the family structure in *Dear Summer Sister?*

Oshima: I don't think that it is a matter of relating this to that. It is not a question of a particular relationship, but rather that the whole psychological atmosphere is saturated with it. It affects everyone and everything. But it is not that the family represents so-and-so, etc.

Mellen: What is the director's view toward the family structure in Japan in *Boy* and *Dear Summer Sister,* to cite two examples?

Oshima: I can't really answer that question because the theme of the film is "the film itself." You can't separate the people in the film from the film.

Mellen: How does the film comment about the people's values and the value of the family as an institution? In *Yojimbo* Kurosawa implies that the rise of capitalism and its competitiveness are destroying the family system, and rampant self-interest is changing human relationships. It doesn't describe only the period in which it is set, although it locates these problems in a historical context. I am asking you the same question. In *Dear Summer Sister* the ending on the beach reveals that the family as an institution is at the center of the film. What is the director's viewpoint toward the people and their relationships, as a family or a semifamily?

Oshima: Both love and hate. I have all possible human emotions for the family.

Mellen: Would you say that the film is a representation of your sense of ambivalence toward the family and family relationships?

Oshima: I am interested in this aspect, but I wouldn't call this my message or the central idea of the film. I don't make films in which I want to send out messages to say something. I start out from very concrete things. I don't start out with the assumption that here we have a certain ideology and construct the story of the film accordingly.

Mellen: I'm not saying that you have an ideology, which is a negative term. But your expression and your concept of things are based upon your sensibility and how you look at the world. Isn't that so? I would like to hear about how you look at the world. What are your values which, if not transmitted in a propagandistic way, are there all the same?

Oshima: [Laughs] My values, my viewpoints—these things may change tomorrow. Perceiving the happenings of life doesn't make films. Many, many elements intervene. An idea goes "through" me before it enters a film. Processing these ideas and reproducing them in the art form are very complicated phenomena. All the elements are intertwined. I reject the notion that a director's particular interpretation concerning one subject is then made into a film.

Mellen: Have there been any Western directors whom you admire besides Godard?

Oshima: Buñuel would be one.

Mellen: Have you seen Makavejev's film *W. R.: Mysteries of the Organism?* Have you noticed any similarity between this film and your *Diary of a Shinjuku Burglar?*

Oshima: Yes, I have seen it. I thought there were definite similarities between the two films. But I saw his film after I had made *Diary of a Shinjuku Burglar.*

Mellen: What is the relation between sexuality and politics in your film? Does the film *Diary of a Shinjuku Burglar* express the idea that sexual liberation must come before political liberation?

Oshima: No, not so much in an order. One doesn't have to precede the other. I think that both are what humanity is after throughout our historical struggles.

Mellen: Since the film doesn't raise the question of political liberation very much, I thought you were talking exclusively about sexual liberation.

Oshima: In either case, liberation itself doesn't mean the end of problem solving. To me liberation is the momentary triumph you feel when you succeed in doing something in a liberated manner. You must challenge the new and reach for another liberation right after. *Shinjuku Burglar* is not a liberated arrival point or anything fixed. It refers to a certain political and sexual liberation attained by the student movement in 1968. It doesn't mean that Shinjuku became a completely liberated place. It was a moment when a step had been made, but these things change again.

Mellen: In what way do you express a progress toward or pursuit of political liberation?

Oshima: At the end of the film when rocks are thrown at the policemen in that big demonstration.

Mellen: What was the issue of the actual demonstration in Shinjuku on which the scene in the film is based?

Oshima: That was the most violent and largest demonstration since 1950. We call the incident "6.29," which refers to its date. It was nothing like a real political demonstration. It was simply a huge gathering of hippies, street people, students, and everybody in the district. To me this incident has a very significant meaning. It was very important that a demonstration, not organized by a political party, should arise.

Mellen: Then the importance of the demonstration lies in its being an expression of the alienation of a large number of people and their spontaneously coming together? What is their level of consciousness? What are they revolting against?

Oshima: I described their conscious level through the two protagonists in the film. These two, the boy and the girl, are a representation of the people I described, the young people who revolted that day.

Mellen: What is the relationship between the fact that those people are a representation of the spirit of the revolt and the fact that they exhibit particular neuroses; the girl is masculine and the boy is effeminate. There would appear to be a specific inversion, a role change, at least at a literal level, or don't you see it that way? It looked like an extreme sexual inversion happening simultaneously with the political spirit of the demonstrations.

Oshima: You have just said a very illuminating thing here. A male being a female figure was the most significant aspect or spirit of that time, the era of the demonstrations from 1968 to 1969.

Mellen: Homosexuality?

Oshima: No, it is rather that the male is not being a male figure at all, but very feminine—a phenomenon at the heart of the spirit of the demonstration.

Mellen: Does bisexuality represent a particular group of people or a particular time?

Oshima: No, not bisexuality. I mean simply that the male figure, rather feminine, is getting weaker and gentler and soft. Before, the male figure was more masculine.

Mellen: Is it that the male is getting away from the old norms defining the so-called male role? To say he is gentle is to suggest that the student demonstration represented something good, something pure?

Oshima: No, not so much as the result of being a gentler figure. I am saying that this psychic change expresses the general sentiment of the younger people.

Mellen: Is this then a criticism of the demonstration? Does it imply ineffectuality?

Oshima: No, it is related to the fact that the boy and girl are representative of the generation who joined in this demonstration. The unmasculine part of the boy was in the whole spirit of the time. It does not mean that I was critical of this demonstration although the boy feels frustration at being weak. It is just that boys are expressing their maleness differently. But it has nothing to do with the result, whether the demonstration was successful or not. Everyone who throws rocks shares the feelings of this boy, the same kind of spirit.

Mellen: Does this say something positive about the people in the demonstration?

Oshima: I don't know if I approve or disapprove. Things were that way at that time. I am describing it as it appeared to me.

Mellen: Why do these two characters, a boy and girl, suffer from sexual inadequacy? The boy is impotent, the girl is frigid.

Oshima: Their relationship doesn't work very well. Don't all of us suffer if we cannot operate very well sexually?

Mellen: Let me see. I am picking up bits and pieces here. Is there then any allegorical connection between their sexual inadequacy and the political situation? Are you separating these two themes—the political and the sexual—as two distinct parts bearing no obvious relation to each other?

Oshima: Their sexual inadequacy is a political inadequacy in itself. You cannot separate them into two distinct problems. These are equal problems.

Mellen: Is there a problem then in the politics of their relationship expressed in their reversal of sexual roles and resulting in their failure to satisfy themselves in either posture?

Oshima: It is a problem not only in the relationship of these two individuals, but in a larger relationship—that of the individual in relation to society as a whole.

Mellen: Why is the therapist in this film portrayed so inadequately, as such an undesirable character?

Oshima: Takahashi-san himself is a psychotherapist and he is that way. He consults his patients in just that way.

Mellen: Did he write his own part?

Oshima: No, it was not even in the script. He just did it himself.

Mellen: Did he know that he was being satirized by you?

Oshima: Yes, I made a slight caricature of him.

Mellen: What was the critical reception of *Diary of a Shinjuku Burglar* in Japan?

Oshima: I had both approval and disapproval, like and dislike.

Mellen: Would you say that your audience is mostly young students?

Oshima: Yes, I think so.

Mellen: I noticed yesterday at the showing of *Dear Summer Sister* at Kinokuniya Hall that the audience was comprised mostly of students. Of course this was in Shinjuku, a student area.

Do you agree with the statement of Donald Richie that *Death by Hanging* is your most important personal statement?

Oshima: I don't understand that very well. I don't agree with the approach of dividing several problems into separate categories, i.e. a sexual problem versus a political problem. These are the same thing. I don't want to be branded a political moviemaker. I am not. Mr. Richie thinks I am a political director because I expressed myself very straightforwardly in *Death by Hanging.* All my films have political subjects, but in *Death by Hanging* it seems very obvious, so it could be used, if one wants to attach labels, to categorize me as a "political" director.

Mellen: Would you explain in what way *Boy* is as equally political in subject matter as *Death by Hanging,* which is about the persecution of Koreans in Japan?

Oshima: To me both are clearly the same thing. I don't see how you can say that one is more political than the other. I understand that if one thinks we should label things in a very limited sense, you might describe these two works as having very different themes, and *Boy* would not then be considered a political film. But to me they are the same. I think people make a mistake in trying to think of these as two different things.

Mellen: What criticism of Japanese culture are you making in *Boy*—a film about a child who throws himself in front of cars so that his family can survive by collecting the insurance?

Oshima: Total criticism. I don't criticize certain social aspects. I am critical of the whole thing. Social phenomena are not the object of my criticism.

Mellen: Are you a nihilist?

Oshima: [Laughs] I don't think so.

Mellen: I asked this because the definition of a nihilist in the historical sense of the term is someone who attacks the total power structure and sets himself against it. The jargon use of nihilist would refer to the cynic who values nothing. But I meant the term in the nineteenth-century Russian sense of the feeling that the whole social fabric is degenerating, and the belief that the society must be destroyed and recreated.

Oshima: Oh, I see. I guess we usually don't use words in their original meaning.

Mellen: Do you have any preference regarding the use of professional versus nonprofessional actors?

Oshima: It is the same to me. It depends on the person, whether professional or amateur. It depends on his personality.

Mellen: Does it take more time for rehearsals and so on when you use amateurs?

Oshima: Not at all. I don't see any difficulty.

Mellen: What accounts, do you think, for the interest in pornography in Japanese films? I don't mean the hard-core sex movies. I am referring to films like Ichikawa's *Kagi* and Imamura's *The Pornographer*. Why does this interest in extremes of sex keep appearing in Japanese films as distinct from other national cinemas?

Oshima: It is a difficult question. I don't know.

Mellen: What is the attitude of the Japanese film industry to women working as writers and directors?

Oshima: We have some female scenario writers.

Mellen: Do they have any difficulty getting work or having their work produced? Are they treated equally with men who do the same jobs?

Oshima: No, I don't think that women writers have any particular difficulties. In the film and television industries I think that writing is a very advantageous profession for women.

Mellen: In the United States there are many women scriptwriters, but they often find that their scripts are changed.

Oshima: Is it because they are women?

Mellen: No, of course they're not the only ones whose scripts are changed, but neither are they given the same privileges as the men. Do you think that the women's liberation movement has had any impact on the image of women in the Japanese film?

Oshima: Do you mean the current movement?

Mellen: Within the last few years.

Oshima: Oh, because we distinguish the current movement from the "bluestocking" movement of the mid-Meiji era. No, I don't think they have had any strong impact on us. I rather think that Japanese women are already liberated. [Laughs] It doesn't seem that this movement is taking much root in Japan and certainly has had no effect in films.

Mellen: Is there any progress in style in your films from one to the next. Do you intend a certain progress in style, in a certain direction, for example, toward a less chronological narrative structure, or could you make a traditionally structured film again?

Oshima: I always try to deny the style I have used in a previous work. So I have many different styles in my films. *Diary of a Shinjuku Burglar* is completely different from *Death by Hanging*. *The Ceremony* is completely different from *Dear Summer Sister*. I never make films in the same style.

Mellen: Then you don't believe that one specific style of filmmaking is especially valuable for your way of looking at the world, i.e. that varying styles may be equally effective in developing a theme?

Oshima: Yes, the style I choose depends on the theme of the film.

Mellen: What is the relation between the thematic development in *Dear Summer Sister* and the techniques you used—close-ups and shallow depth of focus, and the general symbolic, stylized quality of the film?

Oshima: The film itself is the journey, but it is also a dream. That applies to the choice of style.

Mellen: Did you change the depth of field according to whether you wanted to stress the internal or the external journey?

Oshima: A girl going to Okinawa on a trip is not realistic for a girl of that age.

Mellen: In other words, it is a journey into consciousness, an internal journey.

Oshima: Yes, it is. But it is also the external journey. Traveling to Okinawa in the actual sense and also a very dreamlike journey devoid of the weight of reality.

Mellen: So the physical trip is symbolic of the internal journey?

Oshima: Probably, but why should you settle the matter one way or the other? I think it is perfectly all right to think that we have two journeys with the same weight. I always try to consider various things at once.

Mellen: Would you like to discuss a new project you are working on now?

Oshima: We have just finished one. Do you mean the next one? [Laughs] No, perhaps not yet.

FIFTEEN

SHUJI TERAYAMA

INTRODUCTION

Shuji Terayama, at thirty-nine (he was born in 1936), is one of the most productive and provocative creative artists in Japan, working in many media, including poetry, the novel, drama, and film. As an outstanding poet, playwright, and director for theater and film, he considers himself to be "high on the list of dangerous thinkers in Japan." In 1967 he founded the Tenjo-Sajiki Troupe, which has as its message the following:

> We consider theater to be crime.
> We are not working toward the revolution of theater, but we will whip the world with our imagination and theatricalize revolution.
> Tenjo-Sajiki has gone beyond all drama of the past.
> We, as a group, will reform the world through poetry and imagination.
> Take power with Imagination!!

The Tenjo-Sajiki Troupe considers itself the "heretic of Japan's theater world" and is proud of being a place where those who run away from home come to visit. Among the plays Terayama has written for the company are *The Hunchback of Aomori*, *Fatty Oyama's Crime*, *Ulysses of Shinjuku*, *Farewell to Movies!*, *The Crime of Dr. Galigari*, and *Throw Away Your Books, Go Out into the Streets*. The latter was in the style of what the Tenjo-Sajiki call "théatre vérité." Teenagers, who wrote the poems which comprise the play, mounted the stage and addressed the audience as them-

275

selves. Their poems included "The Confessions of a Stammerer," "The Trials of Being Fat," (Before we met, Terayama told me I would easily recognize him because he was considered to be very fat. By Western standards he is of average size.) "Memories of a Criminal," "The Experience of Leaving Home," "First Sexual Experience," and "A Guide to Sodomy." The play has been compared to *Hair*.

Terayama's *Jashumon* condemns the family as an institution, focusing upon Yamataro's suffocation by his mother, Ogin. These two characters enter as if they are puppets at the mercy of the stagehands called *kuroko* who facilitate the action and move the props in the Kabuki theater. They were also used by Shinoda in *Double Suicide*. The *kuroko* pull invisible strings binding the son; they are preconceived bonds enslaving Terayama's people. But Yamataro wants to escape from his mother with his bride, a prostitute named Yamabuki. The mother tries to persuade him to remain with her.

The play includes the son's physical attack on his mother and a song by the *kuroko* entitled "Please Die, Mother," reminiscent of Terayama's scenario for Masahiro Shinoda's film *The Scandalous Adventures of Buraikan*. When Yamabuki refuses to let him touch her, Yamataro returns to his mother for aid. Ogin urges him to kill everyone so they can live together alone. He must strike her down again.

Near the end of the play the actress who plays Yamabuki addresses the audience:

> The writer pulls the wires that control the melancholy of sunset, the smoking of a cigarette, and the fighting. Emotional events are caused by the writer. These things are also determined by time. Time controls history with strings. No! We do not see who controls everything. For example, if I write a script for a play, at that instant I am unable to run away from the play. The play cannot be ended. So in the theater, no play has an ending. It changes its title and characters. Everybody, take off your costumes and come onto the stage!

The actors remove their costumes and makeup and begin to destroy the set. They break down the distinction between actors and audience. They urge the spectators to create their own play—the equivalent to controlling their own lives—by killing the *kuroko* who manipulate their strings.

In *Galigari*, audience participation (their theater seats one hundred) was demanded because from no "seat" in the audience could one see all that was happening on the stage. The set consisted of a bathtub, a table, a children's room, and a study inside a small house. The audience was seated in various places to watch the play taking place in the house. No episode was completed, and, in fact, the person called Dr. Galigari never appears in the play.

At a performance of Terayama's *Origin of Blood* in Iran during the Seventh Festival of Arts, a theatrical agent named Mme. Ninon Tallon Karlweis, who was sitting in the front row, was badly burned in the face by a flame manipulated by one of the actors. It was a less than felicitous result of Terayama's thesis that "the spectators at this play should be thought of as participants at a party." Terayama later sent her roses and a note with "I'm sorry" written on it one hundred times, but other spectators have also been injured at his performances. On one occasion his actors got into a fight with some spectators at the BITEF festival in Belgrade after declaiming to them in Serbo-Croat.

In Amsterdam in 1972 spectators were overcome by claustrophobia during a play of Terayama's designed to provoke precisely that emotion. Terayama is not displeased by these occurrences, given his ambition to eliminate "artificial frontiers" between drama and reality. "When my actors do something outrageous as part of the play, or get beaten up by the spectators," he has declared, "these frontiers are eliminated. I am pleased by this."

In addition to his full-length film version of *Throw Away Your Books, Go Out into the Streets* (1971), Terayama's films include *The Emperor of Tomatocatsup* (1970), a parody of revolution in which children bind and rape adults, and the 1975 Art Theatre Guild production, *Denen ni Shisu,* loosely translated into English as *Cache-Cache Pastoral.* The latter has been described as Terayama's personal version of Fellini's *Amarcord.* Terayama has also written a number of film scenarios, including Susumu Hani's *Nanami* or *Inferno of First Love,* Toshio Matsumoto's *Mothers,* and the previously mentioned *Buraikan* directed by Shinoda, which reflects Terayama's interest in crime as a revolutionary activity.

Terayama has also published a number of books, including: *Dying in the Country,* an anthology of poems; *Postwar Poetry;* a novel called *The Wilderness,* which deals with a boy who becomes a boxer, taking as its premise that boxing is the easiest way for a Japanese without name, status, or money to rise in the world; and a television drama called *The Origin of Lullabies,* which develops the point of view that mothers began to sing lullabies not out of love for their children, but as consolation and solace for themselves.

Typically representative of Terayama's point of view toward

cinema is his play *Farewell to Movies,* written in two parts, "the fan" and "the star." In "the fan" two middle-aged men over forty talk of their admiration for "Hunfry Bogard" and regret their own mediocrity: "Actors can die many times because they have screens. To die many times is to live many times!" One man finally shaves the armpits of the other gently and carefully. In "the star," a famous movie actress who has played more than a hundred characters becomes unable to recognize her own identity. The theme running through both is Terayama's "farewell to movies," by which he means the commercial Hollywood film which shaped both Japanese and American youths of his generation.

Some of the same themes are reflected in Terayama's film *Throw Away Your Books, Go Out into the Streets.* In the following excerpt from the scenario Terayama associates the longing and frustrations endemic to Japanese youth with the distortions visited upon all by movies. The hero, called, simply, "boy," objects not only to the squalid conditions of his life, but also to being made an object for the edification of audiences viewing Terayama's film:

> Sometimes I dream about a man-powered plane. In the dream I'm flying it.
>
> But in real life I'm a poor, nineteen-year-old college flunk-out. I live by the railroad tracks in a cheap apartment that's like a pig sty or a stable. I live with my grandmother, a lonely shoplifter and my father who is forty-eight and still hooked on masturbation. He used to be an Army officer but is now jobless. There is also my younger sister who can't talk and who has a sexual thing for her pet rabbit.
>
> For me, freedom is something I can only find away from home. It's like varsity soccer players. I want to be virile like them.
>
> My grandmother and my sister don't get along. Once my grandmother killed my sister's rabbit when my sister wasn't home. Then she made it into soup and served it at dinner. She even made my sister have some. When my sister found out, she was so upset she ran out of the house. The next morning at dawn she got gang-banged on the soccer field by the whole team. I watched, but I wasn't strong enough to stop them. And while I watched, part of me was sad for my sister but part of me was raping her with the others.
>
> Because I wanted to be strong, I left the pig sty and went out into the streets of the city.

The film keeps turning. It's just a movie. Suddenly I look
out from the empty screen and start talking to the audience.
When the movie's over only a white screen will be left. A
movie can only live in the dark. Even with Polanski or Fellini,
their world disappears when you turn on a light. But I want
movies projected into the bright noonday city streets.
    Good-bye, movies . . . movies, good-bye.

The association of freedom with virility is also a major theme of
Oshima's *Diary of a Shinjuku Burglar*. The recognition of psychol-
ogical ambivalence in the boy's half-incestuous feelings toward his
sister marks Terayama as a member of a generation of Japanese art-
ists whose views have, in part, been shaped by Western thinkers
like Freud. In his vision of the world, Terayama, whose ideas are
much more flamboyant and consciously outrageous, has, nonethe-
less, much in common with directors like Hani and Oshima.

Throw Away Your Books has been reviewed with appreciation in
both Europe and America. Jean A. Gili, writing in the French jour-
nal *Cinema 71*, called it an "oeuvre ambitieuse, foisonnante
d'idées, opera pop . . . le film révèle une personnalité d'une ri-
chesse exceptionnelle''; * Gérard Langlois in *Lettres Françaises*
spoke in equal superlatives, comparing the film to a gigantic hap-
pening:

> Oeuvre remarquable dont on ne manquera pas de parler sous
> peu et qui place son auteur parmi les actuels ténors du jeune
> cinema japonais . . .
> Images acérées comme des couteaux, couleurs provocantes,
> lumières musicales. Sarabande de personnages au centre d'un
> immense happening.†

L'Unità, in Italy, admired the film for its rich political con-
sciousness:

> *Gettiama via i libri, usciamo nelle strade* è, in sintesi, un
> film che nella sua corposa, violenta carica di denuncia e nella
> sua dolorosa passione per la condizione alienata dell 'uomo
> viene ad assumere l'importanza di un documento inoppug-

---

* An ambitious work, abundant with ideas, pop opera . . . the film reveals a per-
sonality of exceptional richness.
    † A remarkable work which we will undoubtedly be discussing before long and
which places its director among the truly pure voices of the young Japanese cinema.
Sharp images like daggers, provocative colors, musical insights. A Saraband of peo-
ple at the center of a gigantic happening.

nabile, sia contro l'attuale societa giapponese fondata sul piu brutalle fruttamento dell 'uomo, sia control l'ingranaggio generale della ferrea logisa del profitto che murove e sorragge lo strapotere capitalistico. Il grosso merito di Terayama è dunque l'essere riuscito a condurre in porto un film dove la passione politica si fonde con la poesia, e la cultura cresce come solidarietà di classe.*

Hank Werba in *Variety* also found the film remarkable:

The film is a virulent blast of outrage and revolt—heightened by apocalyptic colors and symbols—without overclouding the basic family characters of the boy, his sister, their father and grandmother. At times the film resembles a Japanese version of "Mondo Cane" in its grotesque satire of a system to be razed. Included is a magnificent erotic sequence of the young boy learning about sex from a prostie.

A short fantasy film in the surrealist mode, *The Emperor of Tomatocatsup* is a charming anarchist vision about children taking power to create the "Empire of Tomatocatsup." The Emperor, abandoning his "court of short pants," with a gun in his hand, leaves with his regiments for the hunt of the grown-ups.

The Constitution of the New Empire declares that adults who impose physical force upon the children will be suppressed by the civil state. More specifically:

Grown-ups who take away our snacks, those who prevent us from smoking and drinking, those who rob us of our freedom of expression and sexual liberty, those who try to impose their educational prejudices upon us . . . will be condemned to capital punishment or to eighty years in prison.

The Constitution continues:

In the name of God, all children rejoice in their freedom, the freedom to plot, to commit acts of treason, the freedom to

---

* *Throw Away Your Books, Go Out into the Street* is, in synthesis, a film which in its substance assumes the violent task of denouncing with painful passion the alienated condition of man. As such it comes to assume the importance of an incontestable documentary, both against present Japanese society, which is based upon the more brutal exploitation of man, and against the system's control of the logistics of hard profit which motivates and sustains capitalist power.

The great merit of Terayama is consequently his success in directing a film where political passion merges with poetry and culture increases like class solidarity.

practice homosexuality . . . the freedom to use the Bible as toilet paper. . . .

The importance of Terayama's film work has also been recognized in Japan. The brilliant Japanese film critic Tadao Sato has called *Throw Away Your Books* "an important work of which the principal quality is its gaiety, a collection of graffiti" where Terayama does not refrain from revealing "the gamin-like, boyish and irreverent aspect" characteristic of his literary works. Sato calls the film in "Le Jeune Cinéma" published in the French journal *Esprit:*

. . . a potpourri of the raw desires of adolescents lost in the big city, of their sentimentalism, and of their imprecations against power. The images, which at first sight astonish by their seemingly intentional banality and impoverished quality, possess a joy of being, the joy of breaking into a thousand pieces, like the parts of a mosaic, the old-fashioned cinematographic forms which pretend to seriousness and profundity.

For Sato, *Throw Away Your Books* is above all a film where youths make a game of cinema to their heart's content. Sato also places Terayama in terms of the sociology of contemporary Japan:

Terayama, who for several years has launched appeals to youths to leave their families, has often concerned himself with provincial youths who end by following his counsel, leaving for Tokyo. One has the opportunity in this film to understand the confessions of these adolescents grouped around this young poet and partaking of his ideas.

Sato sees the characters of Terayama "scorning traditional morality" and "dreaming of a sexually free utopian universe." Yet, as Sato perceives them, they are also "nostalgic for the traditional life of the countryside." He observes that it is this nostalgia which is ever present behind their professed words; it is a strange disequilibrium in which they, typical of all Japanese youth, flounder.

The interview with Terayama offers but a taste of the richness of his contribution to the arts in Japan and an intimation of his energy and élan as a leading persona in Japan's cultural and political avant-garde.

INTERVIEW WITH
SHUJI TERAYAMA

Mellen: You are considered a member of the avant-garde in both Japanese theater and film. How would you describe your approach to drama and to society?

Terayama: I don't like conservative society or conservative people. I am especially against *Hoshuteki,* * "protecting the status quo," and this is the aim in my work. I wanted to show in *Throw Away Your Books, Go Out into the Streets* that film is a very vain and frail thing. In one part I use only one light and then allow everything to disappear. The light is switched on at one point and not at another. The actor in the film must ask for the lights to be put on because I do not do it willingly.

Mellen: How do your works articulate your feelings about Japan?

Terayama: As one of my primary themes I attack the Japanese family system. I am interested in the *Ie,* a time when there was a community of Japanese, before we had a nation-state called Japan. This was roughly a thousand years ago. Under a clan system there were many activities—religious, entertainment, educational, and protective activities for the group—but they were not institutionalized in the way they are today. Today all these activities belong to society and not to the *Ie,* that is the commonality or the people. But in Japan there remains one vestige of this superior form of social life; we still retain very deeply engrained cooperative feelings, a pervasive sense of group loyalty and mutual dependence. In the center of the *Ie* was a family, which in Japan today has degenerated into the immediate family, quite a different thing. Yet the Japanese conception of the nation still has this concept of *Ie* at its center. The national entity is perceived as a union of many individual *Ie* or communities. My feeling finally is that we need neither *Ie* nor the nation-state.

Mellen: As an independent filmmaker in Japan, how do you fare?

Terayama: I do not do as well as directors like Shinoda or Oshima who have started their own production companies because the truth is that these independent companies are as wealthy as the big companies. Mr. Oshima's company may not be as large as Teshiga-

---
* Literally *Ho* means "maintain" and *shu,* "God."

hara's, but he still has three times the possibility of raising money that I have.

Mellen: How would you compare your problems as an avant-garde filmmaker to those of an experimental filmmaker like Oshima whose films don't reach a mass audience either?

Terayama: Since Oshima has made quite a few commercial films, he now has an accumulation of films which he can use to finance his future work. For example, he can rent his past films out and raise money in this way. Oshima also tries very hard to enter his films at the foreign film festivals like Cannes so that he can increase his market. He wanted to show *Ceremony* in regular competition, but when it was rejected by the selection committee, he brought it to the "Directors' Week," in which less obviously commerical films are shown. He is quite a promoter for his films, although he has the pretention of being a revolutionary.

Mellen: You have been called a revolutionary in your approach to theater and to film. In what sense do you see yourself as a revolutionary? What does revolution mean to you?

Terayama: I don't believe in political revolution at all. Rather, I am interested in a sexual revolution which includes a revolution in language, in touching, in writing. Because of my ideas, the police have often come to raid my theater.

Mellen: Are there any foreign writers or artists whose work you see as parallel to your own?

Terayama: I would name Wilhelm Reich and Makavejev. When I took my theater troupe to Yugoslavia, Makavejev invited us all to his home where he showed us *W. R.: Mysteries of the Organism.* Of course he can no longer make films in his own country and must show them either at festivals or secretly.

Mellen: How would you compare your own film *Throw Away Your Books* to Makavejev's *W.R.?*

Terayama: Technically, my film is not as good as his. I have not had the opportunity to make films the way I would want to. Therefore, I would not like to compare the two films. I don't think it would be fair.

Mellen: How would you account for the sudden interest in the Japanese film in pornography? This appears not only in the hard-core pornographic films which are now flooding the film market, but also in the work of established directors.

Terayama: I am interested in pornography, although I don't know why the whole society has suddenly become so. In this stage of our society, with the amount of repression we still have to confront, it

Shuji Terayama. "I am interested in a sexual revolution which includes a revolution in language, in touching, in writing. Because of my ideas, the police have often come to raid my theater."

is revolutionary to make pornographic movies. There is so much governmental and big-company censorship that one would have to say that the sexual and the political revolutions must go hand in hand. The student movement has been fanatic and radical. The police are trying to turn the interest of the public away from the student movement to sexual things. But, as always in our history, the authorities are devious and subtle. They intensify censorship and overt condemnation knowing that this will produce the opposite of their seeming goal. If there were merely implicit cultural disapproval, people might not care about pornography. The presence of censorship only increases the interest in things sexual. There have also been quite a few sexual scandals in Tokyo, and in general one could say that the authorities are afraid of sexual freedom. Of course they have another problem and this is why the censorship is not as severe or as real as it may seem to be. The authorities are also afraid that if sexual freedom is closed off, the people will turn to political revolution, and this they fear most of all.

Mellen: For whom did you make your films *The Emperor of Tomatocatsup* and *Throw Away Your Books?* What is the audience for your films?

Terayama: My films appeal to the students, but the critics also like my films and they have listed them among the *Kinema Jumpo* list of "best ten." * I think it was a sense of *giri* † on the part of these critics. They felt obligated to recognize my films. So last year my film was number eight and *Eiga Hyōron,* another magazine, named it number two.

Mellen: How do you assess the work of the younger generation of Japanese filmmakers?

Terayama: I don't like most filmmakers at all, but of the directors making movies in Japan today, I would say that Shohei Imamura is the best of all by far. I especially admire his *A Man Vanishes* [*Ningen Johatsu*]. Nobody understands what is real and what is fantasy. Imamura's crime for the Japanese critics and pundits is that he mixes the two indistinguishably. I believe that crime and the criminal are revolutionary responses and so I like this film very much.

Mellen: What do you mean when you say that crime is revolutionary? Do you mean this in the sense of Dostoevski's *Crime and Punishment?*

---

* Equivalent to the American Academy Awards.
† *Giri* means "duty" of the most compelling kind.

Terayama: There are two ways of looking at history—from the point of view of necessity and from the point of view of accident. My conception is that the historical is a result of accident. The laws of a given society and those in power generally decide what is crime and what is not. The law is a function of the nation-state. If you reject this idea of the nation and of nationality, you don't recognize its definition of "law" and then there becomes no such thing as crime. All things are permitted, to quote Dostoevski. The hypocrisy of law may be easily seen in this example. Homicide is generally considered to be a crime, both in your nation and in mine. Outside the nation, however, for example in Vietnam, it is permitted. So crime becomes a national problem. Each time a person commits a crime, he breaks away from the narrowness of nationality and in so doing he approaches the revolutionary.

Mellen: What did you mean when you said that history is a result of accident?

Terayama: Political science instructs us that history is a science and therefore that history is a result of necessity. My opinion is that history is accidental and that historical "accidents" are organized in our imaginations. Thus we come to have recorded history. And through the imagination we can transcend history and what our history has been. I am very interested in the work of Lao Tze, whose writings are parables of the limits of the real as defined by any given present, any specific society, and any particular historical period.

Mellen: Your view of crime is also quite unique. How far would you go with this view?

Terayama: You know, sometimes crime can be very gentle, very tender. That style of crime should be seen as a possibility—a new kind of response that would be liberating and that we should cultivate. Violence too can sometimes be very tender, an obvious example of which would be fornication. Incest is considered to be a crime, yet it can be tender and sweet.

Mellen: Could you name one Western artist whose sensibility echoes your own?

Terayama: Andy Warhol would be one, although I have had very few chances to see his work. What I have seen I like very much.

Mellen: Are you interested at all in the idea of women's liberation since your concern seems to be personal liberation in general?

On the set of *Denen ni Shisu* (*Cache-Cache Pastoral*), 1974. "Each time a person commits a crime, he breaks away from the narrowness of nationality and in so doing he approaches the revolutionary."

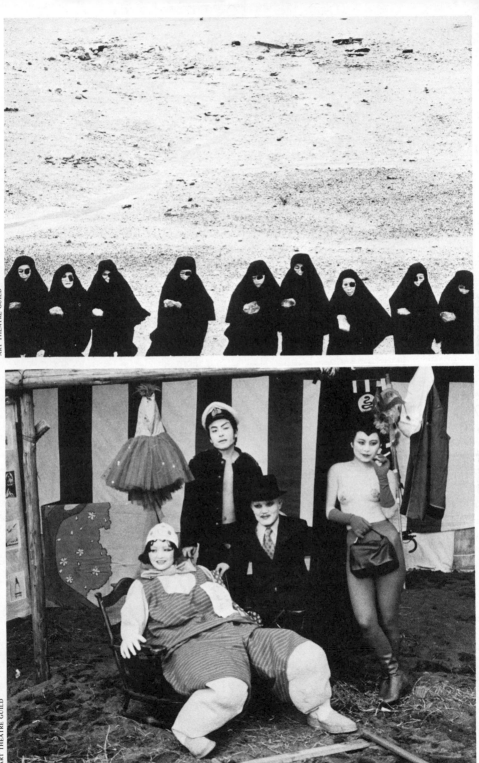

Terayama: Yes, although sometimes the women's liberation people can cut a man to pieces. The most interesting group are the "Fighting Women" led by Mitsu Tanaka, who has taken a job as a bar hostess in Okinawa in order to organize and recruit women to her movement and as a way to experience the life of the women whom she hopes to influence with her ideas.

Mellen: Do you have any future plans in the field of filmmaking?

Terayama: I have gone back to theater work because I have no money to make films. My troupe has toured Europe and the United States and we plan to make another trip to the United States. I also have an idea for a film. I would like to shoot a picture to be called *The Last Movie in the World*.

Mellen: How then do you see the condition of the Japanese film in general today? The answer is almost implied in the title of your projected new movie.

Terayama: About fifty years ago there was a major renaissance in Japanese film. Many of the actors who played in the early films are now living in an old-age home for men. I would like to film them. Kinugasa,* who played women's parts in early Japanese films, because, as in the Kabuki theater, there were no women actresses, is one of them. My final view is that there should be no more movies. At twenty-four I liked the work of Kurosawa very much. Now I don't hate it, but I felt pity when I saw *Dodes'ka-den*. Oshima and Shinoda say they hate Kurosawa, but I don't hate Akira Kurosawa.

---

* Known abroad as the director of *Gate of Hell*.

INDEX